STUDIES IN SOUTH INDIAN JAINISM

STUDIES
IN
SOUTH INDIAN JAINISM

BY

M. S. RAMASWAMI AYYANGAR, M.A.

Chief Lecturer in History and Economics, Maharaja's College, Vizianagram

AND

B. SESHAGIRI RAO, M.A.

Chief Lectuer in English, Maharaja's College, Vizianagram and Sometime Reader in Dravidian Philology to the University of Madras.

GYAN

Published by

GYAN

Gyan Publishing House
5, Ansari Road
Daryaganj, New Delhi-110002
Phone: 011-47034999, 9811692060
E-mail: books@gyanbooks.com

Distribution Network
gyanbooks.com
India, USA, Canada, UK, Australia, France

ISBN : 978-81-212-22808 (PB)
First Published, 1922

2nd Impression 2021

Printed at: Gyan Press, Delhi.

Studies in South Indian Jainism
Author: M. S. Ramaswami Ayyangar & B. Seshagiri Rao

STUDIES

IN

SOUTH INDIAN JAINISM

BY

M. S. RAMASWAMI AYYANGAR, M.A.,

Chief Lecturer in History and Economics, Maharaja's College, Vizianagram

AND

B. SESHAGIRI RAO, M.A.,

Chief Lecturer in English, Maharaja's College, Vizianagram
and
Sometime Reader in Dravidian Philology to the University of Madras.

MADRAS:

PRINTED BY HOE & CO. AT THE "PREMIER" PRESS.

1922.

DEDICATED

BY

GRACIOUS PERMISSION

TO

SAHEB MEHARBAN

DOSTAN MUSHPAK KADARDAN

KADAMPHARMAYE MOKHALISHAN

SREE SREE SREE

MIRJA PUSAPATI

ALAKH NARAYAN GAJAPATY RAJ

MAHARAJ MANYASULTAN BAHADUR,

PADSHA-HI-KALINGA MAHARAJAH SAHEB

BAHADUR OF VIZIANAGRAM

BY

HIS HIGHNESS'S MOST LOYAL

AND HUMBLE SERVANTS

THE AUTHORS.

FOREWORD.

When about a year ago a course of lectures on South Indian History was instituted at the Maharaja's College, the authors of this monograph undertook the teaching of the subject in addition to their other studies; and both of them devoted the summer recess of 1921 to investigations, the results of which are now placed before the public.

The history of Jainism in South India and its influence on the life and thought of the people is a fascinating subject. As the authors themselves point out, all the materials for a final verdict are not yet available and the conclusions reached can only be tentative and provisional. This, however, does not detract from the value of this study which opens out a most interesting field of thought and will, it is hoped, stimulate further research.

I congratulate the authors on the monograph and trust that it will be followed in the near future by studies of other aspects of South Indian Civilisation.

VIZIANAGRAM,
30th Sept. 1922.

V. T. KRISHNAMACHARI.

PART I

SOUTH INDIAN JAINISM

BY

M. S. RAMASWAMI AYYANGAR, M.A.,

Chief Lecturer in History and Economics,
Maharaja's College,
Vizianagram.

INTRODUCTION.

Indian Culture is a web of many threads. The subtle and fearless intellect of the Hindus, the illumination of the Buddha, the abounding humanity of the Jain, the commercial genius and the responsive adaptibility of the Dravidian, and the fierce zeal and organizing energy of the Arabian Prophet, have all entered into the inner sanctuaries of the people's life and even to-day shape their thought, energy and aspiration in curious and unsuspected ways. Nations rise and fall; kings conquer and pass away in the dust; the forms of political life and social effort have their day and cease to be; religious systems and strange rituals move for a brief hour their adherents;—but in this vast process of Becoming, there are elements of permanent value, which remain our inheritance and the inheritance of our children for evermore. In the following pages an attempt is made to trace the history of a people, sincere and great in their day and to estimate, in however tentative and fragmentary a fashion, the value of their contribution to the rich and fruitful stream of South Indian Culture.

I owe a deep debt of gratitude to the Trustee of Vizianagram Samasthanam, M.R.Ry. Rao Bahadur V. T. Krishnamachariar Avl., B.A., B.L., whose zeal for true learning aud culture alone enabled me to carry on my studies,. the results of which are embodied in this little volume and to our revered Principal M.R.Ry. Y. Narashimham Pantulu Garu, M.A., F.M.U., whose inspiration and love of research, encouraged me at every step in my undertaking. If I have, therefore, failed in my purpose to throw light on one of the sequestered corners of South Indian History and trace the early history of one of the innumerable religious sects of India—that, alas! now occupy an obscure position, it is not due to lack of support, financial or otherwise, on the part of the College management.

To my readers I have to offer a word of explanation. These "Studies" do not, by any means, pretend to be a final or full account of the Jains in South India. The time is not yet when such a work can be confidently undertaken. If the Brahmi and cave inscriptions of the Madura and Ramnad Districts can be correctly and incontrovertibly interpreted, if milestones in the long history of Tamil literature, admittedly the oldest of the Dravidian literatures, can be firmly planted and if the vague mass of tradition about the existence and activities of the famous Madura Academy, known as the Tamil Sangam, can be proved to be true and its date fixed even approximately beyond doubt or controversy, one may claim to be proceeding on the right road towards true historical reconstruction. As it is, the information available on the subject of these " Studies " is sketchy and meagre and I have done my best to whet the desire of scholars for further research on this and kindred topics.

I have to thank my brother Mr. M. S. Sundara Rajan of the Income-tax Office, Madras. for invaluable help rendered in preparing the volume for the press.

MAHARAJA'S COLLEGE,
VIZIANAGRAM,
August 1922.

M. S. RAMASWAMI.

TABLE OF CONTENTS.

PART I.

SOUTH INDIAN JAINISM.

CHAPTER I.

EARLY HISTORY OF THE JAIN SECT.

Sources of Information.

No topic of ancient South Indian History is more interesting than the origin and development of the Jains who, in times past, profoundly influenced the political, religious and literary institutions of South India. It has sometimes been thought that a connected account of the Jains could never be written. But the patient and laborious researches of great oriental scholars such as Burnell, Bühler, Burgess, Hœrnle, Jacobi, Mackenzie and Wilson, to mention only a few of them, have placed in the hands of the student of the Ancient History of India enough materials to construct a true and authentic account of the early Jain sect. Of special value and importance to us are the elaborate articles and authentic notices of the Jains from the pen of eminent scholars like Colebrooke, Weber and Bühler. The student of Jain history is especially indebted to Lewis Rice whose splendid services in the field of epigraphy can never be over-estimated. The *Epigraphia Carnatica* and many other valuable historical documents brought to light by the Epigraphical Department of the Mysore State are veritable mines of historical information. But, in accepting the conclusions arrived at by some of these eminent scholars, considerable caution has to be exercised. At the time when they wrote and formulated their opinions, epigraphy was in its infancy. Since then, new facts have been unearthed : the science of epigraphy itself has progressed by leaps and bounds : theories once considered indisputable have to be considerably modified. The vernaculars of the country, again, presented a serious obstacle to European scholars, who, it must be admitted, are not all Beschis and Popes, in arriving at a correct estimate of some aspects of South Indian history. Specially true is the statement with reference to the history and influence of the Jains, materials for which lie deeply embedded in the vernaculars of the country—Tamil, Telugu and Canarese.

Origin of Jainism.

In spite of the fact that a good deal of information is available about the Jains, scholars are still sceptical and speak with caution of the origin of the Jain sect. Almost all oriental scholars, with a few exceptions, had maintained, and some of them still continue to maintain, that Jainism was an offshoot of Buddhism. Certain coincidences in minute details between the lives of the Buddha and Mahāvīra led scholars to believe that Jain records were untrustworthy and that the Jain sect had no early and separate existence. In fact a rich crop of literature has grown round this knotty point and the whole of the introduction of the *Acharanga Sutras* by Hermann Jacobi has been written with a view to remove the deep-rooted prejudice in the minds of European scholars, the prejudice that, because the two sects have so much in common, one should have branched off from the other. It is beyond the scope and aim of this work to enter into an examination of the various theories propounded in connection with the origin of Jainism. But we shall briefly indicate the opinions arrived at by Jacobi to whose researches, enthusiastically assisted by Drs. Bühler and Hœrnle, Jainism owes its rehabilitation as one of the earliest of home religions in India. We may consider Prof. Weber and Prof. Lassen as representing those who attacked the theory of the higher antiquity of the Jain sect, mainly on the ground of certain important coincidences in the tradition of either sect regarding its founder.[1]

Views of Weber and Lassen examined.

Prof. Weber in his learned treatise (*Indische Studien* XVI, 26) writes that, even admitting that the Buddha and Mahāvīra were contemporaries, he still regards the Jains "merely as one of the oldest sects of Buddhism." Relying too much on "the tradition of the origin of its founder having made use of another person than Buddha Sakhyamuni," he boldly suggests "that the Jainas had intentionally disowned Buddha," the animosity of the sect being so great as to drive them out of the pale of Buddhism. But the chief argument in support of his theory rests on the coincidences which are numerous and important in the traditions of the sects regarding their founders. Prof. Lassen[2] also adheres to

[1] Jacobi, Introduction to *Jaina Sutras*, pp. xvii & xix.

[2] *Indische alterthumskunde* IV, p. 763 Slq.

the same argument and adduces four points of coincidence which, he thinks, would establish the priority of Buddhism. That both the sects applied the same titles or epithets to their prophets, that both the sects worshipped mortal men like gods and erected statues to them in their temples, that both the sects laid stress on *Ahimsa* (not killing living beings), that the five vows of the Jains and the precepts of the Buddhas nearly coincide, these were the main points relied upon by Prof. Lassen to prove that Jainism must have branched off from Buddhism. Both Drs. Hoernle and Jacobi have, in a convincing manner, proved the unsoundness of this view. It has been established beyond doubt that neither sect can lay any claim to originality, regarding its moral code. "The Brahmanic ascetic was their (orders) model from which they borrowed many important practices and institutions of ascetic life."[1] In fact both Jainism and Buddhism were not religions at all in the strict sense of the word.[2] They were simply monastic organisations, orders of begging fraternities, somewhat similar to the Dominicans and Franciscans in medieval Europe, established at the end of the sixth and the beginning of the fifth century B.C., a period of great religious activity in northern India. This period is characterised by the springing up of various monastic orders, the most important of

The fifth century B.C., a period of spiritual revolt.

[1] For this and other interesting information, *vide* the inspiring address of Dr. Hoernle delivered in 1898 as President of the Asiatic Society of Bengal.

[2] Introduction to *Acharanga Sutras*, p. 24.

them being Jainism, Buddhism and a quite distinct order of monks, the Ajivakas, established by one Gosala, sometime disciple of Mahāvīra. After an existence of some centuries, the order of Ajivakas suffered a total decay in the confusion of religious ideas which then pervaded the country. This institution of monasticism was nothing new to the religious practices of the day. Already the religion of the Hindus, especially the Brahmins, had ordained that every man should spend his life in four successive stages called, *Asramas*. The first stage was that of a *Brahmachari* or a religious student, the second of a *Grahasta* or a householder, the third of retirement from active life and the last that of a mendicant or *Sanyasi*. It however became the custom for a Brahmin, as a rule, to pass through four, a nobleman through three, a citizen through two and a sudra through one, of the four *Asramas*.[1] This tendency of the Brahmin to limit the entry into the stage of a religious mendicant to those belonging to the Brahminic caste, led to the formation of non-Brahminic orders which, though originally intended for the Kshatriyas, were ultimately thrown open to all castes. Thus Dr. Hoernle[2]:—"It is easy to understand that these non-Brahminic orders would not be looked upon by the *Sanyasins* as quite their equals, even when they were quite as orthodox as themselves and, on the other hand, that this treatment by the Brahminic ascetics would beget in their

Brahmin exclusiveness.

[1] Maxmuller, *The Hibbert Lectures*, p. 343.

[2] Hoernle, *Presidential Address*, Asiatic Society of Bengal, 1898.

rivals a tendency to dissent and even to opposition. Thus the Buddhists and the Jains were not only led to discard the performance of religious ceremonies which was also done by the Brahminic mendicants, but to go further and even discontinue the reading of the Vedas. It was this latter practice which really forced them outside the pale of Brahminism. The still very prevalent notion that Buddhism and Jainism were reformatory movements and that more especially they represented a revolt against the tyranny of caste is quite erroneous. They were only a protest against the caste exclusiveness of the Brahminic ascetics. But, caste as such, and as existing outside their orders was fully acknowledged by them. Even inside their orders, admission, though professedly open to all, was practically limited to the higher castes. It is also significant for the attitude of these orders to the Brahminic institutions of the country, that though in spiritual matters their so-called lay adherents were bound to their guidance, yet with regard to ceremonies such as those of birth, marriage and death they had to look for service to their old Brahminic priests. The Buddhist or Jain monk functionated as the spiritual director to their respective lay communities but the Brahmins were their priests."

Views of M. Barth criticised by Jacobi.

This theory has also received considerable support at the hands of Prof. Maxmuller.[1] Prof. Bühler in the *Bōdhāyana Sūtra* and Prof.

[1] *Hiblert Lectures*, p. 351.

Kern in his *History of Buddhism* have stated a similar opinion. It has, however, been attacked by M. Barth who doubts the authenticity of Jain records and literature which were not reduced to writing till the fifth century A.D. The Jains had not, for many centuries, Barth says, become distinct from the numerous groups of ascetics who had only a sort of floating existence. Therefore they must have been careless in handing down their sacred lore. Jacobi refuted this assumption by saying that the small sect of the Jains, like the Jews and Parsis, carefully preserved their original tenets : that, far from having only vague recollections of their traditions and beliefs, they denounced, as founders of schisms, those who differed from the bulk of the faithful even in the minutest detail.[1] The division of the Jains, into two sects, the Digambaras and the Svētāmbaras, about which mention will be made later on, is a point in illustration.

Not only Jacobi [2] but other scholars also believed that Jainism, far from being an offshoot of Buddhism, might have been the earliest of home religions of India. The simplicity of devotion and the homely prayer of the Jain without the intervention of a Brahmin would certainly add to the strength of the theory so rightly upheld by Jacobi.[3] Another important testimony is that of the eminent oriental scholar Mr. Thomas who, in his article *Jainism or The*

[1] Introduction to *Acharanga Sutras*, p. 36.

[2] See Note 1, p. 154.

[3] *The Journal of the Royal Asiatic Society*, Vol. XV, pp. 376 and 377.

Early Faith of Asoka, inclines to the same belief.[1] The views of the various scholars and their respective positions in regard to this matter have thus been ably set forth by Bühler.[2]

Bühler's summary of scholars' opinions.

" Apart from the ill-supported supposition of Colebrooke, Stevenson and Thomas, according to which Buddha was a disloyal disciple of the founder of the Jainas, there is the view held by H. H. Wilson, A. Weber, and Lassen, and generally accepted till twenty-five years ago,that the Jainas are an old sect of the Buddhists. This was based, on the one hand, upon the resemblance of the Jaina doctrines, writings, and traditions to those of the Buddhists, on the other, on the fact that the canonical works of the Jainas shew a more modern dialect than those of the Buddhists, and that authentic historical proofs of their early existence are wanting. I was myself formerly persuaded of the correctness of this view and even thought I recognised the Jainas in the Buddhist school of the Sammatīya. On a more particular examination of Jaina literature, to which I was forced on account of the collection undertaken for the English Government in the seventies, I found that the Jainas had changed their name and were always, in more ancient times, called Nigrantha or Nigantha. The observation that the Buddhists recognise the Nigantha and relate of their head and founder, that he was a rival

[1] *The Journal of the Royal Asiatic Society*, Vol. IX, (New Series) Art 8.

[2] Bühler's *Indian Sect of the Jainas* will ever remain a standard authority on the early history of North Indian Jainism.

of Buddha's and died at Pāvā where the last Tīrthakara is said to have attained Nirvāna, caused me to accept the view that the Jainas and the Buddhists sprang from the same religious movement. My supposition was confirmed by Jacobi, who reached the like view by another course, independently of mine (see *Zeitschrift der Deutsch Morg. Ges.* Bd. XXXV, S. 669. Note 1), pointing out that the last Tīrthakara in the Jaina canon bears the same name as among the Buddhists. Since the publication of our results in the *Ind. Ant.* Vol. VII, p. 143, and in Jacobi's introduction to his edition of the Kalpasūtra, which have been further verified by Jacobi with great penetration, views on this question have been divided. Oldenberg, Kern, Hoernle, and others have accepted this view without hesitation, while A. Weber (*Indische Studien* Bd. XVI, S. 240) and Barth (*Revue de l' Histoire des Religions,* tom. III, p. 90) keep to their former standpoint. The latter do not trust the Jaina tradition and believe it probable that the statements in the same are falsified. There are certainly great difficulties in the way of accepting such a position especially the improbability that the Buddhists should have forgotten the fact of the defection of their hated enemy. Meanwhile this is not absolutely impossible as the oldest preserved Jaina canon had its first authentic edition only in the fifth or sixth century of our era, and as yet the proof is wanting that the Jainas, in ancient times, possessed a fixed tradition. The belief that I am able to insert this missing link in the chain of argument and the hope of removing the doubts of my two honoured friends has caused me to attempt a connected statement of the whole question although this necessitates the repetition of much that has already been said, and is in the first part almost entirely a recapitulation of the results of Jacobi's researches."

Jainism not an offshoot of Buddhism.

From the above summary of the opinions of scholars, it is clear that Jainism was not only distinct and separate from Buddhism, but that it had an earlier existence. If so, what was the position of Mahāvīra ? That he could not have been the founder of the faith is evident. He is therefore to be considered as a *reformer* of the Jain faith.

As a matter of fact, the traditions of Mahāvīra's own sect speak of him as one who from the beginning had followed a religion established long ago. This position is in perfect accord with Jain theology according to which Mahāvīra Vardhamāna is the twenty-fourth and the last Tirthankara, twenty-three Tirthankaras having preceded him. His immediate predecessor was Parsvanāth. He was born in 877 B.C. and is supposed to have reached *Moksha* in the hundredth year of his age in 777 B.C. Thus Parsvanāth seems to have better claims to the title of "the founder of Jainism" and only two centuries have intervened between the death of the founder of the Jain Church and the rise of its reformer. But here stops the credible element in the canonical history of the Jains. For, Parsvanāth's predecessor, Arishtanemi, is stated to have died 84,000 years before Mahāvīra's *Nirvāna*. We are here concerned only with Mahāvīra from whom the real history of the Jain Church commences. It is from Mahāvīra that we trace those illustrious lines of preachers and *gurus* who played an important part in moulding the religious and political life of many ancient Hindu states.

Mahāvīra: his life and career.

The son of the chief of the Natha clan of the Kshatriyas (Nātaputta), Mahāvīra Vardhamāna was like the Buddha, of high aristocratic descent, his father Siddarta being the head of a Kshatriya clan and the governing king of an oligarchic republic consisting of Visali, Kundaggama and Vaniyaggama. Born in or about 599 B.C., he entered the spiritual career at the age of thirty; and addressing himself mainly to mombers of the aristocracy, joined the order of Parsvanāth.

The observances of this order did not seem to have satisfied Mahāvīra's notions of stringency, one of the cardinal points of which, we are told, was absolute nudity.[1] He therefore remained only for one year within the order of Parsvanāth and then separated from it. Discarding then completely his clothes, he wandered about for a period of twelve years through the country of

[1] This seems to be the Svētāmbara view.

North and South Bihar, Allahabad, visiting the cities of Kausāmbī and Rājagriha.[1] The last thirty years of his life were spent in teaching his religious system and organising his order of societies which were patronised chiefly by those princes with whom he was related through his mother, the kings of Videha, Magadha and Anga. In the towns and villages of these parts he spent almost the whole period of his ministry though he extended his travels as far north as Sravasti near the Nepalese frontier and as far south as the Parsvanāth hill. It is important to note that the area of his ministry practically coincides with that of his late contemporary, the Buddha. During the last days of his life, he was able to gain large numbers of adherents in the course of his perigrinations. It was then that he was acknowledged to be a *Jina* or *Kevalīn*. It is this title of ' Jina ' from which the names, Jains and Jainism, are derived, and his early connection with the order of Parsvanāth accounts for the fact that the latter saint is reckoned as the immediate predecessor of Mahāvīra. Mahāvīra's death took place in the seventy-second year of his life in the small town of Pāvā in the Patna district. Modern research has assigned 527 B.C.[2] as the date of his *Nirvāna*.

[1] *Wilson's Works*, Vol. I, p. 303.

[2] Thus Jacobi in Hastings' *Encyclopædia of Religion and Ethics* (p. 467): "This event (Mahāvīra's Nirvāna) took place, as stated above, some years before Buddha's death, and may, therefore, be placed about 480 B.C. The Svētāmbaras, however, place the Nirvāna of Mahāvīra, which is the initial point of their era, 470 years before the beginning of the Vikrama era, or in 527 B.C. The Digambaras place the same event 18 years later. In the Preface to his edition of the

Mahāvīra's title as the reformer of the Jain Church consists in the fact that he was able to bring the entire order of Parsvanāth to his way of thinking especially in the matter of wearing clothes. As has been stated already, Mahāvīra stood for complete nudity.[1]

Early North Indian Jainism; its development.

Let us next trace the development of this new order of Nigrantha monks founded by Mahāvīra Vårdhamāna. From the statement of the various Buddhistic chronicles, we learn that during the first century after the death of the Buddha the Jains were prominent in various places in the north. An important piece of information is conveyed to us by Hiuen Tsang, the Chinese traveller who visited India in the seventh century A.D. In his *Memoirs* are to be found extracts from the ancient annals of Magadha. One such extract relating to the great monastery of Nālandā, the high school of Buddhism in Eastern India which was founded shortly after the Buddha's death, mentions that a Nigrantha who was an astrologer, had prophesied the great success of the new building.[2] This shows that Jainism was then prevalent in the kingdom of Magadha. The next important evidence of the development of Jainism was the famous Asoka Edict.[3] " My

Parisista Parvan (*Bibl. Ind.*, Calcutta, 1891), p. 4ff., the present writer criticizes the Svētāmbara tradition, and, by combining the Jain date of Chandragupta's accession to the throne in 155 after the Nirvāna with the historical date of the same event in 321 or 322 B.C., arrives at 476 or 477 B.C. as the probable date of Mahāvīra's Nirvāna."

[1] According to the Digambaras all the twenty-four Tirthankaras advocated nudity; the Svētāmbaras hold that only Mahāvīra insisted upon it in his time.

[2] Turner, *Mahāvamsa*, pp. 66-67 and pp. 203-206.

[3] *Pillar Edict* No. VII, 2nd Part. See also Bühler's *The Indian Sect of the Jainas*, pp. 37 and 39.

superintendents", says Asoka, "are occupied with various charitable matters, they are also engaged with all sects of ascetics and householders. I have so arranged that they will also be occupied with the affairs of the Samgha. Likewise I have arranged that they will be occupied with the Ajivika Brahmans. I have arranged it that they will also be occupied with the Nigantha." Thus, during the time of Asoka the Jains who in earlier records are always known as Nigranthas or Niganthas, were deemed worthy and influential enough to be specially mentioned in Asoka's Edicts. The next great progress that was made by Jainism was in the south-eastern part of its original home. The famous Kharavēla inscription of the second century B.C. for the meaning of which we are specially indebted to Dr. Baghavan Lal Indraji, testifies to the advance of Jainism as far as Kalinga. In fact, after the missionary zeal displayed by Asoka in the cause of Buddhism, the centre of Jainism had shifted from Magadha to Kalinga where the faith prevailed, down to the time of Hiuen Tsang.[1] At the same time, the equally famous Mathura inscriptions of the II century A.D. reveal the fact that Mathura was one of the chief centres of the Jain religion long before the I century A.D. Thus, for nearly five centuries after the death of Mahāvīra, Jainism was making rapid progress in the various parts of Upper India. Interesting as it must be

[1] Beal, *Life of Hiuen-Tsang*, Vol. II.

to trace the main lines of development of North Indian Jainism, materials are wanting to fill the lacunæ. It is not our purpose here to deal with North Indian Jainism. We may, therefore, close this outline with the remark that, with the rise of Buddhism during the early Asokan period and the progress of Brahminism in the early centuries of the Christian era, Jainism found it hard to maintain itself in the north and showed rapid signs of decay after the seventh century.

After the death of Mahāvīra, our interest and attention are directed to his disciples who carried aloft the torch of Jain culture far and wide. He had altogether eleven disciples who remained faithful to him and who are said to have instructed among them 4,200 *Munis*. Of them two deserve special mention, Sudharman[1] who, however, died before his master, and Gautama who survived his master but a month; these with Jambusvāmi, the pupil of Sudharman, formed the three *Kevalīs* or possessors of true wisdom. Mention has next to be made of the six teachers who followed in the wake of the *Kevalīs*, the *Sruta Kevalīs* or hearers of the first masters, who in their turn, were followed by seven others, *Dasapūrvis*, who were so called from having been taught the work so named.[2] The names of the *Sruta Kevalīs* as mentioned in the inscriptions are Vishnu, Nandimitra, Aparājita,

The disciples of Mahāvīra.

[1] Hoernle would have us suppose that Sudharman survived his master and that it was through him that Jainism has been continued to the present day.

[2] *Wilson's Works*, Vol. I, p. 236.

Govardhana, Stulabhadra and Bhadrabāhu. The last mentioned *Sruta Kevalī* is of more immediate interest to us as the sage who led a great Jain migration to the south, and who was thus responsible for the spread of Jainism in the Tamil and Canarese countries. We shall, in the next chapter, examine the importance to South Indian religious history of the advent of this sage into the Mysore country.

CHAPTER II.

THE JAIN MIGRATION TO THE SOUTH.

Bhadrabāhu: his career.

Bhadrabāhu, the last *Sruta Kevalī*, is, from the view point of Jain history, a most important figure. Born of a Brahmin priest, the saint was destined to play a great part in the religious history of India. His father was a Brahmin, Sōmasarma by name. From an inspection of the child's horoscope, the father perceived that he would become a great upholder of the Jain faith and so named him Bhadrabāhu. The child was, in due course, brought up in the Jain faith in the house of Akshashrāvaka. Through the instructions of this Svāmi and other *Sruta Kevalīs*, the boy soon acquired a knowledge of the four great branches of learning, *Yogini*, *Sangini*, *Prajnyani* and *Prajlatkena* of the *Veda*, of the four *Anuyoga* of grammar, and the fourteen sciences. Eventually, with the consent of his parents, he took the *Dīksha* and by the practice of *Jnāna*, *Dhyāna*, *Tapas* and *Samyama*, became an *Acharya*. It was this *Acharya* that, during the days of Chandragupta Maurya, led a great migration to South India, so important and fruitful of consequences. The main incidents regarding the advent of this Jain sage into Mysore are graphically narrated in Sravana Belgola Inscription No. 1. The story is told that Bhadrabāhusvāmi " who by virtue of severe penance had acquired the essence of knowledge, having, by his power of discerning the past, present and future, foretold in Ujjain, a period of twelve years of dire calamity and famine, the whole of the Sangha living in the northern regions took their way to the south." The Jain traditions of the country not only make mention of this fact but also give a graphic account of the meeting of Bhadrabāhu and Chandragupta Maurya in the court of the latter at Pātaliputra.[1] Having had during the previous night sixteen dreams, Chandragupta communicated them to Bhadrabāhu. The last of the dreams was of the approach of a twelve-headed serpent which Bhadrābābu interpreted to mean the approach of twelve years of dire calamity and famine. As foretold by him, a terrible famine broke out in the country. The Mauryan emperor, abdicating his throne in favour of his son Simhasēna, took *Dīksha* and joined Bhadrabāhu who, collecting a body of twelve thousand disciples, started on a grand exodus towards the south. In their march southward, the *Sruta Kevalī* had a strange perception that he would die and at once ordered a halt on "the mountain of a populous country completely filled with the increase of people, money, gold, grain, cow, buffaloes and goats, called Katavapra." He then gave *Upadēsa* to one Visākhamuni and entrusted the disciples to his care, sending them on under his guidance further south to the Chola, Pandya and other countries. Chandragupta sought special permission to stay with Bhadrabāhu, which was granted. Very soon, the *Sruta Kevalī* died and

The Jain migration.

[1] The *Rājāvalikathe*, a compendium of Jain history, legends and chronology, compiled in the 19th century by Dēva Chandra of the Jain establishment at Meleyur for a lady of the Mysore Royal family, furnishes a good deal of information regarding early Jain history.

the funeral rites were performed by Chandragupta Maurya. Such is the legendary account of the advent of the Jain sage into the south. There is here no element of improbability and yet scholars have doubted not merely the traditions prevailing in the country, but the very inscriptions at Sravana Belgola that give us a complete picture of the whole story.

That Chandragupta, the Mauryan king, was a Jain and attended on Bhadrabāhu during his last days and died twelve years after, doing penance on the Chandragiri hill, may be taken as historical facts. Evidence in favour of such a theory is overwhelming. We know that scarcity due to drought or floods, is frequently mentioned in *Jātaka Stories.* Sometimes the famine extended over the whole kingdom but, more often than not, it was confined to small tracts. Megasthenes' testimony as to the immunity of India from famine is well known, but his statement perhaps refers to a general scarcity.[1] There is, therefore, absolutely no reason to discredit the story of a twelve years' famine. We shall next consider whether Chandragupta was a Jain. Dr. Fleet has persistently maintained that the Chandragupta referred to in the tradition as well as in the inscription was one Gupti-gupta, a name which however does not occur in any of the inscriptions. The Sravana Belgola inscriptions are, no doubt, late in origin; yet there is no reason to doubt their authenticity

Was Chandragupta a Jain?

[1] *The Journal of the Royal Asiatic Society* 1901 Vol., p. 861.

and accuracy. Lewis Rice was the first to discover these inscriptions and render them easily accessible to scholars. His view that Chandragupta was a Jain and that he came south was strongly supported by eminent scholars like Mr. Thomas. In the course of his article, '*Jainism or the Early Faith of Asoka*', he says[1], "that Chandragupta was a member of the Jain community is taken by the writers as a matter of course and treated as a known fact which needed neither argument nor demonstration. The documentary evidence to this effect is of comparatively early date and apparently absolved from suspicion by the omission from their lists of the name of Asoka, a far more powerful monarch than his grandfather, and one whom they would reasonably have claimed as a potent upholder of their faith, had he not become a pervert. The testimony of Megasthenes would likewise seem to imply that Chandragupta submitted to the devotional teaching of the Sermanas as opposed to the doctrine of the Brahmins." Prof. Kern, the great authority on Buddhist Scriptures, has to admit that nothing of a Buddhistic spirit can be discovered in the state policy of Asoka.[2] "His ordinances concerning the sparing of life agree much more closely with the ideas of the heretical Jains than those of the Buddhists." Thus there is a general consensus of opinion among scholars that Chandragupta was a Jain.

[1] *The Journal of the Royal Asiatic Society*, Vol. IX, (New Series) Article 8.

[2] *Indian Antiquary*, Vol.V, p. 275

The Legend about Chandragupta.

The legend that Chandragupta abdicated his throne and died a Jain ascetic at Sravana Belgola has been discredited by Dr. Fleet.[1] Apparently the late Dr. V. A. Smith,[2] in his first edition of the *Early History of India,* supported him. Referring to the death of Chandragupta, Smith himself says that Chandragupta ascended the throne at an early age and, inasmuch as he reigned only twenty-four years, he must have died before he was fifty years of age. Thus there is an air of uncertainty about the time of his death. Historians do not tell us how he met with his death. If he had died in the battle-field or in the prime of life, mention would have been made of the fact. To discredit the Sravana Belgola inscriptions discovered by Lewis Rice is to discredit the whole tradition and the legendary account of the Jains enshrined in Rājāvalikathe, and it is highly hazardous for the historian to go so far. Are we then wrong in believing with Lewis Rice that Chandragupta who had taken a Jain vow retired with the great Bhadrabāhu to the Chandragiri hill ?

To sum up, Bhadrabāhu, the last *Sruta Kevalī,* led a great Jain migration from the north to

[1] *Epigraphia Indica,* Vol. III, p. 171, and *Indian Antiquary,* Vol. XXI, p. 156.

[2] V. A. Smith, *Early History of India,* First Edn., p. 106. He has, however, changed his view as can be seen from the following extract from the recent edition of the same book, p. 146. "In the second edition of the book I rejected the tradition and dismissed the tale as 'imaginary history'; but, on reconsideration of the whole evidence and the objections urged against the credibility of the story, I am now disposed to believe that the tradition probably is true in its main outline and that Chandragupta really abdicated and became a Jain ascetic. * * * Nevertheless, my present impression is that the tradition has a solid foundation on fact."

the south. After staying some time at Chandragiri hill, he died there. Chandragupta, the founder of the Mauryaṇ greatness, himself a Jain, proceeded to the same place with his *Acharya* and, after surviving him twelve years, died there.

The death of Bhadrabāhu took place, according to the Digambaras, 162 years after Vardhamāna or, according to Svētāmbaras, 170 years after Vardhamāna,[1] which also is the date arrived at by Jacobi and that is 297 B.C.

This fact of the Jain migration is important, as it furnishes us the starting point for an account of the Jains in the south, as otherwise, we would be left in the dark as to the cause and course of the Jain migration. Dr. Leumann says that this migration of the Jains to the south is the initial fact of the Digambara tradition. It is from this epoch that the Jain community which was undivided before separated into two sects, the Digambaras and the Svētāmbaras.[2] As this is one of the important points in the early history of Jains, we shall briefly notice it.

The Jain Church: its schisms.

The history of the Jain Church is full of references to the various schisms that had taken place from time to time. According to Svētāmbaras, there were eight schisms, the first of which was originated by Mahāvīra's son-in-law, Jamali, and the last, occurring 609 years after the death of Vardhamāna (83 A.D.), gave rise to

[1] *The Sacred Books of the East*, Vol. XXII, p. xliii.

[2] *Indian Antiquary*, Vol. XXI, pp. 59 and 60.

the Digambara sect. Of the earlier schisms, the Digambaras do not seem to know anything. But they say that under Bhadrabāhu rose the sect of Ardhaphālakas which in 80 A.D. developed into the Svētāmbara sect. Writing of this schism, Jacobi says[1], " It is probable that the separation of the sections of the Jain Church took place gradually, an individual development going on in both groups, living at great distance from one another and that they became aware of their mutual difference about the end of the 1st cent. A.D." The first great schism probably took place during the time of Mahāvīra who organised his own order of monks distinct from that of Parsvanāth. This is evident from the fact that even to-day there are Jains who trace their spiritual descent from Parsvanāth and not from Mahāvīra. The same schism reappears in a more elaborate form and in a more acute manner during the time of Bhadrabāhu. As has been pointed out by Dr. Hoernle, the essential point of difference between the order of Parsvanāth and that of Mahāvīra was on the question of wearing a modicum of clothes. The final separation took place about the year 82 A.D. This involved the rejection by one sect of the canonical literature of the other.

Dr. Hoernle on the schisms.

The whole circumstance has thus been clearly indicated by Dr. Hoernle. " In the second century after Mahāvīra's death, about 310 B.C., a very severe famine lasting twelve years took

[1] Hastings, *Encyclopædia of Religion and Ethics*, Vol. VII, pp. 465 & 466.

place in the country of Magadha, the modern Bihar, beyond which, as yet, the Jain order does not seem to have spread. At that time Chandragupta, of the Mauryan dynasty, was king of the country and Bhadrabāhu was the head of the still undivided Jain community. Under the pressure of the famine, Bhadrabāhu with a portion of his people emigrated into the Karnātaka or Canarese country in the south of India. Over the other portion that remained in Magadha, Stulabhadra assumed the headship. Towards the end of the famine, during the absence of Bhadrabāhu, a council assembled at Pātaliputra, the modern Patna, and this council collected the Jain sacred books, consisting of the 11 angas and the 14 pūrvas, which latter are collectively called the 12th anga. The troubles that arose during the period of famine produced also a change in the practice of the Jains. The rule regarding the dress of the monks had been that they should ordinarily go altogether naked, though the wearing of certain clothes appears to have been allowed to the weaker members of the order. Those monks that remained behind felt constrained by the exigencies of the time to abandon the rule of nakedness and to adopt the white dress. On the other hand, those who out of religious zeal chose to exile themselves rather than admit of a change of the rule of nakedness made that rule compulsory on all the members of their portion of the order. When on the restitution of peace and plenty, the exiles returned to their country, the divergence of practice which had in the meantime fully established itself between the two parties made itself too markedly felt to be overlooked. The returned exiles refused to hold fellowship any longer with the (in their opinion) peccant portion that had remained at home. Thus the foundation was laid of the division between the two sections, the Digambaras and Svētāmbaras."

Svētāmbara sub-sects.

Now each of these main divisions is subdivided into different minor sects, according to the difference in acknowledging or interpreting the religious texts. The principal divisions of the Svētāmbara sect are[1] :—

(1) Pujera, who were thorough worshippers.

(2) Dhundias, who although they recognise the images of Tirthankaras, yet do not indulge in worshipping with formal rites and formulas.

(3) Terapanthis, who do not believe in images or their worship in any form whatever.

Digambara sub-sects.

The Digambaras, in their turn, are also subdivided into various sects. The most important of them are :—

(1) Bispanthi, who allow worship to a certain extent.

(2) Terapanthi, who acknowledge images but do not allow any sort of worship.

[1] For a detailed account of the Jain Gachchhas *vide* Nahar and Ghosh, *An Epitome of Jainism*, Ch. XXXVI.

(3) Samaiyapanthi, who do away entirely with image worship and who merely acknowledge the sanctity of the sacred books which alone they worship.

(4) Gumanpanthi, an eighteenth century sect, calling itself from its founder Gumanpam.

(5) Totapanthi.

The Digambara Church is further divided into four Sangas or monastic orders :—

(1) Nandi Sanga, (2) Sena Sanga, (3) Deva Sanga and (4) Simha Sanga.

Ganas and Gachchhas.

Each of these Sangas was still further divided into Ganas, such as the Punnata, Balathkara, Kotiya. Each of these, again, was sub-divided into Gachchhas, such as Pushtaka, Sarasvati and others.

The Svētāmbaras are generally classified further into 84 Gatchas or divisions. Most of these Gatchas are now extinct.

Digambaras and Svētāmbaras: points of difference.

So far as the main division is concerned, there is very little difference in the essentials of doctrine between the Svētāmbaras and the Digambaras. For example, the most authoritative book of the Digambaras, *Tattvārthādhigama Sūtra* by Umāsvāmi, is one of the standard books also of the Svētāmbaras. The Digambaras, however, might be said to differ from the Svētāmbaras in the following points[1] :—

[1] Hastings, *Encyclopædia of Religion and Ethics*.

(1) According to the Digambaras, *Kevalīns* are perfect saints, such as the Tirthankaras who live without food.

(2) The embryo of Mahāvīra was not removed from the womb of Dēvānanda to that of Trisala, as the Svētāmbaras contend.

(3) The Digambaras believe that a monk who owns any property, *i.e.*, wears clothes, cannot reach *Nirvāna*.

(4) No woman can reach *Nirvāna*.

(5) The Digambaras disowned the canonical books of the Svētāmbaras, as has already been pointed out by Dr. Hoernle.

Chandragupta's successors.

The Jain heirarchy and succession of *Gurus* after Chandragupta can be ascertained from Sravana Belgola Inscriptions Nos. 47, 145, 108 and 54. First comes Yatindra Kunda[1], a great Jain *Guru*, "who, in order to show that both within and without he could not be assisted by *Rajas*, moved about leaving a space of four inches between himself and the earth under his feet." Umāsvāmi,[2] the compiler of *Tattvārtha Sūtra*, Griddhrapinchha, and his disciple Balākapinchha follow. Then comes Samantabhadra,[3] 'ever fortunate', "whose discourse lights up the palace of the three worlds filled with the all meaning Syadvada." This Samantabhadra was

[1] Sravana Belgola Inscription, No. 105.

[2] From a paper read by Mr. K. B. Pathak, *vide* the *Journal of the Bombay Branch of the Royal Asiatic Society*, Vol. XVIII, p.213.

[3] Sravana Belgola Inscription, No. 105.

the first of a series of celebrated Digambara writers who acquired considerable predominance, in the early Rāshtrakūta period. Jain tradition assigns him Saka 60 or 138 A.D.[1] Sravana Belgola Inscription No. 44 records some interesting accounts of Samantabhadra's activities. "At first, in the town of Pātaliputra,[2] was the drum beaten by me.[3] Afterwards in the Malava, Sindu and Thaka country,[4] in the far off city of Kāñchi[5], arrived at Karhātaka[6], strong in warriors, great in learning, small in extent, I roam about. Oh! King: like a tiger in sport!" From the above statement of Samantabhadra, it is evident that he was a great Jain missionary who tried to spread far and wide Jaina doctrines and morals and that he met with no opposition from other sects wherever he went. Samantabhadra's appearance in South India marks an epoch not only in the annals of Digambara tradition, but also in the history of Sanskrit literature.[7] He is also the author of an important Jain work *Apta Mimamsa*, the most authoritative exposition of the Syādvāda doctrine. After Samantabhadra a large number of Jain *Munis* took up the work of proselytism. The more important of them

[1] Dr. Bhandarkar's *Report on the Search of the Sanskrit* MSS. in 1883 & 1884, p. 320.

[2] Patna on the Ganges.

[3] To beat a drum fixed in a central place in the city is a peculiar form of challenge and invitation extended to religious disputants.

[4] Cunningham in his *Ancient Geography* identifies Thaka country with the Punjab.

[5] The *Rājāvalikathe* mentions Samantabhadra as having gone to Kāñchi a number of times.

[6] Kolhapur in South Mahratta country.

[7] *Bombay Gazetteer*, Vol. I, part 2, p. 406.

have contributed much for the uplift of the Jain world in literature and secular affairs. There was, for example, Simhānandi, the Jain sage, who, according to tradition, founded the state of Gangavādi.[1] Other names are those of Pūjyapāda, the author of the incomparable grammar, *Jinēndra Vyākarana*, and of Akalanka who, in 788 A.D., is believed to have confuted the Buddhists at the court of Himasītala in Kāñchi, and thereby procured the expulsion of the Buddhists from South India. An account of some of these Jain missionaries will, no doubt, be interesting but we cannot pursue the subject further.

[1] See Chapter VII, *The Jains in the Deccan.*

CHAPTER III.

THE JAINS IN THE TAMIL LAND.

Paucity of materials for Jain History.

It is impossible to fix with any tolerable certainty the date of the introduction of the Jain faith into the Tamil land. Few records exist to enable us to write any consistent account of the Jains in the extreme south of India. The Rājāvalikathe, references to which have been made in the foregoing pages and the trustworthiness of which has been in more than one instance illustrated, mentions that Visākhamuni, in the course of his wanderings in the Chola and the Pandya countries, worshipped in the Jain *Chaitālyas* and preached to the Jains settled in those places. This would show that the Jains had already colonised the extreme south even before the death of Bhadrabāhu, *i.e.*, before 297 B.C. The matter rests, however, on the solitary evidence of Rājāvalikathe, and there is no other trustworthy record to show that the Jains had migrated to these places at this early period.

Evidence from Mahāvamsa.

It is common for writers of South Indian History to derive information, in order to find support for their statements, from *Mahāvamsa*. It is well known that *Mahāvamsa* was composed by Monk Mahānāma, a great literary artist, during the reign of Dhantusēna, a king of Ceylon (461—479 A.D.). Written in Pāli verse, it covers the period, 543 B.C.—301 A.D. Its value as containing authentic materials for a true history has often been doubted. Nevertheless, for our purposes, it may be pointed out that during the reign of King Pandugābhaya, the fifth in Vijaya's line, the capital was transferred to Anurādhapura (about 437 B.C.). The *Mahāvamsa* gives us a detailed description of the various buildings in the new city. Among these was a residence allotted to a Nigantha devotee named 'Giri.' In the same quarters, many Pāsandaka devotees dwelt. The king built also a temple 'for the Nigantha Kumbandha,' which was called after him. Provision was also made in the new capital for residence for 500 persons of various foreign religions and faiths.[1] If this information could be relied upon, it would mean that Jainism was introduced in the island of Ceylon, so early as the fifth century B.C. It is impossible to conceive that a purely North Indian religion could have gone to the island of Ceylon without leaving its mark in the extreme south of India, unless like Buddhism it went by sea from the north.

Brāhmī Inscriptions the only epigraphical records.

Let us next see if epigraphy aids us in fixing the date of the origin of Jainism in South India. The earliest lithic records in the Tamil country are the famous Brāhmī inscriptions discovered in the districts of Madura and Ramnad, and published a few years ago by the Government Epigraphist. These inscriptions written in the alphabet of the Asoka Edicts are assigned

[1] P. Arunachalam, *Sketches of Ceylon History*, pp. 14 & 15: see also *Mahāvamsa*, p. 49.

to the end of the third and the beginning of the second century B.C. They are found scattered in the following places :—1. Marugāltalai, 2. Anaimalai, 3. Tirupparankunram, 4. Arittapatti, 5. Kīlavalavu, 6. Karungālakkudi, 7. Muttupatti, 8. Siddharmalai, 9. Kongar-Puliyañgulam, 10. Alagarmalai, 11. Sittannavāsal. No one has succeeded in deciphering these inscriptions. Looking carefully into the characters, one finds such Tamil words as *Pāli, Madhurai, Kumattur*.[1] The identification of a few Tamil words written nevertheless in Brāhmī characters has led scholars to propound the view that these characters were perhaps in use in the Pandyan country even in that early period, and that these may have developed into the Tamil Vatteluttu just as they developed into the present Tamil, Grantha, Canarese and Telugu characters. We are not just now concerned with these questions. These records are, perhaps, Jain in character, for, not far off from the places where these inscriptions are found, we have ruins of Jain temples, with mutilated statues of Jain *Tirthankaras*, with their respective iconographic symbols such as the hooded serpent or the triple umbrella. If the date of the inscriptions is the beginning of the third century B.C., as has been conceived by specialists,[2] the inference may perhaps be made

[1] The following words can also be identified:—Nādu (நாடு,) Kāyipan (காயிபன்), Kudumbihan (குடும்பிகன்,) Pōlāliyan (போலாலையன்), Kānyan (காணியன்), Chirya (சிறிய), Challēhanai (சல்லேகனை).

[2] *Madras Epigraphical Reports* 1907, pp. 60-61. *Madras Epigraphical Reports* 1910, pp. 77-78.

that, even then, Jain sages had commenced their work of preaching the Jain doctrine to the Tamils. Other than these, there are no records that illumine the obscure history of early South Indian Jainism. It is astonishing that, for some of the brightest periods of South Indian History, neither copper-plate grants nor inscriptions on stone are available. Such inscriptions as have been published by Government epigraphists deal more largely with medieval than the early history of South India. For further information as regards early South Indian Jainism, we are therefore forced to depend mainly on the literature of the Tamils.

The literature of any country is the expression in memorable poetry and prose, of the life and character of the people inhabiting it. Tamil literature is no exception to this, and the long succession of books that make up the Tamil literature is a record of the inner life of the people, and of the hopes and beliefs of each succeeding generation. And any student who patiently examines it may glean much information for the reconstruction of South Indian History. An attempt is, therefore, made in the following pages to present, in a connected narrative, an account of the Jains based on such authentic evidence as can be gathered from Tamil literature. **Tamil literature: its value.**

The whole of the Tamil literature may roughly be divided into three periods :—1. The Sangam or the Academic period. 2. The period of Saiva **Periods of Tamil literature.**

Nāyanārs and Vaishnava Alvars. 3. The Modern period. The works published during each of these periods throw a flood of light on the life and activities of the Jains in the Tamil kingdoms. It, therefore, becomes necessary for us to examine each period separately. In this task we are assisted by the combined labours of the great Tamil scholars whose antiquarian researches have enabled us to fix some milestones in Tamil literature.

I. SANGAM PERIOD.

Sangam Age: a vexed question.

According to Tamil writers, there were three Sangams or Literary Associations :—the first, the intervening, and the last. The date and history of these Academies are to-day the subjects of keen controversy among scholars entitled to form opinions on them. The late Mr. Kanakasabhai Pillai and Prof. S. Krishnaswami Ayyangar have more or less fixed the date of the last Sangam as the second century A.D. Convincing as some of the arguments of these scholars are, it is, however, quite possible to hold different opinions in the matter of interpretation of some of the Sangam poems, from which mainly Prof. Krishnaswami Ayyangar, at any rate, has sought to establish that the Sangam existed in the second century A.D. These points are discussed in this work elsewhere and the attention of scholars to that portion is respectfully invited. It is here tentatively assumed that the II century A.D. is the period of the last Sangam.

At the same time, it must be mentioned that no progress can be made in the reconstruction of Early South Indian History, unless the vexed question of the Sangam Age is finally solved.

To Nakkīrar[1], one of the forty-nine poets of the last Sangam, we owe much of the legendary information regarding the history of the three Academies. According to him, Tolkāppiyar, the grammarian, was a member of the first and second Academies. The date of this ancient author might, therefore, give us a starting point for an account of the Jains in the south. It would appear, that during the time of the second Sangam, a great tidal wave passed over the extremity of the peninsula, as a result of which portions of the Pandyan country were submerged. Dim traditions of this occurrence are known to the third Sangam.[2] Mention is made of it in *Silappadikāram* also.[3] From these two sources, we learn that that portion of the Pandyan country which was submerged was the land between the two rivers

Fact and Tradition, about the two Sangams.

[1] *Iraiyanār Kalaviyal.*

[2] "மலிதிரை யூர்ந்துதன் மண்கடல் வௌவலின்
மெலிவின்றி மேற்சென்று மேவார்நா டிடம்படப்
புலியொடு வின்னீக்கிப் புகழ்பொறித்த கிளர்கெண்டை
வலியினான் வணக்கிய வாடாச்சீர்த் தென்னவன்."

Kalit-tokai....(104).

[3] "வடிவே லெறிந்த வான்பகை பொறாது
பஃறுளி யாற்றுடன் பன்மலை யடுக்கத்துக்
குமரிக் கோடுங் கொடுங்கடல் கொள்ள."

Silappadikāram ....XI—18-20.

Kumari and Pahruli. The traditions, however, give us an exaggerated idea of the extent of the land that was thus destroyed. Both Adiyār-kunallār and Nachchinār-kiniyar, the famous commentators of Sangam works, evidently believed in the traditions and have stated that forty-nine countries, to the extent of nearly 1,400 miles, were lost in this swelling of the sea. This seems, however, to be an exaggeration. A more sober reference to this incident is to be found in the commentary of *Silappadikāram*. The information here supplied is that the river Pahruli was quite close to Kumari.[1] From this it is evident that the tract of land lost as a result of this tidal wave was but a strip comprising perhaps, forty-nine plots of ground. We are further told that the Pandyan king, in order to recoup the loss, took forcible possession of two small districts, Kundur and Muttur, belonging to the Chola and Chera kings and that, for this reason, he was known as Nilantaru Tiruvir Pandyan. When did this tidal wave pass over the country ? If we are able to fix its date, we may fix also the age of Tolkāppiyar ; for it was during the days of the second Academy, of which Tolkāppiyar was a member, this incident happened.

The probable age of Tolkāppiyar.

In Tennent's *History of Ceylon*, mention is made of three such disasters that effected con-

1 "பஃறுளியாறு—குமரிப்பக்கத்தோர் யாறு."

siderable change in the geography of the island. The first is stated to have occurred in 2387 B.C., when the island of Ceylon got itself separated from the mainland ; the second in 504 B.C. during the reign of Pānduvāsa which involved considerable loss of Ceylonese territory ; the last, comparatively a minor one, in 306 B.C., during the time of Dēvānāmpriya Tissa. Taking, this last encroachment of the sea as the one alluded to in *Iraiyanār Ahapporul*, some fix III century B.C. roughly as the lower limit for the date of Tolkāppiyar and contend that the evidence of *Rājāvali* of Ceylon and that of *Mahāvamsa* tend to confirm this view. It is also contended that Tolkāppiyar's mention in his work, of *Hora*, for a knowledge of which it seems we are indebted to the Greek astronomers that accompanied Alexander the Great in the course of his Indian raid, would fix the age of Tolkāppiyar as III century B.C.[1] Again the mention in the colophon to Tolkāppiyam, of the Sanskrit grammar of Indra, coupled with the fact that Indra's date has been ascertained as 350 B.C.[2] makes it plain according to some that 350 B.C. is the latest date that can be assigned for Tolkāppiyar[3], the earliest known grammarian

[1] Colebrooke, *Miscellaneous Essays*, Vol. II, p. 29.

[2] Macdonnell, *History of Sanskrit Literature*, p. 11.

[3] In an interesting article in *Sen Tamil*, the organ of the Madura Tamil Sangam (Vol. XVIII, 1919-20, p. 339), Mr. S. Vyapuri Pillai suggests that Tolkāppiyar was a Jain by faith. His chief argument rests on the fact that Panambāranār a contemporary of Tolkāppiyar, calls him 'பல்புகழ் நிறுத்த படிமையோன்.' *Padimai* is from the Prakrit *Padima*, essentially a Jain word referring to Jain rules of conduct. The following extract from the article referred to above deserves to be studied by all interested in the

and Sangam author, whose work was an authority for all later literary productions.[1]

Kural: its date and the faith of its author.

The next work of considerable importance in Tamil literature is the famous *Kural* of Saint Tiruvalluvar. Various opinions are held regarding the date and the religious faith of its author. Of him all sorts of wild traditions exist. Most of these are more fanciful than real. What is the date of *Kural?* It is common knowledge that *Kural* is quoted in *Silappadikāram* of

history of religious movements in South India :—

"மோக்ஷ மெய்தற்குரிய மார்க்கத்தில், பதினான்கு நிலைகள் உள்ளனவாக ஜைன சமயத்தவர்கள் கருதுகின்றார்கள். இந்நிலைகளைக் குணஸ்தானகங்களென்று கூறுவர். இவற்றுள் முதலைந்து நிலைகளும் இல்லறத்தோர் துறவறத்தோரென்ற இருதிறத்தார்க்கும் உரியன. ஆறு முதல் ஏனை நிலைகள் துறவறத்தோர்க்கு மட்டுமுரியன. இல்லறத்தில் நிற்பார் முதலைந்து நிலைகளும் கைவரப் பெற்ற பின்னர், உண்மைத்தீர்த்தங்கரர் மாட்டும், உண்மையாசாரியர் மாட்டும், உண்மை நூலின் மாட்டும், துளங்காதபக்திவைத்து, பஞ்ச அதிசாரங்களையும் நீத்துப் பன்னிரண்டு விரதங்களையும் அனுஷ்டித்தல் வேண்டும். இங்ஙனம் நின்றோரினும் மிக்குச் சிறப்பெய்த விரும்பும் இல்லறத்தோர் பதினொரு தவவொழுக்கங்களை மேற்கொள்வர். இவ்வொழுக்கங்கள் 'படிமா' என்று பிராகிருதத்திற் பெயர் பெறும். 'தவம்' என்ற சொல் இல்லறத்தார்க்கும் உரியதாதல் 'நற்றவஞ் செய்வார்க்கிடம் தவம் செய்வார்க்கும் அஃதிடம்' என்ற (சீவகசிக்-77) மேற்கோள் நோக்கி யுணரலாகும்.

இதனால் 'படிமை' யென்பது ஜைனசமய வழக்குச் சொல்லென்பதும், அச்சொல் 'தவவொழுக்கம்' என்றதனை யுணர்த்துதல் அவ்வொரு சமய நூலின் கண்ணன்றிப் பிறசமய நூல்களில் இல்லையென்பதும் தெளியக் கிடக்கின்றன.

ஆகவே 'பல்புகழ் நிறுத்தபடிமையோன்' என்று சிறப்பிக்கப் பெற்ற தொல்காப்பியனார் ஜைன சமயத்தவராவரென்பதும், அதன்கண் இல்லற நெறி நின்று சிறந்த தவவொழுக்கங்களை யனுஷ்டித்தவராவரென்பதும் உணரலாகும்."

[1] I wish it to be understood that this section merely summarises the views of others and does not represent my own views. My attitude is one of extreme scepticism in regard to these early dates claimed for *Tolkāppiyam* and *Kural*; for it is doubtful whether Tamil had attained a uniform standard so early as the beginning of the Christian era. (Please see my article "Misconceptions about Sangam Chronology", Appendix D.)

Ilangōvadigal; he was the brother of Senguttuvan whose date is said to fall in the second century A.D. It is contended by some that the *Kural* must have been written at least a century before *Manimēkalai* and *Silappadikāram*, that is in the beginning of the I century A.D. It is astonishing that the author of *Kural*, who is undoubtedly recognised as one of the great geniuses of the world, should have remained without a name. Almost every religionist has claimed the author as belonging to his faith. Tamil literary tradition attributes the authorship of *Kural* to Valluvar; but there are strong reasons for believing that the author was a Jain. The late Prof. Seshagiri Sastriar[1] held that Valluvar was a follower of Arhat.

Was Valluvar a Jain?

Evidences in favour of the Jain origin of *Kural*.

Certain references in *Kural* to *Malarmisai yēginān* (மலர்மிசை யேகினான்) and *Yengunathān* (எண்குணத்தான்) are held to be sufficient evidence to prove that the author was a Jain. Hindu scholars have pointed out, however, that these expressions are equally applicable to Vishnu. But one who has read or is acquainted in the least, with Jain canonical scripture will have no hesitation in agreeing with Mr. Seshagiri Sastri. The expression *Malarmisai yēginān*, i.e., 'He who walked on lotus' is a very common epithet applied to Lord Arhat. According to the Jain scriptures, when the *Tirthankara* attains omniscience there gather around him a vast crowd of men, animals, birds and

[1] Seshagiri Sastriar, *Essay on Tamil Literature*, p. 43.

other living beings to hear his teachings. Indra and many other Dēvas, according to them, worship the Lord, praise Him and honour Him by manifesting wonderful phenomena. One such wonder is the formation of a beautiful lotus under the feet of the Jina, which moves along under his feet as he goes to several countries to preach his doctrine. This is the special significance of the expression *Malarmisai yēginān*. Then again the reference to *Yengunāthan* (*i.e.*, he who has eight qualities) has a special significance to the Jain. God, according to Jainism, has the following eight qualities :—1. Perfect faith, 2. Infinite knowledge, 3. Infinite cognition, 5. Extreme fineness, 6. Interpenetrability, 7. Stationariness (quality of being neither light nor heavy) and 8. Undisturbable bliss. It is, therefore, difficult to join with those who say that Valluvar referred to the Hindu Gods and not specially to the qualities of the Jina.

An objection answered.

Another expression that was held to be destructive of the theory that the author was a Jain, is what is supposed to be contained in the 4th couplet of Chapter III in *Kural*. Dr. Pope, in pointing this out, says that a Jain would not believe that Valluvar was a follower of his faith, because a Jain sage would have neither wife nor the emotion of anger, nor the power to inflict punishment. But we know that one of the Tirthankaras married and begot children.

Another evidence in favour of the Jain origin of *Kural*.

One other evidence in favour of the Jain origin of *Kural* might be adduced. The commentator of *Nīla-*

kēsi, a Jain work, calls *Kural*, *Emmottu* (எம்மோத்து), our own Bible. That shows that the Jains generally believed that Valluvar was a member of their community. The tradition is that one Elacharya, a Jain sage, was the author of *Kural*. This Elacharya, some say, was no other than Sri Kunda Kunda, a great Jain *Muni*, well versed in Sanskrit and Prakrit, who carried on the work of propagating Jainism in the Tamil land, in or about the first century A.D. A sage of great intellectual attainments, he is supposed to have written for the instruction of Sivaskandha, a ruler of Conjeeveram, the *Panchāstikāya*, which has been recently edited by Prof. Chakravarti, a prominent member of the Jain community. In the historical portion of the introduction to that book, the learned Professor identifies the author of the *Kural* with Kunda Kunda whose other name was Elacharya. From the *Pattāvalis* edited by Hoernle and Klatt, the date of Kunda Kunda can be ascertained as I century A.D.[1] One other point may be briefly noticed. If, as has been contended, the author of *Kural* was a low caste Valluvar, what is there in the history of ancient social institutions in the Tamil land to warrant the belief that a low caste man could obtain such a high education not only in the vernacular but also in the sacred language of Sanskrit, which is essential for producing such a work as *Kural*; for it must be remembered

Was Elacharya Kunda Kunda himself?

Yet another point.

[1] *Indian Antiquary*, Vols. XX and XXI.

that *Kural* represents not only what was best in South Indian culture but also it has given to the Tamils the quintessence of North Indian wisdom contained in such works as the *Artha-sāstra* of Kautilya. No one, therefore, who had not a sound knowledge of Prakrit and Sanskrit literature could have attempted the writing of *Kural* and such a one was Kunda Kunda. If this supposition is true, the inference is inevitable that the Jains had penetrated into the extreme south of India so early as, if not earlier than, the I century A.D. and that they had actively taken up the work of propagating their faith through the medium of the vernacular of the country namely Tamil.

The spread of Jainism in the early centuries of the Christian era.

The first two centuries of the Christian era saw, therefore, the appearance in the Tamil countries of a new religion which, with its simple moral code devoid of elaborate exegetics, appealed to the Dravidian and was destined to play an important part in the religious history of South India. Fostering the vernaculars of the country out of opposition to the Brahmins, the Jains infused Aryan thought and learning among the southern people, which had the effect of awakening Dravidian literature to proclaim the new message it had received from northern lands.[1] A consideration of the literary history of India led Mr. Frazer[2] to write " It was through the fostering care of the Jains that the south seems

[1] *The Journal of the Royal Asiatic Society*, Vol. XXII, p. 249.

[2] Frazer, *Literary History of India*, pp. 310 & 311.

to have been inspired with new ideals and literature, enriched with new forms and expressions." A knowledge of the then Dravidian methods and forms of worship would easily make us understand why Jainism had taken root in the soil. The Dravidian had developed a civilization of his own. His religion consisted in sacrifices, prophecies, ecstatic dances and demon-worship. This was open to the attacks of the first batch of Brahmin immigrants from the north who settled at Madura and other cities and tried to introduce Hindu notions of caste and ceremonial but met with much opposition, the caste system then being 'inchoate and imperfect.' Nevertheless, the Brahmins succeeded in introducing their notions of religion. Sacrifices were performed under royal patronage and horses or cows were sacrificed with elaborate ceremonies, the flesh of the victims not being disdained by the Brahmins.[1] Though anxious to spread vedic religion among the masses, the Brahmin kept the Vedas a sealed book to them. As in the north of India, so in the south, the non-Aryan races began to cultivate a contempt for the Brahmins whose worship of the elements did not find favour with the masses. It was at this period that the non-Brahminic orders, Jainism and Buddhism, entered the country, and no wonder that these, with their less complex forms of worship and

[1] Kanakasabhai Pillai, *Tamils Eighteen Hundred Years Ago*, p. 230.

embodying in their doctrines some of the highest and noblest principles of human conduct, found favour among the ancient Dravidians who not only tolerated them in their midst but even accorded them in their religious life a position of great honour and trust.

The Tamil Epics: their value to Jain History.

The period immediately following the age of *Kural* is characterised by the growth of classical literature, mainly under the Jain auspices. This age is generally called the Augustan age of Tamil literature, the period of the predominance of the Jains in intellect and learning, though not in political power.[1] It was during this period *second century A.D.* that the famous Tamil epic *Silappadikāram* is supposed to have been written. The author of the work was Ilangōvadigal, a brother of the Chera prince, Senguttuvan, and, perhaps, a member of the Jain Church. From this epic and its companion volume, *Manimēkalai,* can be gleaned a graphic account of the state of the Dravidian society at that time. It would appear that there was then perfect religious toleration, Jainism advancing so far as to be embraced by members of the royal family. Religious conversion did not, as it does now, destroy the bonds of society and family. Thus, for example, Ilangōvadigal, the author of the epic *Silappadikāram,* was a Jain, while his brother, Senguttuvan, was a Saivite. In short, the fervent manner in which Jain beliefs and morals are depicted, the copious

[1] V. A. Smith, *Early History of India* (1914), p. 445; Dr. Pope in *Journal of the Royal Asiatic Society,* 1889 Vol, p. 242.

references to Jain centres of learning, and the description of the society in general, leave no doubt in the minds of the readers of the epics, the impression that the religion of Arhat was embraced by large and ever increasing numbers of the Dravidians.

The position of the Jains in the Academic age.

We shall next examine the position held by the Jains during this Academic age with the help of references to them in *Silappadikāram* and *Manimēkalai*. These epics are specially valuable as records of the extent to which the non-Brahminical religions, Jainism and Buddhism, had spread in South India in the early part of the second century A.D. The epics give one the impression that these two religions were patronised by the Chola as well as by the Pandyan kings. The Nigranthas, as the Jains were called, generally lived outside the towns "in their own cool cloisters, the walls of which were exceedingly high and painted red and which were surrounded by little flower-gardens"; their temples were situate at places where two or three roads met ; they erected their platforms or pulpits from which they generally preached their doctrine. Side by side with their monasteries, there also existed nunneries showing thereby the vast influence exercised over the Tamil women by Jain nuns. There were Jain monasteries at Kavirippoompattinam, the capital of the Cholas, and at Uraiyur on the banks of the Cauvery. Madura, however, was the chief centre of Jainism. When

Kōvalan and his wife were on their way to Madura, they met a Jain nun who warned them to be on their guard against causing pain or death to living creatures as, at Madura, it would be denounced as a heinous sin by the Nigranthas there. The Nigranthas of this period did not appear to have been hated so much as those who flourished in the sixth or seventh century A.D. The Jains in this period, we further learn from the epics, worshipped the resplendent image of Arhat who is generally represented as sitting underneath the Asoka tree with the triple umbrella held over him. That these Jains were the Digambaras is clearly seen from their description. Judging from the account of the society as depicted in *Manimēkalai*, the Tamil sovereigns appear to have been generally tolerant towards all the foreign faiths in the country. Thus, on the occasion of the annual festival held in the city of Puhar in honour of Indra, the king asked all preachers of virtue belonging to all religious sects to ascend the public halls of debate and preach their respective doctrines to the people. The Jains took every advantage of the opportunity and large was the number of those that embraced this faith.

Popularity of Jainism: its causes.

There are certain reasons why Jainism was so popular in those days. The masses of the Dravidians were remnants of the great Nāga race that held the sovereignty of the land before the Tamils conquered it. The Tamils themselves borrowed from the Nāgas some of their elements of worship. Traces of the *Tree and Serpent Worship* so eminently characteristic of the Turanian race are also to be seen in Jainism that was introduced in the Tamil country. Buddhism had no such charm at this period[1] as the worship of the Buddha had not yet been introduced. The worship of a pair of feet is too abstract for a people already accustomed to worship idols of some of the Aryan and non-Aryan deities. To these reasons may be added the comparative simplicity of Jain worship and the exclusive character of Brahminical rites. These tended to make the Nigrantha system more popular than either Brahmanism or Buddhism. The fact that the Jain community had a perfect organisation behind it shows that it was not only popular but that it had taken deep root in the soil. The whole community, we learn from the epics, was divided into two sections, the *Srāvakās* or laymen and the *Munis* or ascetics. The privilege of entering the monastery was not denied to women and both men and women took vows of celibacy.

We shall close this part of the subject with a quotation from *Manimēkalai*, which illustrates the Nigrantha system as was preached to the Tamils. *Manimēkalai*, being a Buddhistic work, one may not expect an ideal representation of the Jain system at the hands of its author

[1] Throughout the epic *Manimēkalai*, no reference is made to any statue of the Buddha. A pair of feet representing the Buddha was the only object of worship by the Buddhists.

Chāttanār, a staunch Buddhist. But enlightened Jain opinion is, that excepting *Dharmāstikāya*, every other point of the Jain system is fairly represented.

Nigrantha system as preached to the Tamils.

"Leaving this confusion of words, she (Manimēkalai) asked the Niganta (Nigranta) to state who was his God, and what he was taught in his sacred books, and to explain correctly how things exist and are formed or dissolved. He said that his God is worshipped by Indras: and that the books revealed by him describe the following: The wheel of Law, the axle of Law, Time, Ether, Soul, Eternal atoms, good deeds, bad deeds, the bonds created by those deeds and the way to obtain release from those bonds. Things by their own nature, or by the nature of other objects to which they are attached, are temporary or everlasting. Within the short period of a Kshana (second), they may pass through the three unavoidable stages, appearance, existence and dissolution. That a margosa tree sprouts and grows is eternal: that it does not possess that property is temporary. Green gram when made into a sweetmeat with other ingredients does not lose its nature, but loses its form. The wheel of Law (Dharma) pervades everywhere and moves all things in order and for ever. In the same way the axle of Law retains everything (and prevents dissolution). Time may be divided into seconds or extend to Eons. Ether expands and gives room for everything. The soul entering a body will, through the five senses, taste, smell, touch, hear and see. An atom may become a body or assume other forms. To stop the origin of good and evil deeds, and to enjoy the effect of past deeds, and to cut off all bonds is release (salvation).[1] "

The third and fourth centuries a perfect blank.

The third and fourth centuries of the Christian era seem to be a perfect blank in the history of the Jains in the Tamil kingdom. What little information we have been able to gather about the Jains in the Sangam period is from non-Brahminical sources, the Brahmin as well as the other Hindu poets of the Sangam having ignored their very existence. Just as the literature of the north refused to take cognizance of the great raid of Alexander, so the Brahminical literature of the south had not cared to shed any light on the history and activities of the Jains. But we can, more or less, follow the probable course of the development of Jainism in the light of their later history, particularly of the seventh and eighth centuries A.D. Second century A.D. is a great age in Jain history ; not merely Kunda Kunda but other Jain scholars as well evinced the greatest activity during this period in spreading their gospel. The necessary impulse and resource for an undertaking of such magnitude must have come from Sravana Belgola. The Gangas who ruled the Gangavādi for nearly nine centuries, second to eleventh century A.D., had been great patrons of Jainism and must have aided the spread of the faith in the

[1] *The Tamils Eighteen Hundred Years Ago*, pp. 215-16.

Tamil land. In fact, a closer study of Indian religious movements, particularly those in the Peninsula, would reveal that for nearly four centuries, second to the beginning of the seventh century, Jainism was the predominant faith. We can merely indicate here, in a general way, the course of its development.

Formation of a Jain Sanga.

To revert to our subject, Brahmin literature, when it condescended to take notice of the Jains at all, showed considerable animosity to them in the fourth and the beginning of the fifth century. This resulted in the formation of a separate Sangam by the Jains themselves. An information of greatest consequence is given in a Jain religious work, the *Digambara Dharsana.*[1] The book states that in the year 526 of Vikrama Saka, *i.e.*, 470 A.D., a Dravida Sangam was formed at the Southern Madura by Vajra Nandi, a disciple of Pūjyapāda. We further learn from the same source that the Sanga was an association of Digambara Jains who migrated south with a view to spread Jainism. Unless the reigning kings of Pandyan country patronised them, the Jains would never have dared in those days of cruel punishment to establish a Sangam. We see in the formation of this Sangam the extension of royal patronage to Jainism which excited the jealousy of the leaders of Brahminism. The conflict was bound to come. For the time being it was postponed. The Sangam, as we have seen, was formed at the

[1] *Journal of the Bombay Branch of the Royal Asiatic Society* Vol. XVII, p. 74.

end of the 5th century A.D. and when the 6th century opens, the political fortunes of the Tamil country undergo a rapid change. It is the period of the Kalabhra invasion and occupation of the Pandyan kingdom.

Kalabhras: who were they?

Who were these Kalabhras? And what is the relation between them and the Jains of South India? The Kalabhras are frequently mentioned in the Pandyan as well as the Pallava inscriptions. These speak of them as the conquerors of Tamil kings, the Cholas, the Cheras and the Pandyas. Since they are not mentioned in any inscription outside South India, the presumption is strongly in favour of their Dravidian origin. At any rate there is nothing to show that they were Aryans. The same Kalabhras are mentioned in the Vēlvikudi grant, as having conquered the Pandyan country and ruled there for a short time, till they were defeated by Kadungōn who got back the country. In the account of Mūrti Nāyanār in *Periyapurānam,* we learn that, during the time of the Nāyanār, a large Carnatic force raided the country, defeated the Pandyan king and established its sway in the land. We are not aware of any other foreign invasion of the Pandyan country. Taking the information in the Vēlvikudi grant and the historical matter furnished by *Periyapurānam,* we are forced to equate the Kalabhra interregnum of the Vēlvikudi grant with the Carnatic rule of Madura in the period of Mūrti Nāyanār.

This conclusion is further supported by what are known as Sendalai inscriptions published by the late Mr. T. A. Gopinatha Rao in *Sen Tamil*, Volume VI. Sendalai is a village two miles off Trichinopoly. The old name of the place is Chendralēghai Chaturvēda Mangalam. There is in that village a great Saiva temple dedicated to Meenākshisundarēsvarar. The pillars of one of the *Mantapams* in the temple contain beautiful inscriptions. According to Mr. Gopinatha Rao these pillars originally belonged to another temple dedicated perhaps to a Sylvan deity by one of the kings. Coming to the point, the pillars contain inscriptions which together give us the family genealogy of one Perumpidugu Muttaraiyan. It is as follows :—

Perumpidugu Muttaraiyan I
alias Kuvāvan Māran
(his son)
|
Ilangōvati Araiyan
alias Māran Paramēswaran
(his son)
|
Perumpidugu Muttaraiyan II
alias Suvaran Māran.

The other names of the last-named king as mentioned in the inscriptions are Sri Māran, Sri Kalvarakalvan, Sri Satrukēsari, Sri Kalbharakalvan, Sri Kalvakalvan ; sometimes he is spoken of as Pandāram. The titles Māran and Nedumāran clearly show that he was a conqueror of the Pandyas, at any rate, that he was a Pandyan king. The three other titles, viz., Kalvarakalvan, Kalbharakalvan, and Kalvakalvan indicate their origin. These three mean the same thing, *i.e.*, thief of thieves or king of thieves, showing thereby that the 'Kalabhras' of Vēlvikudi grant were Kallars in their origin. Kalvarkalvan might also be read as Kalvarakalvan (கள்வரகள்வன்), but in the inscriptions it is common to read Kalvarakalvan as Kalavarakalvan (களவரகள்வன்). In its Canarese form the 'v' is easily interchangeable with 'b' and we have Kalabharakalvan and from that, the Kalabhras of the Vēlvikudi grant. When they conquered the Pandyan country they assumed the title of Muttaraiyan. The word might mean either 'Lord of Pearls' (muttu + araiyan) or as the 'Lord of Three lands' (mū + ttaraiyan) which latter interpretation corresponds more closely with the description given of them in the inscriptions as conquerors of Chola, Pandya and Chera countries.

Kalabhras and Jainism.

Having thus established the identity of the Kalabhras with the Carnatic king of *Periyapurānam*, we shall next inquire what light this information throws on the history of the Jains. The same *Periyapurānam* account of Mūrti Nāyanār tells us that the Kalabhras, the moment they came to the country, embraced Jainism and influenced by the Jains who were innumerable, began to persecute the Saiva saints and disregard the worship of Saiva gods. It looks as though the Jains had themselves invited the Kalabhras with a view to establish Jainism more firmly in the country. The period of the Kalabhras and that which succeeds it must, therefore, be considered as the period when the Jains had reached their zenith. It was during this period that the famous *Nāladiyār* was composed by the Jains. There are two references[1] in *Nāladiyār* to Muttaraiyar indicating that the Kalabhras were Jains and patrons of Tamil literature. We would fain know more about these Muttaraiyar but unfortunately, the book, presumably treating about them and mentioned in *Yāpperumkalaviruti*, viz., *Tamizhmuttarayar-kōvai*, is entirely lost.[2]

Nāladiyār and the Jains.

A word about *Nāladiyār*. It consists of 400 quatrains of moral and didactic sayings, each one composed, according to tradition, by a Jain ascetic. Dr. Pope styles it as the *Vellālar Vēdam*,

1 The base feed full of rice and savoury food,
That men, great lords of the triple lands,
With generous gladness give ;
But water won with willing strenuous toil
By those who know not savoury food by name even,
Will turn to nectar. Q. 200.

Poor are the men that *give not*,
Even though deemed wealthiest
Of all that flourish on the teeming ample earth !
They who even when they are poor seek not as
Suppliants wealthy men are, 'Lords of the three mighty lands.'
Pope's *Nāladiyār*. Q. 296.

2 Where are the descendants of these *Muttaraiyar*, the Kalabhras of the Vēlvikudi grant ? In Trichinopoly district we have even to-day *Muttaraiyar*. They seem to be petty chiefs. In the Andhra country they are known as *Muttu Rajakkal*. This is quite in keeping with the description of Kalabhras in *Periyapurānam* as Vadugakarnātaka people. The *Muttaraiyar* of the Melur taluq, Madura district, are known as *Ambalakārans*. They are Kallars by caste. This is a very interesting subject for investigation. It is noteworthy that in Sangam literature, Pulli, the Chief of Vēngadam, is known as Kalvarkōman (king of thieves).

that is, the Bible of the Vellālar or Agriculturists. "These epigrams, drawn sometimes from Sanskrit sources and often forming the ground of ornate Sanskrit verses written in imitation or rivalry, have become household words throughout all South India." When the two facts, the formation of a Digambara Jain Sangam at Madura and the large Sanskrit borrowings in composing *Nāladiyār* are examined together we are led to conclude that the work must have been written after the formation of the Jain Sangam and that, exactly at the time when it was composed, the rivalry between the two sects Jainism and Brahminism was becoming keener and keener. Quatrain 243 pretty clearly illustrates the spirit of rivalry between the two sects and, as has been already remarked, this period is that which immediately succeeded the Kalabhra interregnum.

Thus the works published during what we have called the *Sangam* or *Academic period* clearly indicate the following points in the life and history of the Jains in the Tamil kingdoms :—

1. That the Jains had probably not entered the extreme south of India during the days of Tolkāppiyar who must have flourished before 350 B.C.
2. That they must have colonised and permanently settled in the extreme south of India during and before the first century A.D.

3. That what is known as Augustan age of Tamil literature was also the age of the predominance of the Jains.
4. That after the fifth century A.D. Jainism became so very influential and powerful as to even become the state-creed of some of the Pandyan kings.

CHAPTER IV.

THE PERIOD OF SAIVA NAYANARS AND VAISHNAVA ALVARS.

Revival of Brahminism and decline of Jainism.

This period which begins from the sixth century A.D. is characterised by a great revival of Brahminism which shook the heretical sects of Buddhism and Jainism to their very foundations. Buddhism had already lost its hold in South India, but the latter was, as we have seen, at its zenith. The Jains had played their role well ; but they had stayed in the Tamil country too long. The mild teachings of the Jain system had become very rigorous and exacting in their application to daily life. The exclusiveness of the Jains and their lack of adaptability to circumstances soon rendered them objects of contempt and ridicule, and it was only with the help of state patronage that they were able to make their influence felt. No longer did the Tamilians embrace the Jain faith out of open conviction ; force and religious persecution were resorted to by over-zealous state officials who were always ready to execute the commands of bigoted Jain kings.

The growth and strength of any faith depend to a large extent upon the support it receives at the hands of the rulers. When they cease to patronise it or become converts to rival faith, large numbers secede from the movement. No wonder, therefore, that the followers of the

Brahminical religion looked forward eagerly to the day, when their religious leaders would be able to bring erring monarchs round to the true path of *Dharma* and thus wipe the Nigranthas out of the Tamil country.

The Hymnal period in Tamil literature. With the rise of Saiva temples in South India (5th century A.D.) there came into existence a kind of Saiva religious literature in Tamil, mainly consisting of hymns in praise of the various local shrines. Each hymn is made up of ten or eleven stanzas in what is known as Asiriyam metre, a composition peculiar to the early hymnologists. These hymns celebrate the miraculous deeds and sports of Siva. The superiority of Siva over the other Indian Gods is sought to be established therein. The importance of these hymns and their great superiority over the secular literature have been set forth by Umāpati Siva Chārya (1320 A.D.) in the following verse:—"Lo! They cannot be consumed by fire, will go up the current, vivify even bones, take out poison, subdue the elephant, make the stone float, and make the crocodile vomit the child it devoured." By the time of Rāja Rāja Chōla (984-1013 A.D.) the Saiva religious literature became so enormous and scattered that it was deemed urgently necessary to collect and arrange it. This important task was entrusted to Nambiāndār Nambi (975-1035 A.D.) a *Gurukkal* or Audisaiva Brahmin of Tirunaraiyur in South Arcot District. He collected and edited all the Saiva works into eleven *Tirumurais* or series. Later on, during the reign of Kulōttunga or Anabāya Chōla 1150 A.D., a mass of tradition about the Saiva saints was collected from all sources and an extensive hagiology entitled the *Tirutondar Purānam or Periyapurānam*, was written by Sēkkizhar, a Vellāla poet of the Pallava country. This legendary biography of Saiva Nāyanārs consisting of about 4,306 stanzas was later on added to the Saiva religious literature as the twelfth *Tirumurai*. It is to these, Sekkizhār's *Periyapurānam* and the compilation of Nambiāndār Nambi, that we are indebted for an account of the Jains during, what we have called, the period of Saiva Nāyanārs and Vaishnava Alvars. The information that could be gleaned from Saiva religious literature is to a little extent supplemented by the Vaishnava Prabandhams. Elaborate as are the details of the lives of Saiva saints, they are yet useless for purposes of history, as no dates are assigned to any of the Nāyanārs; and being based on legends, the *Periyapurānam* is replete with fanciful accounts of miraculous incidents which no modern student of history would care to accept. Hence not a little difficulty is felt in tracing the various epochs in the religious history of South India. Among the 63 saints an account of whose lives is given in *Periyapurānam*, the names of Appar, Siruttondar and Tirujñānasambandar are important, as they alone furnish us some information about the Jains. Of these three, Sambandar is a very important figure, as it was during his time that Jainism received a mortal blow, from the effects of which it never recovered.

Sambandar: his life and career.

Born of a Brahmin priest at Shiyali in the Tanjore District, Saint Sambanda began to sing hymns in praise of Siva, when only three years old! Well versed both in the Vedas and Vedāngas, he had no equal in Tamil learning also. Proud of his birth as a Brahmin, he spoke highly of his caste and the Vedas. He made extended pilgrimages to different Saiva shrines in South India, singing hymns in praise of Siva and working out miracles by the grace of that deity. His one object in life seems to have been the putting down of heretical faiths, such as Jainism and Buddhism. With huge crowds of devotees and worshippers accompanying him, he constantly peregrinated the Tamil land creating unbounded enthusiasm among the people for the cause of Saiva religion. A bitter opponent of Jainism, every tenth verse of his soul-stirring songs was devoted to anathematize the Jains. We are not here concerned with the various details of his life, but it is interesting to note the manner in which Jainism which took such a deep root in the Madura country was driven out of it. The ruler of the Pandyan kingdom at this time was the famous Ninrasīr Nedumāran, the conqueror of Nelvēli, otherwise known as Sundara Pandyan, who, from all accounts we know was a staunch Jain. He had for his wife Mangayarkarasi, the daughter of the Chola king and a devoted worshipper of Siva. The Pandyan king's minister who played a great part in the religious history of the time was Kulachchirai who was also a worshipper of Siva. These two contrived to bring Tirujñānasambandar to Tiruvālavāi (Madura) with a view to convert the king to their own faith and thus establish Saivism in the land. The invitation was readily accepted by the saint to the great consternation of the Jain ascetics of Madura. The facts and circumstances concerning the saint's visit to Madura may be considered historical, though the miracles attributed to Sambandar are obviously legendary. It would appear from the account given in *Periyapurānam* that the Jains attempted to set fire to the building occupied by the Saiva saint and his Brahmin followers. The plot was discovered and the danger averted. The king suddenly fell ill and his Jain advisers were asked to cure him. They failed in the attempt and the pious queen and the minister begged the king's permission to allow Tirujñānasambandar to treat him. Sambandar sang a hymn or two and the king soon recovered. Elated with success, the clever Sambanda took full advantage of this opportunity to prove to the king the utter futility of Jain *Mantras* and the uselessness of the Jain religion. The doubting sovereign ordered the Jains to accept the challenge thrown by the Brahmin saint. Two tests were employed, by mutual agreement, to decide the superiority of their

The struggle commences.

respective faiths—the ordeals of fire and water. A fire was kindled and into it were thrown the sacred books of the Jains and the leaf containing the hymns of Sambanda. The latter instead of being burnt shone quite green in the flames, while the Jain books were reduced in no time to ashes. Blushing with shame, and fuming with anger, the Jains hoped for better luck in the other test. This time, the books were thrown into the river Vaigai, famous for its swift current. The leaf containing the hymns of the Saiva saint swam against the current, while the Jain books drifted along with it. This was a great blow to the Jains. From this time on, they not only lost the confidence of the king but hundreds of them were impaled. Such is the legendary account of Tirujñānasambandar. Amidst fables and mythical accounts there stands the historic personality of Tirujñānasambandar who brought about the conversion of the king of Madura from Jainism to Saivism. This was a death blow to Jainism in the south.

The Age of Tirujñānasambandar.

The date of Tirujñānasambandar and therefore of Kūn Pandya[1] is very important, as it fixes the age of the downfall of Jainism in South India. Mr. Taylor[2] assigned 1320 B.C. as the date of Kūn Pandya, while Dr. Caldwell[3] contended that he flourished in 1292 A.D. Thus,

[1] He is otherwise known as Ninrasīr Nedumāran and Sundara Pandya.

[2] Nelson, *Madura Country*, part III, Ch. III, p. 55.

[3] Caldwell, *Comparative Grammar of Dravidian languages*.

in fixing the date of Kūn Pandya, individual opinions drift at pleasure from 14th century B.C. to 13th century A.D. The late Professor Sundaram Pillai[1] has maintained that the opening of the seventh century A.D. was the latest period that could be assigned to Sambandar. From the internal evidence furnished by Saiva literature, the learned Professor has proved that Jñānasambandar should have preceded by a few centuries Kandarāditya, one of the authors of *Tiru-Isaippa*, the ninth book of the Saiva Bible of the Tamils. This Kandarāditya should have flourished about the close of the ninth century, as he is known to have preceded by several generations Rāja Rāja Dēva, the constructor of the Tanjore temple (984 A.D.). As the renowned Sankaracharya (8th century) referred to Jñānasambandar as "the Dravida child" it is evident that Sambandar flourished before him. From his hymns it is known that Sambandar was a great friend of Siruttondar who was a generalissimo and fought for the Pallava King, Narasimha Varman I, at Vātāpi (Badami). Happily, the date of the destruction of Vātāpi by the Pallava king was discovered by the late Mr. Venkiah (642 A.D.) and this fixed the age of Tirujñānasambandar. For, it must be remembered, Tirujñānasambandar, Siruttondar and another saint of whom we shall have to speak presently, Tirunāvukkarasar, popularly known as Appar, were all contemporaries.

[1] *Tamilian Antiquary* No. 3. *Some Milestones in the History of Tamil literature.*

And thus they must have flourished in the first half of the seventh century A.D. which is the period of the decline and downfall of Jainism in Southern India.

Appar and Jainism.

In this holy task of Hindu revival in the south, there was associated with Sambandar another great saint Tirunāvukkarasar, an elder contemporary of Sambandar. If Sambandar brought about the downfall of Jainism in the Pandyan Kingdom, Appar drove the Jains out of the Pallava country. Appar [1] was born of Vellāla parents at Tiruvāmur in the South Arcot District. He had an elder sister, Tilakāvati by name. She was betrothed to Kalippakai who, however, died in the war between the Pallava king, Paramēswara Varma, and the Chalukyas (660 A.D.). After the death of her husband, she devoted her life to the service of Siva, while her brother Appar became a Jain and spent his life in the Jain cloisters at Tiruppāpuliyur under the name of Dharmasēna. In his later years, as a result of the prayers of his sister, he became a convert to the Saiva faith and with all the zeal of a new convert, he began to persecute the Jains in the Pallava country. He is also credited with having converted to Saivism the Pallava king, Mahēndra Varman, son of Narasimha Varman I, from Jainism. Most of his hymns are of an autobiographical nature and from them we learn that he repented his past company and association with the Digambara

[1] See note 2, p. 154.

Jains. His account of the Jains is interesting; but unfortunately, the value of the poems is to be discounted much, as the vindictive spirit of a neophite is displayed throughout. According to him Jainism was put down in the Tamil country by the strenuous preaching of Saint Jñānasambandar and Vaishnava Apostles, Tirumaẓhisai and Tirumangai.

Thus, during the middle half of the seventh and the beginning of the eighth centuries A.D., the Jains sustained a series of reverses both in the Pallava and the Pandya country. The Chola kings did not encourage during this period the Jain religion, as they were devoted to the worship of Siva. But it is a mistake to suppose that the Jains were rooted out of those territories. The 8,000 Jains who were impaled at the instance of Tirujñānasambandar, the arch-enemy of Jainism, were all of them leaders and not followers. From the *Periyapurānam* account of the saints, it is evident that both in the Pallava and Pāndya countries they were cruelly persecuted. The hymns of Appar are full of references to such a religious persecution. Making ample allowance for exaggeration, there is no reason to doubt the fact. The Jains in the sixth and seventh centuries A.D. had vast political influence in the Tamil country, especially in the Pandyan kingdom. From the time of the Kalabhra invasion down to the period of Kūn Pandya's conversion, the Jains must have controlled the policy of that state. They took

The decadence of Jainism.

every advantage of the opportunity thus presented and rigorously carried on a crusade against Vedic religion. This soon brought about a reaction. The conversion of Kūn Pandya, therefore, is not a mere episode in the religious history of the Madura kingdom. It is nothing less than a political revolution, the fruits of which the Brahmin Saint, Tirujñānasambandar, reaped to the full. Not only hundreds and thousands of recalcitrant Jains were driven out of the country, but many were forced by circumstances to embrace Saivism.

References to the Jains in *Tēvāram*.

Before considering the part the Vaishnavaite Alvars took in this general movement against the Jains of the Tamil land, let us inquire what light the *Tēvāram* hymns throw on the life and activities of the Jains, in the seventh or eighth centuries A.D. The stronghold of the Jains in the south was Madura and the ascetics who guided the movement generally lived in the eight mountains surrounding Madura, such as Anāimalai, Pasumalai and so on.[1] They kept themselves severely aloof, not caring to mix with the society at large. If women happened to meet them in the streets, they rushed in and bolted their doors, out of shame.[2] They seem to have spoken

[1] "ஆனைமாமலை யாதியாய விடங்களிற்பல வல்லல்சேர் ஈனர்கட்கு"
தேவாரத் திருமுறை, சுவாமிநாத பண்டிதர் பதிப்பு, 1911, பக்கம் 858, ஞானசம்பந்தர், ஆலவாய் 'மானினேர் விழி' 1.

[2] "பூவையாய்த் தலைபறித்துப் பொறியற்ற சமணிசர் சொல்லே கேட்டு
காவிசேர் கண்மடவார் கண்டோடிக் கதவடைக்குங் கள்வனேன்"
தே. தி. 698, அப்பர், திருவாரூர், 'மெய்யெலாம்' 8.

Prakrit and other mantrams with a nasal twang.[1] Ever bent upon denouncing the *Vedas* and the Brahmins[2], they went from place to place in the hot sun, preaching against the *Vedas* and carrying in their hands an umbrella, a mat and a peacock feather.[3] These Jain ascetics whom Sambandar compares to monkeys[4] were very fond of theological disputations[5] and delighted in vanquishing, in debate, leaders of other religions. Pulling out the hair from their head[6], these naked ascetics stood unabashed before women.[7] They did not clean their body before eating.[8] These cruel monsters who undertook the most brutal vows of self-mortification [9] ate very frequently

1 "சங்கத பங்கமாப் - பாகதத்தொடிரைத்துரைத்த"
தே. தி. 858, ஞா.சம்., ஆலவாய், 'மாணிநேர்விழி' 2.
"மூக்கினான் முரன் றோதியக்குண்டிகை-தூக்கினார்."
தே. தி. 423, அப்பர், பழையாறை வடதளி, 'தலையெலாம்' 2.

2 "வேதவேள்வியை நிந்தனை செய்துழல்-ஆதமில்லியமணொடு"
தே. தி. 865, ஞா.சம்., ஆலவாய், 'வேதவேள்வி,' 1.

3 "பெரிய வாகிய குடையும் பீலியுமவை வெயிற்கரவார்."
தே. தி. 836, ஞா.சம்., மறைக்காடு, "பொங்குவெண்மணல்," [10.

4 "மந்திபோற்றிரிந்து."
தே. தி. 859, ஞா.சம்., ஆலவாய், "மாணிநேர்விழி" 4.

5 "போதியார் பிண்டியாரென்ற வப்பொய்யர்கள் வாதினாலுரை யவை மெய்யல."
தே. தி. 376. ஞா.சம்., மேலைத்திருக்காட்டுப்பள்ளி 'வாருமன்னும்,' 10.

6 "குருளையெய்திய மடவார் நிற்பவே குஞ்சியைப் பறித்துத் திரளைகையிலுண்பவரும்."
தே. தி. 1138, ஞா.சம்., அரசிலி, 'பாடல்வண்,' 10.

7 "குண்டாக்களாயுழன்று கையிலுண்டு குவிமுலையார் தம்முன்னே நாணமின்றி - உண்டியுகந்தமணே நின்றார்."
தே. தி. 962, அப்பர், அதிகை, "வெறிவிரவு," 7.

8 "குளித்துணாவமணர்."
தே. தி. 1063, ஞா. சம்.

9 "காவியநற்றுவராடையினார் கடுநோன்பு மேல்கொள்ளும் பாவிகள்'
தே. தி. 510, ஞா. சம்., வலம்புரம், "கொடியுடை," 10.

dried ginger and the leaves of *marutha* tree [1] (*Terminalia Arjuna*) and besmeared their body with gallnut powder.[2] They were well versed in black magic [3] and chanted *mantras*, the efficacy of which they ever praised.

Such is the account of the Jains as preserved for us in the immortal hymns of Tirujñāna-sambandar and Appar. At the same time, it must be noted that it is the description by avowed enemies. The main object of Sambandar was to rouse the prejudices of the people against the Jains, and to depict their practices in the blackest colour possible. Abuse, as is well known, is no argument and as the hymns contain nothing but terrible invectives, we are forced to conclude that the methods employed by Appar and Sambandar to defeat the Jains were not only crude but also cruel. On the other hand, it must be admitted that the Jains took unfair advantage of their friendship with, and influence over, ruling sovereigns by having recourse to forcible conversion.

The part of Vaishnava Alvars.

Thus during the middle half of the seventh century A.D.. the Jains sustained a series of reverses, both in the Pallava and the Pandya

1 "இலைமருதே யடகாக நாளுமிடுதுவர்க்காயொடு சுக்குத்தின் னும், நிலைய மண்டேரரை"
தே. தி. 660, ஞா.சம்., மருகல், "அங்கமும்," 10.

2 "கடுப்பொடி யட்டிமெய்யிற் கருதியோர் தவமென்றெண்ணி வடுக்களோடிசைந்த நெஞ்சே."
தே. தி. 288, அப்பர், ஐயாறு, "குண்டனாய்," 5.

3 "பிச்சச் சிறுபீலிச் சமண் குண்டர் முதலாயோர்
விச்சைக் கிறையென்னு மவ்விறையைப் பணியாதே."
"தூய்மையில்லாச் சமணர்க்கும்".
திருமங்கை ஆழ்வார், பெரிய திருமொழி.

country. But they were not rooted out of those territories, for, Tirumangai Alvar, the famous Vaishnava saint and the feudal chieftain of a small group of villages called Ali Nadu in the north-eastern part of the Chola country, and who flourished in the earlier half of the eighth century A.D., has frequent notices of the Jains. He shared with his predecessor, Tirumazhisaipirān, the bitter hatred of the Jains and other heretical sects. Another Alvar, Tondaradipodi, a contemporary of Tirumangai, joined this general movement against the Jains and his hymns are terrible invectives against the Jain faith, as the following quotations will show :—

1. "அறியார் சமண ரயர்த்தார் பவுத்தர்."
(நான் முகன்திருவந்தாதி 6.)

2. "இலிங்கத்திட்ட புராணத்தீருஞ் சமணரும்
சாக்கியரும், மலிந்து வாது செய்வீர்களு
மற்றுநுந் தெய்வமு மாகிநின்றான்"
திருவாய்மொழி 5-10-5.

This clearly shows that the Jains lingered long in the country and that Tirumangai Alvar, a great religious disputant, came in conflict with them, in the course of his pilgrimages to the eighty eight Vaishnava temples scattered throughout South India. By the time of Nammālvār, perhaps the last of the Vaishnava saints, Jainism and Buddhism had nearly died out of

[1] புலைபற மாகிநின்ற புத்தொடு சமணமெல்லாம்
கலையறக் கற்றமாந்தர்காண்பரோ கேட்பரோதான். திருமாலை. 7

வெறுப்பொடு சமணமிண்டர் விதியில் சாக்கியர்கள் நின்பால்
பொறுப்பரி யனகள்பேசிப் போவதே நோயதாகிற்
குறிப்பெனக் கடையுமாகிற் கூடுமேற்றலையை யாங்கே
யறுப்பதே கருமங் கண்டா யரங்கமா நகருளானே. திருமாலை. 8

South India, as he makes only a few references to the Jains.

We may now indicate the main conclusions arrived at in the course of our discussion.

1. That the Jains who weilded powerful influence in the 5th, 6th and 7th centuries underwent deterioration.

2. That the rise of Saiva Nāyanārs and their organised efforts to stamp out Jainism, the conversion of Kūn Pandya by Tirujñānasambandar and that of the Pallava King by Appar, led to the downfall of the Jains in the Tamil land about 750 A.D.

3. That the Jains were subjected to further persecution at the hands of Vaishnava Alvars till, in the 9th and 10th centuries, they do not seem to have enjoyed any prominence in the land.

CHAPTER V.

MODERN PERIOD.

The rise of Acharyas.

After the Saiva Nāyanārs and Vaishnava Alvars, there came the great Acharyas or theological doctors who aided the evolution of Hindu religion a great deal. The earliest of these Acharyas, Sankarachārya (8th century A.D.), turned his attention towards the north, thus indicating that the Jains had ceased to be an important factor in the religious life of South India. The Jains, after their persecution in the Pallava and Pandyan kingdoms, migrated in large numbers to their favorite religious centre, Sravana Belgola, in Mysore. There they sought refuge under the Ganga Rajas who patronised them. The few that remained in the Tamil land led an obscure life devoid of all political influence in the country. Nevertheless they retained in full their intellectual vitality which had in earlier times produced such classical works as *Kural* and *Silappadikāram*. Thus during this period of Jain decadence, *Chintāmani*, one of the *Mahākāvyās*, was composed by the Jain saint, Tirutakkadēvar. The famous Tamil grammarian and Jain, Pavanandi, published his *Nannūl* in the 13th century A.D., the patron who supported him being Seeyagangan, evidently a Ganga prince. Besides these they were also responsible for the publication of many books on grammar, lexicon, and astronomy. A detailed account of the literature of the Jains is given elsewhere. A perusal of some of these treatises indicates that the Jains generally lived in large numbers in Mylapore, Nedumbai and Tirumalai. In modern times the Tamil Jains are found in groups in the following places; Chittamur and Perumandur near Tindivanam, Tirumalai, Tirunarunkondai and Tipangudi. The life and times of the last of the Acharyas, Madhvachārya, synchronised with the Mahomedan conquest of the south, which at once arrested all literary, intellectual and religious activities and the Jains shared with other religious sects persecution and humiliation at the hands of the idol-breakers. Referring to the condition of the Jains at the time, M. Barth observes, "It was thus able to hold on till the period of Mahomedan domination, the effect of which was to arrest the propagation of Hinduism and which, while it evidently contributed to the religious, political and social dismemberment of the nation everywhere, showed itself conservative of minorities, small associations and small churches."

Scanty evidence.

The origin, development and decay of the Jains in the extreme south of India have thus far been traced with the aid of Tamil literature. A detailed account, however, of the Jains in the Tamil country, cannot be written, as records are scanty. Indeed, there is some truth in what Mr. Frazer said, "So far, history traces the fluctuating fortunes of the rulers, who in the early ages held the sovereign power, south of the Vindhyas. The literature of the South like that of the North takes but little note of the political history of the time."[1]

What little knowledge we now possess regarding Jain history is mostly due to the records left by antiquarians and travellers who were most of them Europeans.[2] Moreover, we are always obliged, as M. Barth truly observes,[3] to refer to Brahminical sources for a general view of Jain history and they are not likely, considering the animosity that existed between the two sects, to give a true account of the Jains. Hence no little difficulty has been experienced in distinguishing various epochs in the development of Jainism.

It is beyond the scope of this work to describe Jain society—the manners and customs of Jains. The subject has received adequate attention at the hands of Col. Mackenzie and Colebrooke.[4] Nor is it possible to deal at length with Jain architecture.[5] But an attempt is made here to examine how far Hindu society has been affected by its long contact with Jainism.

[1] Frazer, *Literary History of India*, p. 309.

[2] Buchanan, for example, has preserved in his *Travels* (2 Vols.) interesting accounts of the Jains in Malabar. He notes that the Tuluva country was once occupied by Jain chiefs, the Jain family of Byrasudayar being particularly powerful. This family underwent disruption at the hands of Sivappanayakar of Ikkeri who, after dividing the country into petty districts, placed over each of them a Jain Raja. But Tippu Sultan hanged the last man who held any such title. The Tuluva Jain kings and their descendants degenerated gradually into mere cultivators of the soil. One of them became a pensioner of the East India Company. *Travels*, Vol. 3, Chapter XIV, p. 19.

[3] Barth, *Religions of India*, p. 140.

[4] Vide *Asiatic Researches*, Vol. IX, Chapters 4 and 5. See also Beauchamp, *Hindu Manners and Customs*, pp. 685—700.

[5] Fergusson devotes one whole book to Jain Architecture, Bk. V.

The Jain contribution to Tamil culture.

The Jains had been great students and copyists of books.[1] They loved literature and art for their own sake. The Jain contribution to Tamil literature forms the most precious possession of the Tamils. The largest portion of the Sanskrit derivatives found in the Tamil language was introduced by the Jains. They altered the Sanskrit words which they borrowed in order to bring it in accordance with Tamil euphonic rules.[2] One great peculiarity of Jain Tamil literature is that in some of the works which have become classical, *Kural* and *Nāladiyār* for example, there is no mention of any particular God or religion. Not only Tamil literature but Canarese literature also owes a great deal to Jains. In fact they were its originators. "Until the middle of the twelfth century it is exclusively Jain and Jaina literature continues to be prominent for long after. It includes all the more ancient and many of the most eminent of Canarese writings."[3] Thus Rev. F. Kittel: "They have not only written from sectarian motives, but also from a love for science and have reproduced several Sanskrit scientific works in Canarese."[4]

The Doctrine of Ahimsa.

Ahimsa or non-killing of living beings has been the essential principle of Jain moral conduct and, as M. Barth observes, "No Hindu sect has carried *Ahimsa* further, that is, respect for absti-

[1] Burnell, *South Indian Palaeography*, p. 88.

[2] Caldwell, *Comparative Grammar of Dravidian languages*, (III Edition) p. 85.

[3] E. P. Rice, *The History of Canarese Literature*, (The Heritage of India Series), p. 12.

[4] *Indian Antiquary*, Vol. IV, 1875, p. 15.

nence from everything that has life. Not only do they abstain absolutely from all kinds of flesh, but the more rigid of them drink only filtered water, breathe only through a veil and go sweeping the ground before them, for fear of unconsciously swallowing or crushing any invisible animalcule." How far this Jain respect for the life of living beings, a respect shown in daily practice, has influenced the Vedic rites and ceremonies can be seen from the fact that animal sacrifices in certain religious functions were completely stopped, and images of beasts made of flour were substituted for the real and veritable ones required in conducting *Yāgams*. Tamil poets have received inspiration in this matter from the Jains and passages might be cited from Tamil literature to indicate the extreme abhorrence with which Dravidians, a large section of them at any rate, regarded eating flesh.

Temples and Institutions.

Idol worship and temple building on a grand scale in South India have also to be attributed to Jain influence. The essence of Brahminism was not idol worship. How came it then that the Dravidians built large temples in honour of their gods ? The answer is simple. The Jains erected statues to their Tirthankaras and other spiritual leaders and worshipped them in large temples. As this method of worship was highly impressive and attractive, it was at once imitated. Especially after the advent of Appar and Sambandar, a period of miracles and piety was inaugurated and it was at this time that the whole country was studded with temples.[1] It is further curious to note that, in the temples so constructed, a niche was given to each of the saints who in any way contributed to the revival of Saivism. In the great temple at Madura, as many as sixty-three Nāyanārs or Saiva devotees have been given a niche, each of them. One wonders if the Saivites had not borrowed this custom from the Jains who worshipped their saints in the way described, long before these Nāyanārs flourished. By far the most important of the Jain influences that led either to the intellectual or moral uplift of the Dravidians was the establishment throughout South India of *Matams* and *Pātasālas* to counteract the effects of Jain centres of learning and propagandism.[2] Such *Pātasālas* or theological seminaries are now scattered throughout South India.

Modern Tamil Jains.

A reference may now be made to the present state of South Indian Jains.[3] According to the Census Report there are nearly 28,000 Jains in the Madras Presidency, the districts South

[1] *Tamilian Antiquary*, No. 3, p.23.

[2] Fergusson, Book V, *Indian Architecture*.

[3] The following note of Mr. Sastram Ayyar, translated by Bower, may be read with interest. "There are about 15 families of Jains in Madras, residing in Muttialpettah and Peddunaikanpettah. They are School-masters, or merchants of whom the writer of this essay was one. Some of the *Souars* from Jeypoor, residing in Mint street, are Jains. There are also Jain families in Royapuram, the Mount, Palaveram, Madavaram, Pondicherry and Tanjore. They have a temple at Chittamoor, 30 miles west of Pondicherry, dedicated to Singapurinada. They have also a Pagoda at *Perrul*."

Kanara, North Arcot and South Arcot alone containing more than 23,000 Jains. The majority of these scattered remnants are poor cultivators, ignorant, illiterate and all unconscious of the noble history and spacious traditions of their fathers. Their brethren in the north who represent a survival of early Jainism are comparatively better off in life, most of them being wealthy traders, merchants and money-lenders.[1]

The vast Jain remains in South India of mutilated statues, deserted caves and ruined temples at once recall to our mind the greatness of the religion in days gone by and the theological rancour of the Brahmins who wiped it out of all active existence. The Jains had been forgotten; their traditions have been ignored; but, the memory of that bitter struggle between Jainism and Hinduism, characterised by bloody episodes in the south, is constantly kept alive in the series of frescoes on the wall of the *Mantapam* of the Golden Lily Tank of the famous Minakshi Temple at Madura. These paintings illustrate the persecution and impaling of the Jains at the instance of the arch-enemy of Jainism, Tirujñānasambandar. As though this were not sufficient to humiliate that unfortunate race, the whole tragedy is gone through at five of the twelve annual festivals at the Madura temple. It is, indeed, sad to reflect that, beyond the

The Jain remains.

[1] *Imperial Gazeteer, Bombay Presidency,* Vol. I, pp. 17, 18 and 227.

lingering legends in secluded spots and the wayside statues of her saints and martyrs, Jainism in the south has left little to testify to the high purposes, the comprehensive proselytizing zeal and the political influence which she inspired in her fiery votaries of old.

CHAPTER VI.

JAINS AND TAMIL LITERATURE.

In one of the earlier chapters, reference was made to the Jain contribution to South Indian learning and culture. The subject is so vast that an attempt is made now to indicate, only in rough outlines, the nature of such a contribution and its permanent influence.

Early Tamil literature.

It is well known that, among the Dravidian tribes of South India, the Tamils were the first to possess a literature. Unfortunately, most of the pre-Sangam works are either lost or not known to us. If they are available, we will be able to know something about the religion, the morals and the civilization of the pre-Sangam age in the Tamil land. Some of the earliest of Tamil poems, however, give us a clue to understand the type of culture that must have prevailed in the country, long before the earliest Brahmin settlers under the leadership of sage Agastyar came to the Podiyil hill. Poems like *Ahanānūru* and *Puranānūru* which have been recently published show that the earliest tribes were a warlike race like the Germanic tribes. They loved war and adventurous life. Their literature, therefore, is full of references to their martial habits. A change in the tone of Tamil literature is noticed after the advent of the Aryans, among whom must be included the Buddhists and the Jains. Under the influence of the Brahmins who were brought in by kings and chiefs for the purpose of ministering to the spiritual needs of the people, Tamil poetry came to be largely panegyric in nature. But the Jains and the Buddhists who entered the Tamil land in large and ever-increasing numbers disliked the military habits and the hunting pursuits of the Tamils, as being contrary to the spirit of their religions which proclaimed, above all else, the message of *Ahimsa*. Their simple life, their intense piety, and the zeal with which they propagated their faith, soon won for them royal patronage and court favour. These they were not slow to take advantage of. Well versed in Sanskrit and Prakrit literature, they imposed their ideals, their expressions and forms of life on the literature of the early Tamils. This largely accounts for the didactic nature of early Sangam literature. Yet, as Mr. M. Srinivasa Ayyangar remarks : "In every department of Tamil literature, we can still perceive a slender veil of Dravidian thought running through. Its groundwork is purely non-Aryan and its superstructure necessarily Aryan." This period in which Aryan thought and learning gained mastery over native sentiments and literature, and in which the second and third Academies are said to have flourished in the city of Madura, is sometimes called the Augustan age of Tamil literature.

The Augustan age of Tamil literature.

It is a matter for fruitful speculation to inquire what would have been the trend of Tamil literature but for the advent of the Jains and the Buddhists, more particularly of the former. In all probability, we would never have had those masterpieces of Tamil literature like *Kural*, *Silappadikāram*, *Manimēkalai* and *Chintāmani*. We would certainly have had brilliant pieces of panegyric poetry composed by intelligent Brahmin bards. But literature of the kind that it' is now the proud boast of the Tamils to possess, we could certainly not have had.

Scholars have divided Tamil literature into broad periods, according to the nature of influences that were predominant in particular periods. It was Damodaram Pillay, the learned editor of *Tolkāppiyam* and other works, that first attempted a division of this kind. His division is as follows :— Damodaram Pillay's classification of Tamil literature.

1. Pre-historic.
2. Alphabetic.
3. Grammatic.
4. Academic from 10150 B.C.—150 B.C.
5. Lethargic 150 B.C.—50 A.D.
6. Jain 50 A.D.—350 A.D.
7. Puranic 350—1150 A.D.
8. Monastic 1150—1850 A.D.

An improvement was made on this division by the late Mr. Suryanarayana Sastri. His Suryanarayana Sastri's classification.

scheme looks quite simple. He has divided Tamil literature into the following periods:—

1. The early 8000 B.C. to 100 A.D. including the age of the Sangams or the three Academies.
2. The Medieval.
3. (*a*) The first half : 100—600 A.D. when the five major and the five minor epics and other works were written.
   (*b*) The second half : 600 to 1400 A.D. the period when, according to him, *Tēvāram*, *Tiruvoimozhi*, *Rāmāyanam*, *Nala Venbā* and other works were written.
4. The Modern : from 1400 A.D.

It would take us far away from the purpose of this work, if we entered into a critical examination of these two schemes of classification. Nevertheless, it may be remarked that the above divisions are based on mere legends about the existence of the three Academies, each extending over several thousands of years, thus taking the beginnings of South Indian History and of Tamil culture to the glacial period. More patriotic than sound, the divisions cannot now stand the test of historic criticism. We shall, therefore, pass on to the classification of Dr. Caldwell.

The learned bishop divides Tamil literature into seven cycles, citing some author or work as representative of each cycle.

Dr. Caldwell's Classification.

No.	Name of Cycle.	Period.	Representative works or authors.
1.	The Jaina cycle or the cycle of the Sangam.	8th or 9th-12th or 13th century.	*Kural, Nāladiyār, Chintāmani, Divakaram* and *Nannūl.*
2.	The Rāmāyana cycle.	13th century ..	Kamban.
3.	The Saiva revival cycle.	13th and 14th centuries.	*Tēvāram* and *Tiruvāchakam.*
4.	The Vaishnava cycle.	Do.	The Vaishnava *Prabandhams.*
5.	The cycle of the literary revival.	15th and 16th centuries.	....
6.	The Anti-Brahminical cycle.	17th century ..	Siddhar school came into existence during this period.
7.	The Modern cycle ..	18th and 19th centuries.	....

That the above classification is defective in many respects needs no mention. Those defects have been pointed out in an able manner by the late Prof. Sundaram Pillai in his *Milestones in Tamil Literature.* And yet the bishop's remarks in regard to the existence of the Sangam about the 8th century A.D. need not be dismissed with such contempt, as has been done by scholars who have criticised him. There are to be found, even to-day, when our knowledge of epigraphy has advanced considerably, students of ancient history of South India, who think that the period of Sangam activity is to be sought in the century prior to the time of the Tamil Vatteluttu inscriptions which begin in the Pandya and the Chera countries in the last quarter of the 8th century A.D. Apart from the question whether or not many Sangam authors flourished in the early centuries of the Christian era, evidences are growing to show that what is known as Sangam literature was perhaps reduced to writing in the 6th and 7th centuries A.D. This consideration need not, however, prevent us from rejecting the classification of Dr. Caldwell as unsound. Other classifications of Tamil literature are those by Sir William Hunter and Mr. Julien Vinson of Paris, both of which are however vitiated by the conclusion of Dr. Caldwell which, in some respects, the two savants had accepted. Of these Julien Vinson's deserves mention, as it approaches accuracy in the sequence of events mentioned. In one respect he has, like Caldwell, grossly erred in attributing the rise of Vaishnavites to the 15th and 16th centuries. According to the French scholar there were—

Julien Vinson's classification.

(1) a period of essays, pamphlets and short poems (6th and 7th centuries);

(2) a period of Jain predominance (8th century);

(3) a period of struggle between Saivas and Jains (9th century) ;

(4) a period of Saiva predominance (10th century) ; and

(5) a period of Vaishnavas (15th and 16th centuries).

As we have already seen, we must look to the middle half of the 7th century A.D. for the period of struggle between the Saivas and the Jains. After that period the Jains were exterminated and their influence was little felt, and yet it is exactly in that century Julien Vinson would have us suppose that the Jains predominated. We have stated the position taken up by the various English scholars as regards periods of Tamil literature merely to show that, so long as we are not able to fix milestones in the history of literature, no such attempt can be considered as either sound or rational. Nevertheless, it had become the fashion for writers on Tamil history and literature to adopt such a plan. The talented author of the *Tamil Studies*, notwithstanding his trenchant and accurate criticism of the views of various scholars in regard to this subject, has himself committed the error which he warned others to avoid. We shall therefore take up for our consideration whether his division of Tamil literature into periods is at all sound. He has exhibited his arrangement thus :— M. Srinivasa Ayyangar's classification.

Period.	Religion.	Literature.	Language.
B.C. 600–200.	I. Animistic ..	I. Academic (Tolkāppiyam, Kural, etc.)	I. Early *Grammar*: Agastyam, Tolkāppiyam.
B.C. 200–150 A.D.	II. Buddhist ..		
A.D. 150–500	III. Jaina ...	II. Classic (Silappadikāram, Manimēkalai, Pattupāttu etc.)	
A.D. 500–950	IV. Brahmanic ..	III. Hymnal (Tēvāram, Tiruvāchakam. Tiruvoimozhi, etc.)	II. Medieval *Grammar*: Tolkāppiyam, Kallādam, Virasoliyam.
A.D. 950—1200.	V. Sectarian ..	IV. Translations—(Kamban's Rāmāyana, Kachiyappar's Skantham, etc.)	
A.D. 1200—1450.	VI. Reformatory.	V. Exegetical (Commentaries by Nacchi-narkiniyar, Adiyarkunallar, etc.)	III. Modern *Grammar*: Virasoliyam and Nannūl.
A.D. 1450—1850.	VII. Modern ..	VI. Miscellaneous.	

According to him, 150—500 A.D. forms a distinct period—the Jain period of Tamil literature. The representative works ascribed by him to this period are *Silappadikāram*, *Manimēkalai*, *Pattupāttu*, etc. Of these only *Silappadikāram* may be considered as a Jain work. More properly, it is a work written by a Jain monk. Can therefore the existence of only one Jain work in a period covering nearly four centuries be considered sufficient enough as to call it the Jain period of Tamil literature ? It cannot also be supposed that the style and diction of *Silappadikāram* were such as to have influenced the other literary productions of the age. Moreover, some of the best books written by the Jains belong to 9th or 10th century A.D. For these reasons, 150—500 A.D. cannot be considered as the Jain period of Tamil literature. Again 200 B.C.—150 A.D. is supposed to be the Buddhistic period and the main works cited for this period are *Tolkāppiyam* and *Kural*. The author of *Tolkāppiyam* is usually supposed to be a Brahmin, but very cogent reasons have been adduced lately for regarding him a Jain, while *Kural* was certainly composed by a Jain. There are no traces of Buddhistic influence in any of these works. The best thing, therefore, seems to be not to divide Tamil literature into periods corresponding to the predominance of religious faiths.

Instead, therefore, of adopting the familiar plan of dividing Tamil literature into periods, we shall attempt to classify Jain works under various groups, such as Didactics, Kāvyas and other treatises.

1. Didactic Works.

Among works of this nature composed by the Jains, special mention must be made of *Tirukkural*, *Nāladiyār* and *Pazhamozhi Nānūru*.

Kural: its importance.

1. *Kural.*—We have already noticed that its author was a Jain. But every rival sect in the Tamil country has claimed *Kural* as its

own. The *Kural* is a masterpiece of Tamil literature, containing some of the highest and purest expressions of human thought. Writing of *Kural*, M. Ariel says: "That which above all is wonderful in the *Kurral* is the fact that its author addresses himself, without regard to castes, peoples or beliefs, to the whole community of mankind; the fact that he formulates sovereign morality and absolute reason; that he proclaims in their very essence, in their eternal abstractedness, virtue and truth; that he presents, as it were, in one group the highest laws of domestic and social life; that he is equally perfect in thought, in language, and in poetry, in the austere metaphysical contemplation of the great mysteries of the Divine Nature, as in the easy and graceful analysis of the tenderest emotions of the heart."

The *Kural* owes much of its popularity to its exquisite poetic form. "It is an apple of gold in a network of silver." It has been translated into various European languages. It is cosmopolitan in its teachings and appeals directly both to the head and heart of every religionist. Even Christians do not neglect *Kural*. On the other hand, they strongly believe that the teachings of Valluvar were more or less borrowed from Saint Thomas who, according to tradition, obtained his martyrdom at Mylapore. Thus, Dr. Pope :—"Mayilapur to us is better known as S. Thome. In this neighbourhood a Christian community has existed from the earliest times. Here are fine old Armenian and Portuguese churches ; and a Christian inscription of the 5th century. Here Pantaenus of Alexandria taught ; and we are quite warranted in imagining Tiruvalluvar, the thoughtful poet, the eclectic, to whom the teaching of the Jains was as familiar as that of every Hindu sect, who was not hindered by any caste prejudices from familiar intercourse with foreigners, whose one thought was to gather knowledge from every source, whose friend, the sea-captain, would bring him tidings of every stranger's arrival (coming from Ceylon, perhaps, in his own dhoney) : we may fairly, I say, picture him pacing along the sea-shore with the Christian teachers, and imbibing Christian ideas, tinged with the peculiarities of the Alexandrian school, and day by day working them into his own wonderful *Kurral*."

2. *Nāladiyār.*—*Nāladiyār*, another Jain work, is an anthology containing 400 quatrains in 40 chapters. It stands in the estimation of the Tamils, next to *Kural*. It treats about the transitoriness of wealth and other vanities of human wishes. It lays special importance on the cultivation of virtue and truth and the possession of saintly character. There is a tradition regarding the composition of *Nāladiyār*. *Nāladiyār : its tradition.* The story goes : Once upon a time, 8,000 Jain sages visited the Pandyan kingdom during a period of famine in their own native place. When the famine ended and when better days

dawned, these Jains prepared to go back to their own country. The Pandyan king was very unwilling to lose the company of these learned men and refused them permission to return. Thereupon, one night, these 8,000 Jains placed under their respective seats, each one quatrain, and gently slipped out of the city. When the king heard of this, he got angry and ordered a search to be made of their residence. The 8,000 quatrains were brought to the king. He ordered them to be thrown into the river Vaigai. Much to the astonishment of the king, 400 of these bits swam against the current and came to the bank. These were then picked up, collated and published.

Apart from traditions, there is no doubt that some Jains of Madura were the authors of these poems containing excellent moral sentiments. The period of their composition must be referred to the time after the founding of the Digambara Jain Sangam at Madura (470 A.D.) ; the references in the anthology to Muttaraiyar would further show that these quatrains were written at a time when the Kalabhras were in occupation of the Madura country.

Pazhamozhi Nānūru.

Pazhamozhi Nānūru.—The author of this work was a Jain king of Munrurai, perhaps a feudatory of the Pandyan kings. As every stanza has a proverb tacked to it in the end, it is called *Pazhamozhi* (a proverb). These proverbs, now little remembered, were current in the days of the last Academy at Madura. A careful study of these proverbs will enable us to form an idea of the ancient Tamil civilisation. As in *Kural* the sentiments expressed are cosmopolitan in nature. Some of the topics treated in the book are learning, great men, perseverance, royalty and household life.

This book has now been edited in a masterly manner by the late Mr. T. Chelvakesavaroya Mudaliar of the Pachiappa's College, Madras.

2. Major Kavyas.

In Tamil literature there are five major kāvyas and five minor ones. The major epics are *Manimēkalai*, *Silappadikāram*, *Valayāpadi*, *Chintāmani* and *Kundalakēsi*. Of these the Jains were responsible for three.

Silappadikāram.

Silappadikāram.—The references to Kountiadigal and to innumerable Jain *stōtras* clearly indicate the Jain origin of the book. As has already been stated, its author was Ilangōvadigal, a brother of the Chera prince, Senguttuvan. *Silappadikāram* is a storehouse of information on the state of Jains in the Tamil land. Being composed at a time when the Jains had just established themselves in the various centres of learning, the work does not naturally contain denunciations of other faiths. The moral sought to be inculcated by the epic is, that as life, youth and riches are evanescent, men should take warning and make the best use of their life in doing good deeds, which alone would be of benefit in their after-life. Divided into three cantos of 30 *Kadais*, the work is dedicated to the three great capital cities of the Tamil land. The story is so well known that it is needless to give a summary of it here.

Valayāpadi is an unpublished Jain work. A study of the 50 and odd poems of this epic published a few years ago in *Sen Tamil* indicate that the epic treats of lives of Jain sages.

Chintāmani: its excellence.

Chintāmani.—The greatest in importance, of the Jain works, is of course *Chintāmani*. The frequent use of the double plural 'kal' in *Chintāmani* indicates that its author belongs to the period of the Alvars whose writings are replete with such a kind of double plural. Tiruttakkadēvar, the author of *Chintāmani*, is an eminent Sanskritist. His work not only contains what was best in Sanskrit literature but also gives us the essence of the Sangam poems. Add to these a thorough and intelligent grasp of the chief tenets of the Jain faith. It treats of the life of a king, Jīvakan, from his birth to the attainment of bliss. The various incidents connected with the life of this hero are intended to preach the following morals :—

1. That a king should not be hasty in his action and that he should consult his ministers several times before determining on final action.

2. Ruin is the ultimate result of the actions of those who keep with women.

3. Preceptor's orders and his advice should be implicitly obeyed.

4. He who wants to conquer his enemy should never utter a word about his designs under any circumstance, till the proper time comes for realising his object.

5. It must be the duty of men to relieve the distress of others.

6. No one should ill-treat those who had never rendered him any injury.

7. A true friend will prove to be a source of great help.

8. Under all circumstances, whether of joy or of sorrow, it is becoming for men not to lose their mental equilibrium.

9. Mercy and tenderness to all animals must be the watchword of all men.

10. Try to rectify the man who is pursuing evil ways.

And, above all, never forget kindness done to you.

It is not easy to determine the original of this Tamil epic. It is conjectured that some of the Sanskrit treatises like *Kshatra Chūdāmani*, and *Kattia Chintāmaṇi* might be the basis of this work.

Tiruttakkadēvar: tradition regarding the composition of *Chintāmani*.

Nothing definite is known of the life of the author Tiruttakkadēvar. But a tradition gives the following account of the circumstance under which the epic was composed. According to this, Tiruttakkadēvar belongs to the Chola country and learned various arts from renowned masters. He studied all the Sangam works with great care and was equally proficient in Sanskrit. Hearing of the fame of Madura, a great centre of Tamil learning, Tiruttakkadēvar went there and spent most of his time in conversing with learned Pundits. One day, the poets of the city made a somewhat disparaging remark about the puritanic nature of Jain compositions and desired to know if Tiruttakkadēvar was competent to write on such subjects as love and luxury. He replied that the Jains cared only for serious poetry and that their religion would not permit of such contemptible things as love and luxury being made subjects of literary compositions. The Sangam poets, persisting in their remark, Tiruttakkadēvar proceeded at once to his preceptor and laid the full case before him. The preceptor, equally anxious to demonstrate the capacity of the Jains to undertake literary work of such kind and willing to test the ability of his disciple, asked him to compose poems on a jackal that was just then passing by. Instantaneously, Tiruttakkadēvar began reciting poems on the subject and produced a work known as *Nariviruttam* of which we shall speak later. The preceptor, perfectly satisfied with the elegance, style and subject matter of the *Nariviruttam*, commanded the pupil to compose a bigger work on the life of Jīvakan and to show it to the Sangam poets of Madura. Such is the traditional account of the composition of *Jīvakachintāmani*.

Be the circumstance of the composition of *Chintāmani* what it may, there is no doubt it has been praised as one of the choicest masterpieces of Tamil literature. Not only the Jains but also scholars belonging to Saiva faith have eulogised it in terms that at once speak of the immense popularity of the Tamil epic. In order to counteract the effect of such a work on popular imagination, Sēkkizhār had to undertake the composition of *Periyapurānam*.

The place of *Chintāmani* in Tamil literature.

The following stanzas extracted from *Sēkkizhār Nāyanār Purānam* explain the high position that *Chintāmani* was occupying during his time.

கலகமிடு மமண்முருட்டுக் கையர்பொய்யே
கட்டிநடத் தியசிந்தா மணியை மெய்யென்
றுலகிலுளோர் சிலர்கற்று நெற்குத்துண்ணு
துமிக்குத்திக் கைவருந்திக் கறவைநிற்க
மலடுகறந் துளந்தளர்ந்து குளிர்பூஞ்சோலை
வழியிருக்கக் குழியில்விழுந் தளறுபாய்ந்து
விலைதருமென் கரும்பிருக்க விரும்பை மென்று
விளக்கிருக்க மின்மினித்தீக் காய்ந்துநொந்தார்.
20

வளவனுங்குண் டமண்புரட்டுத் திருட்டுச்சிந்தா
மணிக்கதையை மெய்யென்று வரிசைகூற
வுளமகிழ்ந்து பலபடப்பா ராட்டிக்கேட்க வுபயகுல
மணிவிளக்காஞ் சேக்கிழார்கண்
டிளவரசன் றனைநோக்கிச் சமணர் பொய்ந்நூ
லிதுமறுமைக் காகாதிம் மைக்குமற்றே
வளமருவு கின்றசிவ கதையிம்மைக்கு
மறுமைக்கு முறுதியென வளவன் கேட்டு. 21

Sēkkizhār's *Lives of the Saints*, inspiring though it was, had not superseded *Chintāmani* in its popularity. On the other hand, both in matter and diction, the Jain epic shone all the brighter, by contrast. That it is so is seen from the fact that, when in the early part of the eighteenth century, Kachiyappa Munivar, the disciple of Sivagñāna Munivar, wanted to compose poems in honour of Saiva saints, he set *Chintāmani* as his model.

As many, even among Tamil scholars, do not appear to know the story of Jīvakan, the following concise account is extracted [1]:—

The story of Jivakan.

"Sacchanthan was the king of Emankatanadu and married Vijayai. So enamoured was he of the queen that he neglected his government and left his minister, Kattiankāran, in charge of it. The latter proved treacherous to his master : he formed a plot against his life and assasinated him. Vijayai was driven out of the realm and the usurper ascended the throne. Advanced in pregnancy, the queen gave birth to Jīvakan in the cemetery amid a wild forest and began the life of a devotee. The child was taken by a rich merchant who brought him up as his own and posted him up in all branches of learning. When he had come of age, a gang of free-booters attacked the city and plundered it. The young hero pursued them and rescued the plunder. In appreciation of his valour, Pasukavalan, a citizen, gave him his daughter, Govindaiyār, in marriage. While enjoying the happiness of wedded life, he competed with Tattaiyār in a *Vīna* performance, and, proving himself far superior to her in the art, gained the hand and

[1] Purnalingam Pillai, *History of Tamil Literature.*

heart of the musical lady. Then he was given certain scented powders of their own manufacture by Gunamālai and Suramanjari and was asked to judge which was of stronger smell. He decided in favour of the former who accepted him in marriage. After exhibiting his skill at metamorphosis, he tamed a rut elephant of the minister. Then he went on a travelling tour and met Padumai, a princess of the Pallava kingdom, in a park in the agony of a venomous snake-bite. At once Jīvakan showed his proficiency in the healing art and rescued her from death. As a mark of gratitude, the rescued lady married him. His next feat was doing wonders at Kema-māpuram and wedding a Vaisya girl, Kemasari. From Takkanadu he proceeded to Susanadesam, and there proved his skill in archery and wedded the princess Kanakamālai. Then he started on his travels, and reached Thandaka-Araniam, where he met his mother and obtained her blessing. Returning to his own city, he fell in love with Vimalai, a merchant's daughter, and took her for wife. He then heard of Suramanjari's dejection and contempt for man and hastened to cure her melancholy. Wearing a mask he played Gita-natakam and so pleased her with his performance that she surrendered herself to him. They became man and wife. The next feat that awaited him was hitting at a target and winning the youngest daughter, Ilakkanai, of the king of Vidēham. Now the fame of Jīvakan spread far and wide and stirred up fears in the mind of the usurper. The latter laid plots for his life, but the young hero slew him and ascended the throne of his ancestors. He then conquered his father's dominions and made them acknowledge him as sovereign. Having regained his lost kingdom, he ruled it wisely and well and married Ilakkanai, his maternal uncle's daughter. With her and his wives he spent his time most happily and had by them a number of sons to whom he partitioned his dominions. Then he and his devoted female associates renounced the world and spent their time in doing charity and performing austerities. Jīvakan attained Moksha."

Nariviruttam: its composition.

Before we leave this part of the subject a word or two might be mentioned regarding *Nariviruttam*. The circumstance of its composition has already been mentioned. It is a small work consisting of 50 stanzas embodying some of the noblest tenets of Jainism. The style is very charming, appealing both to the young and old. The story seems to be based upon *Hitōpadēsa*. The author wants to illustrate the transitoriness of human wishes and the unstability of wealth and enjoyment. The method adopted to illustrate this simple truth is an old and familiar one in the Tamil land. Briefly the story is this:—Once upon a time, a wild elephant was destroying the crops in a field. A brave hunter wanted to kill it. Taking his stand upon an elevated ground, underneath which poisonous cobras lived in their holes, he aimed at the elephant. The arrow struck the animal when with fury it rushed upon him and fell dead on the spot. This disturbed the peace of the cobras and roused them up. One of them came out of the hole and saw the hunter standing. Raising its hood it bit him. The hunter immediately died, not however before cutting the snake into two. Thus the dead bodies of the elephant, the hunter who killed it and the snake that killed the hunter only to be killed in its turn, were all strewn together. A jackal which was observing all this from under a neighbouring bush came out and in great joy exclaimed, "What a huge mass of food for me ! The elephant's body will last for six months, the hunter's will be sufficient for seven days, while the remains of the snake will be sufficient for the day." Thus saying it approached the body of the hunter. Close by, there was his bow. The jackal bit the strings unawares and the bow straightening with all its force struck its body killing it on the spot. The moral of the story is obvious.

3. Minor Kavyas.

We shall now proceed to an account of the minor Kāvyas. Among these must be mentioned *Nīlakēsi*. Properly speaking it is in the nature of a treatise on logic. It is in manuscript form and has not yet been published. The heroine Nīlakēsi is depicted as refuting the arguments of various other sects prevailing in the

The minor Kāvyas.

land, such as Buddha, Ajivaka, Sankhya, Vaisēshika and finally proving the superiority of Jainism. The author of this work is unknown. There is a very good commentary of this minor epic by a great Jain sage, Samaya Divākara Munivar.

Next among the minor works must be mentioned the *Brihathkathā* or *Perunkathai.* It is a 5th or 6th century work. The author of this charming epic is believed to be Konguvēl. It seems to be a translation of the old *Brihathkathā* written in Paisācha language by a great pundit known as Gunādittya. It treats *in extenso* of the life of Udayanakumāra, king of Vatsadēsa. In style and diction it is supposed to transcend even *Chintāmani.* Mahāmahōpādhyāya Swaminadha Ayyar has undertaken the publication of this work and in all probability it is now in the press.

The third minor work of the Jains is *Yasōdarakāvyam.* The author was an unknown Jain sage. It teaches the following precepts :—

(*a*) Under no circumstance the life of living things should be taken away.

(*b*) Lying and deception are bad.

(*c*) Stealing is sinful.

(*d*) Adultery is heinous.

(*e*) One should be content with just the necessaries of life and no more.

Besides indicating these morals, *Yasōdarakāvyam* is an epitome " of useful, polite and entertaining information calculated to facilitate the improvement of youth and to answer the purpose of a text of general ethics to those more advanced in life."

The other two minor epics are *Nāgakumāra-kāvyam* and *Chūlāmani.* We need only mention other Jain works. *Eladi* is a work on didactics composed by a Jain. It is a moral poem by Kanimēthāviyār. Each quatrain is supposed to combine, compare and illustrate five or six points of practical wisdom. *Kalingattupparani* is the well-known poem describing the battle in the Kalinga country between the forces of Kulōttunga Chola and the Northern Kalinga Raja. Selected stanzas from *Kalingattuparani* are translated in the form of verse by the late Mr. Kanakasabhai Pillai in the pages of *The Indian Antiquary.* One peculiarity regarding *Kalingattuparani* [1] is that it is perhaps the only work written by the Jains on things pertaining to war. Besides these there are various *stōtras* composed by the Jains such as *Tirukkalambagam, Tirunūrrandādi* which have recently been published. The Jains had a genius for lexicon work. *Chūdāmani Nigandu* is a work of this kind. It was composed by a Jain, Vīramandala Purushar, disciple of Gunabhadra Acharyar of Tirunarunkunrai. He belongs to the period of Krishnadeva Rāya. In grammatical science the Jains

[1] That the author was a Jain is clear from the following stanza attributed to him, composed in reply to a question by Apayan :—

செய்யும்வினையு மிருளுண்பதுவுந் தேனுநறவு மூனுங்களவும்
பொய்யுங்கொலையு மறவுந்தவிரப் பொய்தீரறநூல் செய்தார்தமதூர்
கையுமுகமு மிதழும்விழியுங் காலுநிறமும் போலுங்கமலம்
கொய்யுமடவார் விழிவாயதரங் கோபங்கமழுந் தீபங்குடியே.

had always excelled. Besides *Nannūl* of the celebrated Pavanandi, there are other treatises such as *Nēmināthum* by Gunavīrapandita, *Yāpparungalakkārigai* by Amritasāgara Muni. *Srīpurānam* in prose and *Mērumandarapurānam* in verse are two other Jain works, expository of religion and theology. The above list is by no means exhaustive. A large number of Jain works treating of various branches of learning unfortunately lie buried in the archives of *Matams*. It is to be hoped that enlightened South Indian Jains will bring them to the light of day and thus enable us to realise what great part the Jains had played in the literary history of South India.

CHAPTER VII.

THE JAINS IN THE DECCAN.

Formation of Sangas.

We have seen how the Jains migrated south from northern India and how Bhadrabāhu sent away all the 12,000 Jains under the leadership of Visākhamuni to the Chola and the Pandya countries. The Jains entered the Carnatic and colonised the country on the borders of the Western Ghats, as well as the southern portion of the Mysore State. By this time, the zeal for proselytism grew and the whole Jain Sangam wandered over the various parts of the south of India and established themselves in North and South Arcot districts and in Madura. Among these religious enthusiasts were great scholars who had enriched the literature of the country. Some of the most learned among them grouped together and formed various Sangas. Each Sangam was sub-divided into many *Ganas*, each of which was again divided into many *Gachchhas*. We further learn from the inscriptions that, of all these Sangams, the Dramila Sanga was the most prominent, the Nandigana within it being particularly noteworthy.[1]

Jains very influential in the past.

The whole of South India was strewn with small groups of learned Jain ascetics who were slowly but surely spreading their morals through the medium of their sacred

[1] *Epigraphia Carnatica*, Shimoga, Vol. II, No. 35.

literature composed in the various vernaculars of the country. But it is a mistake to suppose that these ascetics were indifferent towards secular affairs in general. To a certain extent it is true that they did not mingle with the world. But we know from the account of Megasthenes that, so late as the fourth century B.C., "The Sarmanes or the Jain Sarmanes who lived in the woods were frequently consulted by the kings through their messengers regarding the cause of things."[1] Jain *Gurus* have been founders of states that for centuries together were tolerant towards the Jain faith, but the prohibition of blood-shedding so emphatically preached by the Jain moral code led to the political debasement of the whole Jain race.[2] In this part of the inquiry, an attempt is made to indicate, in rough outlines, the nature of the vast political influence weilded by the Jains in that part of India, represented in modern geography by the Bombay Presidency and the Native States of Mysore, and to trace the steps by which that political ascendancy was lost.

Periods of Deccan history.

It will, perhaps, be better if the general reader remembers the following points regarding the political history of the Deccan :—

(1) The Gangas exercised their sway over the greater part of Mysore from the second century A.D. to the eleventh century A.D., when they were overthrown by the Cholas. The

M'Crindle, *Fragments of Megasthenes.*

[2] *Journal of the Royal Asiatic Society*, Vol. IX, p. 172.

Cholas did not stay in the country for a long time; they were soon expelled by the Hoysalas who established a separate dynasty which continued to exist for three centuries (from the 11th to 14th century A.D.).

(2) The early Chalukyas established their sway about the sixth century and after a vigorous rule divided themselves into several branches (about 615 A.D.), the Eastern and the Western Chalukyas.

(3) The Eastern Chalukyas ruled from 750 A.D. to the eleventh century A.D., when their dominions were annexed by the Cholas.

(4) The Western Chalukyas succumbed to the Rāshtrakūta power in about 750 A.D.

(5) The Rāshtrakūtas who thus succeeded to the power of the Western Chalukyas maintained their independence down to 973 A.D., when they were defeated by the Western Chalukyas who once again established their rule, albeit for a short period (973 A.D.—1156 A.D.).

(6) In 1156 A.D., the Western Chalukyas fell a prey to a new power, the Kalachuris, who ruled for 30 years (1156 A.D.—1186 A.D.).

(7) The Hoysalas, as already mentioned, established their dynasty and their sway extended over the whole of Mysore, the modern districts of Salem, Coimbatore, Bellāry and Dharwār.

The various periods may, for convenience, be thus indicated :—

(1) The period of the Gangas (2nd century to 1000 A.D.).

(2) „ Early Chalukyas (500 A.D.—630 A.D.).

(3) „ Eastern Chalukyas (630 A.D.—1000 A.D.).

(4) „ Western Chalukyas (630 A.D.—750 A.D.).

(5) „ Rāshtrakūtas (750 A.D.—973 A.D.).

(6) „ Revival of Western Chalukyas (973 A.D.—1156 A.D.).

(7) „ Kalachuris (1156 A.D.—1186 A.D.).

(8) „ Hoysalas (eleventh century to 1326 A.D.).

Gangavādi: tradition *re* its founding.

According to tradition, Simhānandin, was the founder of Gangavādi (or the 96,000 country) which comprised a large extent of territory bounded on the north by Marundale, east by Tondanād, west by Cochin and Travancore and south by Coimbatore and Salem. The Nagar and Shimoga inscriptions[1] have legends to narrate in connection with the establishment of the Ganga kingdom. It would appear that Simhānandin met at Gangapērur in the Cuddapah district, two young boys Dadiga and Mādhava, sons of one Padmanābha, of the race of Ikshvāku and ruler of the original kingdom from which Gangavādi derived its name. Padmanābha was for some reason or other suddenly attacked by Mahipāla, the ruler of Ujjain. The two young princes, therefore, were sent away for safety to the South of India. On their way they met Simhānandin who, moved by pity on hearing the story of these Ganga princes, took them under his protection, instructed them in all arts and finally procured for them a kingdom. Of course, it was obtained by a miracle. Whatever might be the truth of the legend, there seems to be no doubt that the Ganga kingdom was established under Jain auspices.

This kingdom, according to Lewis Rice, lasted for more than seven centuries. The first king was Mādhava, called Kongani Varma. His date has been ascertained from the Nāgamangala inscription and from the Tamil chronicle called *Kongudēsa Rajākkal* to fall in the second century A.D.[2] Herewith is annexed a table[3] of the Ganga kings of Mysore, compiled entirely from the inscriptions and published by

[1] N. R. 35, Sh. 10.

[2] *Epigraphia Carnatica* N. G. 110.

[3] *Mysore and Coorg from the Inscriptions*, p. 49. See Appendix A., page 155.

Lewis Rice. Jainism became the state creed during the time of Mushkāra or Mukhāra. His predecessors certainly countenanced the Jain faith except the third and fourth kings in the line of Mādhava, who were devotees of the puranic gods. His successor Avanīta was a Jain, the learned Vijayakirti being his preceptor. Durvanīta who succeeded Avanīta was a disciple of the famous Jain grammarian and guru, Pūjyapāda. Of the other Ganga Rajas special mention must be made of Rachamalla Satyavākya, the twenty-first in succession, who tried to revive the waning influence of the Jains. It was during his reign that the famous Chamundarāya, his minister, erected the colossal statue of Gomatēswara, which in daring conception and gigantic dimension stands unrivalled in India.[1] The Chola clouds were at this time hanging over the whole

[1] The following tradition about the famous Chamundarāya will be read with interest. :—

"Chamundarāya, after having established the worship of this image, became proud and elated at placing this God by his own authority at so vast an expense of money and labour. Soon after this, when he performed in honour of the God the ceremony of *Panchamritasnana* for washing the image with five liquids — (milk, curds, butter, honey and sugar), vast quantities of these things were expended in many hundred pots ; but, through the wonderful power of the God, the liquid descended not lower than the navel, to check the pride and vanity of the worshipper. Chamundarāya, not knowing the cause, was filled with grief that his intention was frustrated of cleaning the image completely with this ablution. While he was in this situation, the celestial nymph Padmavati, by order of the God, having transformed herself into the likeness of an aged poor woman, appeared, holding in her hand the five amritas in a Beliya Gola (or small silver pot) for washing the statue, and signified her intention to Chamundarāya, who laughed at the absurdity of this proposal, of accomplishing what it had not been in his power to effect. Out of curiosity, however, he permitted her to attempt it ; when, to the great surprise of the beholders, she washed the image with the liquid brought in the little silver vase. Chamundarāya, repenting his sinful arrogance, performed a second time, with profound respect, his ablution, on which they formerly wasted so much valuable liquids, and washed completely the body of the image. From that time this place is named after the silver vase (or Beliya Gola) which was held in Padmavati's hand."

of the east of the Peninsula and burst with terrific force on the Gangas who, along with the Eastern Chalukyas and Rāshtrakūtas, were swept away by king Rājarājadēva I and his successor. Thus fell, in the ninth century A.D., an important South Indian Jain state, a prey to the militant Cholas.

Chalukyas and Jainism.

The Jain religion seems to have enjoyed considerable patronage at the hands of the early Chalukyas. Pulakēsin II patronised a certain poet, Jain Ravikīrti. Vinayāditya, the eighth in succession from Jayasimha of the early Chalukyas, had for his spiritual adviser Niravadya Pandita.[1] We also learn from an inscription[2] that Vikramāditya II after repairing a Jain temple gave a grant in connection with it to the great disputant, Vijayapandita. But the Chalukyas were tolerant towards other religions, as is evident from the large number of temples built during this period in honour of the Puranic Triad—Brahma, Vishnu and Mahēswara. Nevertheless, Jainism was just then rising to predominance during the time of the Rāshtrakūtas, as will be mentioned presently.

Rāshtrakūtas patronise Jainism.

That Jainism was largely prevalent among the Rāshtrakūtas and that it was the professed creed of many kings are evident, as a good many extant Digambara works were composed during their sway.[3] Thus, the Harivamsa of the Digambara Jains is stated to have been composed by

[1] *Bombay Gazetteer*, Vol. I, Part 2, p. 191.

[2] *Indian Antiquary*, Vol. VII, p. 197.

[3] *Bombay Gazetteer*, Vol. I, Part 2, p. 208.

Jinasēna in the Saka year 705 or 783 A.D., during the reign of Govinda II. Amōghavarsha I was the greatest patron of the Digambara Jains and there is no reason to doubt that he became a convert to the faith. The authorship of *Ratnamālika* has been assigned to Amōghavarsha, while the introductory portion of a Jain mathematical work by Virāchārya, called *Sārasamgraha Ganita*[1] speaks of Amōghavarsha as a follower of the Jina. But the power of the Rāshtrakūtas was rapidly waning and, owing to a quick succession of weak rulers, the Ganga king, Narasimha, had to interfere,[2] and at last succeeded in getting the crown to his own nephew, Indra IV. The latter, evidently a Jain, died about 974 A.D., taking the Jain vow of *Sallēkhana*.[3] After Indra, the political power passed into the hands of the Western Chalukyas.

Jainism and Western Chalukyas.

Jainism, during the period of Western Chalukya revival, ceased to be the conquering faith that it was once. If the traditions of the country are to be believed in, the Jain statues and idols in *bastis* were thrown away and the idols of the puranic gods were substituted. The rule of the Chalukyas was, however, shortlived; for, they were soon

[1] *Bombay Gazetteer*, Vol. I, Part 2, pp. 200-201. This work has been edited and translated in a masterly manner by the late Prof. M. Rangacharya.

[2] *Mysore and Coorg from the Inscriptions*, p. 72.

[3] *Sravana Belgola Inscriptions*, No. 57. The following reflection of Lewis Rice regarding this Jain vow will be of great interest: "The bitterest satirist of human delusions could hardly depict a scene of sterner irony than the naked summit of the bare rock dotted with emaciated devotees both men and women in silent torture awaiting the hour of self-imposed death. The irony is complete when we remember that avoidance of the destruction of life in whatever form is a fundamental doctrine of the sect."

overthrown by the Kalachuris in 1126 A.D. These in their turn had only an ephemeral existence (1126 A.D.—1186 A.D.); yet, the short period of Kalachuri sway furnishes some points of interest to the student of Jain history. We find that Vijjala, the greatest Kalachuri prince, was a Jain by faith. This period is remarkable for the revival of the worship of Siva and for the rise of the Lingāyat sect which, under the leadership of a treacherous minister of Vijjala, Basava, persecuted the Jains.

Whatever the expounders of *Basava Purāna* might say, the fact seems to be beyond doubt that this Basava brought about the assassination of his own master, the Jain king, Vijjala. According to *Vijalarāja Charita*, Basava was hunted out of the country and in despair he threw himself into a well. But, he soon obtained martyrdom at the hands of his followers who flooded the country with literature written in elegant and simple prose, expository of their new creed, Lingāyatism. Myths and legends gathered round the name of Lingāyat leaders, which helped considerably the extermination of the Jains in the Kalachuri Empire. One such legend is noted by Sir Ramakrishna Bhandarkar in an undated inscription of the time of Mahāmandalēswara Kāmadēva (1181 A.D.—1203 A.D.). The story runs thus:

Extirpation of Jainism in the Kalachuri Empire:

God Siva and Pārvati with a host of Saiva saints were enjoying themselves at Kylāsa, when Nārada came and informed the assembly of the its legendary account.

rising power of the Jains and Buddhists. Siva then commanded Veerabhadra to be born in this world in human form, in order to subdue them. In obedience to the order, Veerabhadra appeared in a dream to one Purushōttama Patta and informed him that he would soon beget a son. The dream was realised. The babe was christened Rama and was brought up as a Saiva. Owing to his extreme piety and devotion for Siva, he was called Ekāntada Rāmayya. This was the man who, according to the legend, was responsible for the suppression of Jainism in that country. The story is further narrated that, while the Saiva devotee, Rāmayya, was worshipping, the Jains challenged him to prove the superiority of his god. He took up the challenge. The Jains promised to leave their *bastis* and the country, if Ekāntada Rāmayya agreed to do a miracle. They stipulated that his head must first be cut off and that he must get it back with the help of Siva. Rāmayya agreed. He was beheaded ; but, lo ! next morning he appeared again before the Jains who, however, refused to fulfil their part of the contract. Enraged at this, Ekāntada Rāmayya began to destroy Jain places of worship. The matter was reported to Vijjala who was wroth at the action of the Saivites. But Rāmayya undertook to repeat the miracle. Vijjala was convinced of the superiority of Saiva faith and, dismissing the Jains from his presence admonished them to remain on peaceful terms with the Saivites.

Such is the interesting legend in connection with the extirpation of the Jains in the Kalachuri empire. The story best proves that the Jains sustained a series of reverses in their attempt to revive their faith.

Jainism and early Hoysalas.

There seems to be no doubt that the early Hoysalas of Mysore had been Jains. They came to power on the subversion of the Gangas by the Cholas, in 1004 A.D. Gradually expelling the Cholas from the country which they had occupied, the Hoysalas became supreme in the land by the 12th century. They retained possession of the Bēlūr taluka of the Hasan district. The following story is narrated relating to the origin of the name Hoysala. One Sala, the supposed progenitor of the family, was receiving instruction in the temple of Vasantikadēvi from a certain Jain *Yati*. At that time a tiger was about to pounce upon the *Yati*. The latter observing this handed his rod to Sala exclaiming "Hoy ! Sala !" ("Oh Sala! strike"). Immediately the tiger was killed. From this we have the name Poysala or Hoysala.

The origin of the name 'Hoysala': its story.

Little is known of Sala, but, his successor Vinayāditya seems to have been the disciple of Santidevamuni, a Jain ascetic.[1] Next in importance was the Hoysala king, Bittidēvabittiga, the famous Vishnuvardhana (1111 A.D.—1141 A.D.) who, it is said, had been converted to Vaishnavism by Rāmānujāchārya. As to the cause and history of his conversion, there exist many

[1] *Epigraphia Carnatica*, S. B I, Vol. II, p. 139.

legendary accounts.[1] Vishnuvardhan's first wife was Santaladēvi, a lady disciple of the Jain sage, Prabachandra. This conversion of the king to Vaishnavism was a serious blow to the cause of the Jains in South India, for, it should be noted, that, at any rate, in ancient times, regal religions alone prospered. Cruelly persecuted by the Lingāyats, hated by the powerful Cholas and devoid of the mighty support of the Hoysalas, Jainism naturally succumbed, just as any faith might have, under such distressing circumstances. Nevertheless, attempts were not wanting to restore the faith to its original greatness. Thus Gangarāya, the minister of king Vishnugōpa, and after him Hula, the minister of king Narasimha Dēva, tried in vain to get back the lost influence of the Jains. But the rapid rise of Vaishnavism patronised by Hoysala kings, the systematic and organised opposition of Rāmānuja and a number of Saiva leaders and, last but not least, the severe attacks of the Lingāyats contributed to the downfall of Jainism in the Mysore country. It must not be supposed that Jainism was entirely rooted out of the soil. It was simply losing its vitality, being absorbed gradually in the rising sects of Vaishnavism and other Vedic faiths. A respectable number of persons still followed the faith but they no longer obtained any political influence. The later Rajahs of Mysore not only did not persecute the Jains

[1] *Asiatic Researches*, Vol. IX, Chapters 4 and 5 contain an extensive collection of such legends.

but supported them. Even foreign rulers such as Hyder Naik granted villages to the Jain temples, though, owing to the oppressive nature of the Government, the great festivals at Sravana Belgola and other places were stopped.[1]

Patronage of Jainism by the Kingdom of Vijayanagar.

The Hoysala power lasted to 1326 A.D., when the dynasty was overthrown by Mahomedans. Out of the disorder and anarchy that arose out of Mahomedan rule, the Hindu kingdom of Vijayanagar arose. Not that Jainism expected a great revival under the *aegis* of Hindu rulers of South India who were most of them controlled in their state policy by the Brahmins. But it is pleasing to note that the kings of Vijayanagar never persecuted the Jains. On the other hand, evidences tend to show that they patronised the Jains in a way. Take, for example, the famous Jain-Vaishnava compact of the time of Bukkarāya, 1353 A.D. to 1377 A.D. The reconciliation was effected in this way. After summoning the leaders of both sects, he declared that, as no difference existed between the two sects, they should remain friends. Then, taking the hand of the Jains and placing it in the hands of the Vaishnavas, he gave the injunction that each should pursue his religious practices with perfect freedom. The Sri Vaishnavas were further ordered to get engraved on stone this decree in all the temples throughout the kingdom. "As long as the Sun and Moon endure, the Vaishnava

[1] *Asiatic Researches*, Vol. IX, Ch. 4.

Samaya will continue to protect the Jain Darsana. The Vaishnavas cannot (be allowed to) look upon the Jains as in a single respect different." We cannot say that this order of Bukkarāya was implicitly obeyed by the quarrelling sectarians. One thing, however, seems to be certain. The support given to Jainism gave some stimulus to their activities. For, we find that the son of a general of Harihara II (1307 A.D.—1404 A.D.), as well as one Prince Uga, became converts to the Jain faith.[1] Another inscription mentions that Dēvarāya II (1419 A.D.—1446 A.D.) built a stone temple of Arhat Parsvanātha in a street of the *pan supari* bazaar, at his residence in Vijayanagar. These incidents are sufficient evidence to prove that the ruling families of Vijayanagar not only patronised but some of them also professed the Jain faith.

[1] *South Indian Inscription*, Nos. 152 & 53.

CHAPTER VIII.

THE SANGAM AGE.[1]

Sangam chronology: its importance.

It will be readily admitted by all scholars that no progress can be made in the attempt to resuscitate the ancient history of South India, unless the date of the Tamil Sangam can be fixed. Realising this, several distinguished scholars have been making elaborate researches to find out the true date of the famous Madura Academy. It was the late Professor Seshagiri Sastriyar that first contributed materials for a clearer understanding of the various epochs in the long history of Tamil literature. A certain 'officer of the Ceylon Rifles' wrote a small history of the island of Ceylon. In the list of kings which he furnished and which he prepared from the Sinhalese chronicles, there were two Gajabāhus. One of them existed in 113 A.D., while the date assigned to the other was about 1127 A.D. For obvious reasons, the learned Professor identified the Kayavāhu of *Silappadikāram* with the Gajabāhu of Ceylon, and thus was able to fix the age of *Silappadikāram* and hence of Senguttuvan as second century A.D. This, however, did not mean that the Professor believed that the third Sangam existed during the time of Senguttuvan, for he seriously doubted the very existence of the Academy. The credit of having established the identity of Kayavāhu with Gajabāhu of Ceylon belongs to Mr. Seshagiri Sastriyar.

The Gajabāhu-synchronism.

[1] The contents of this chapter originally appeared in the 'Hindu' dated 14th, 15th and 17th April 1922 and have now been reproduced here with the kind permission of the editor after some elaboration.

Views of Kanakasabhai Pillai.

The next to enter the field was the late Mr. V. Kanakasabhai Pillai. Following up the clue thus presented by Mr. Sastriyar, he not only maintained, with greater insistence, the Gajabāhu-synchronism, but also brought in additional evidence to prove that the Sangam must have flourished in the second century A.D. As his *Tamils Eighteen Hundred Years Ago* is out of print and as the views of many scholars are mere elaborations of what he had stated, we need offer no apology for quoting him *in extenso*.

"The Chilappadikaram also mentions the fact that Chengudduva Chera paid a friendly visit to the kings of Magadha on the banks of the Ganges. It gives the name of the Magadha King as *Nurruvar Kannar* or the 'Hundred Karnas' and this expression was long a puzzle to me, until it struck me that it was a translation of the Sanskrit title, 'Satakarnin.' Several kings of the Karna or Andhra dynasty bore the epithet Satakarnin, and coins and inscriptions of these kings have been found, in which the Pali form of the word 'Satakani' occurs. Sanskrit scholars have however misread the name as Sâtakarnin, instead of Satakarnin. The Tamil rendering of the name into 'Hundred Karnas' in a contemporary poem leaves no doubt of the fact that the name is correctly Satakarnin, made up of the words Sata (hundred) and Karna (ears), the epithet evidently meaning a king who employed one hundred spies, or had one hundred sources of information. The Vayu,

Vishnu, Matsya and Bhagavata Puranas state that the Mauryas ruled the Magadha Empire for 137 years, and after them the Sungas 112 years, and after them the Kanvayanas, 45 years: and that after them there were 30 kings of the Andhra dynasty who reigned 456 years; but none of the Puranas gives a complete list of the names of the Andhra kings. The Matsya, which appears to be the oldest of the Puranas, furnishes the fullest list, which contains the names of only 29 kings and the number of years during which each of the kings reigned. In the early history of the emperors of Magadha, the only date which may be safely relied upon is that of Chandragupta, the contemporary of Seleucus Nicator, who began his reign in B.C. 310, and concluded a treaty with him in B.C. 305. The year of accession of Chandragupta may be fixed at B.C. 312, two years earlier than that of Seleucus Nicator, and, calculating from that year, the reign of the first Satakarnin ought to have extended from A.D. 77 to A.D. 133, according to the Matsya Purana, as shown below:

Ten Mauryas for 137 years, B.C. 312—175.
Ten Sungas for 112 years, B.C. 175—63.
Four Kanvayanas for 45 years, B.C. 63 to 18.
Thirty Andhras of whom the first six are—
Sisuka for 23 years, B.C. 18—A.D. 5.
Krishna for 18 years, A.D. 5—23.
Simalakarnin for 18 years, A.D. 23—41.
Purnotsunga for 18 years, A.D. 41—59.
Sirivaswami for 18 years, A.D. 59—77.
Satakarnin for 56 years, A.D. 77—133.

"The reign of this Satakarnin covers the entire period of the reign of Gajabāhu, king of Ceylon, which lasted 12 years from A.D. 113 to 125, according to the Mahawanso. Satakarnin, Emperor of Magadha, who is alluded to in the Chilappadhikaram as the contemporary of Chengudduva Chera and Gajabāhu, is therefore doubtless the first Satakarnin in the list of the Matsya Purana, who reigned from A.D. 77 to 133. The synchronism of the Puranas and the Mahawanso is perfect, at least from the reign of Chandragupta up to that of the first Satakarnin; and this coincidence is a strong proof of the general accuracy of the traditional history preserved in Puranic accounts and in the Mahawanso.

" The Mahawanso was composed in the fifth century A.D. and the Dipavanso still earlier; and both these historical works mention Gajabāhu I. It appears that during the reign of his father, 'crooked nosed' Tissa, a Chōla king had invaded Ceylon, and carried away several thousands of captives; and that in retaliation Gajabāhu invaded the Chōla dominions soon after his accession to the throne in A.D. 113. The tradition is that the captives were carried away to work on the banks of the river Kaviri, which were then under construction. This is quite in accordance with later Tamil poems and inscriptions which speak of Karikal Chōla as the king who commenced the construction of the high banks along both sides of the bed of the Kaviri. The construction of the Kaviri banks which extended along its course to a distance of about 100 miles from its mouth, was an undertaking of such magnitude that it could not have been completed during the reign of Karikal. The Chōla king, who invaded Ceylon in order to procure captives to work at the banks, might have been, therefore, Karikal or his immediate successor. This tradition is further evidence of the fact that Chengudduva Chera was contemporary with Gajabāhu I who lived in the early part of the second century A.D. Chengudduvan's grandfather Karikal Chōla should have, therefore, reigned in the latter half of the first century A.D. or, in other words, about *eighteen hundred years ago*. It will appear further on, from my account of Tamil literature, that the poets of the last Sangha at Madura, many of whom allude to the Chēra kings, Athan and Chengudduvan—should be assigned to the same period."

S. K. Ayyangar in *Ancient India.*

The third great effort to fix South Indian chronology was by Professor S. Krishnaswami Ayyangar. Writing many years before the publication of his *Beginnings of South Indian History*, he had arrived at the following conclusions :—

1. That there was an age of great literary activity in Tamil to warrant the existence of a body like the traditional Sangam.

2. That the period of the greatest Sangam activity was the age when Senguttuvan Chera

was a prominent character in South Indian politics.

3. That this age of Senguttuvan was the second century of the Christian era.

4. That these conclusions find support in what is known of the later history of South India.

Collecting the various evidences then available, he has maintained Kanakasabhai Pillai's theory with slight modification in the dates of a few kings. This view, however, was not accepted by a section of scholars among whom Diwan Bahadur Swamikannu Pillai and Mr. K. V. Subramania Ayyar deserve special mention. They maintain that the date of the Sangam is to be sought in the seventh century A.D.

It is not our object to critically examine here the views expressed by the two latter scholars. But we shall take up for our serious consideration the theories of Professor S. Krishnaswami Ayyangar and Pundit M. Raghava Ayyangar of the Tamil Lexicon Office.

Conclusions of Pundit Raghava Ayyangar.

Pundit Raghava Ayyangar, in a work which he published a few years ago in Tamil, entitled *Cheran Senguttuvan*, has devoted a chapter for the examination of the date of the hero. His conclusions are important, as they present a view of South Indian History not to be easily brushed aside. They may be briefly set forth thus :—

1. That the age of the Sangam must be 5th century A.D., as Māmūlanār refers in *Aham* 265, to the destruction of Pātaliputra by the Ganges, which event took place in the period

intervening the visits of the two Chinese travellers, Fa-hien and Hiuen Tsang.

2. That the Palayan of Mōhoor who was vanquished by Senguttuvan was the Mōhoor chieftain, whose territory according to Māmūlanār was attacked by the Mauryas in the course of their southward march.

3. That, therefore, the Mauryan invasion must have taken place during the time of Senguttuvan.

4. That, since the Mauryan power decayed in the second century A.D., the Mauryas referred to by the Sangam poets must be the Guptas who held imperial sway in the 5th century A.D. and whom Māmūlanār expressly refers as 'Vamba Moriar.' (New Mauryas.)

S. K. Ayyangar in his *Beginnings of South Indian History*.

The publication of *Cheran Senguttuvan* at once arrested the attention of scholars. Rao Bahadur K. S. Srinivasa Pillai of Tanjore and Mr. K. G. Sesha Iyer of Trivandrum have controverted the Pundit's views in the pages of *Sen Tamil* and the *Madras Christian College magazine* respectively. Later on, Professor S. Krishnaswami Ayyangar took up the subject for re-examination of evidences and rightly concentrated his attention on this important topic. His *Beginnings of South Indian History* published a few years ago, was intended, perhaps as a final reply to the various theories propounded, regarding the date of the Sangam. His position in that work of his may be summarised by a series of statements thus :—

1. That the Mauryas carried their invasions to the farthest south of India.

2. That they were in hostile occupation of forts in the northern borders of the Tamil land.

3. That the Aryans were beaten back, when the central Mauryan power became feeble, and their dislodgment from the south must be referred to the period which included that of Māmūlanār and others of the third Tamil Academy of Madura.

In other words, the learned Professor has attempted to evolve a series of connected events for the Sangam period with the help of contemporary literature, such as *Ahanānūru* and *Purānanūru* and the writings of foreign travellers, and has thus endeavoured to strengthen his old position regarding the age of the third Sangam.

Purpose of this chapter.

The purpose of this chapter is merely to press for the Professor's reconsideration certain aspects of the Pundit's theory which further can stand the test of true historic criticism. It is not our object to maintain 5th century as the date of the third Sangam, much less to enunciate new theories regarding the subject: nevertheless, the attention of scholars should be drawn more prominently to the fact that there are great difficulties to be overcome before Professor Krishnaswami Ayyangar's views regarding South Indian History can be accepted as final. To the subject we shall now revert.

Of the many poets who adorned the Sangam Age, Māmūlanār is the only bard who interests students of history by giving them intelligent information regarding contemporary works and past events. He seems to have travelled widely in South India and his poems are full of allusions to several ancient kings. They are, therefore, very useful as trustworthy materials for the reconstruction of South Indian History. The first to use them extensively for the purpose of pure history is the learned Pundit, Raghava Ayyangar, who has thereby rendered a signal service to the cause of Tamil Historic Research, the value of which can never be overestimated. **Poems of Māmūlanār: their importance.**

Two of the poems of Māmūlanār containing what is undoubtedly a historic reference are the following :— **Reference to the Mauryas**

"முரண்மிகு வடுகர் முன்னுற மோரியர்
தென்றிசை மாதிர முன்னிய வரவிற்கு
விண்ணுற வோங்கிய பனியிருங் குன்றத்
தொண்கதிர்த் திகிரி யுருளிய குறைத்த வறை."

(*Aham.* 281)

"வெல்கொடித்—
துனைகா லன்ன புனைதேர்க் கோசர்
தொன்மூதாலத் தரும்பணைப் பொதியில்
இன்னிசை முரசங் கடிப்பிகுத் திரங்கத்
தெம்முனை சிதைத்த ஞான்றை மோகூர்
பணியா மையிற் பகைதலை வந்த
மாகெழு தானை வம்ப மோரியர்
புனைதேர் நேமி யுருளிய குறைத்த அறைவாய்."

(*Aham.* 251)

Māmūlanār is not the only poet who has referred to the Mauryas. Two of his contemporaries make similar references to the coming in of the Mauryas. Thus, Parankorranār :—

"விண்பொரு நெடுவரை யியறேர் மோரியர்
பொன்புனை திகிரி திரிதரக் குறைத்த வறை."

(*Aham.* 69).

Referring to the same incident, Attiraiyanar mentions the following :—

"விண்பொரு நெடுங்குடைக் கொடித்தேர் மோரியர்
திண்கதிர்த் திகிரி திரிதரக் குறைத்த
உலக விடைகழி."

(*Puram.* 175).

Putting these poems together, the following account of the Mauryan invasion can be constructed:—"The Mauryas started southwards on a great career of invasion, pushing the Vadugar and the Kōsar in front. The Kōsar, ever victorious and with their war-drums beating, appeared suddenly before the chief of Mōhoor, who not yielding, the Mauryas themselves had to come with a large army. This they did cutting a path across a mountain that stood in their way." The information thus furnished by Māmūlanār is in substance corroborated by the other two poets, Parankorranār and Attiraiyanar.

The first point requiring consideration is whether the incidents referred to took place in the time of our poets, or whether the poems merely give us an account of events that took place centuries before. According to Professor S. Krishnaswami Ayyangar, the various references to the Mauryas in Māmūlanār, as well as the reference to their cutting their way through the rock, are to a great southward invasion of the Mauryas. He further thinks that this conquest of the South by the Mauryas took place during the time of Bindusāra. He imagines that the term 'Mōhoor' in the text refers to some chieftain of Mōhoor and not necessarily to 'Palayan Maran.'[1] "All the passages of Māmūlanār", finally he says, "referring to these incidents refer to them as past occurrences and not as contemporary events." Mr. S. K. Ayyangar has however adduced no satisfactory argument to show why the passage should necessarily refer to the incidents that took place in the time of Bindusāra. From the text it is clear that "சிதைத்த ஞான்றை" is the only expression that can possibly express remoteness, but it need not necessarily indicate such high antiquity as is claimed for by the Professor. After all, the word ஞான்று merely means 'at that time.' It is difficult to conceive if the poets, even supposing the incidents were contemporaneous, could have described them in any other language.

It is a well-known fact that Seran Senguttuvan won a great victory over the chief of Mōhoor.[2] This Mōhoor was known as Palayan.[3] This Palayan was a great warrior who was very much feared by the neighbouring kings. We have next to see if this Palayan was the same as the Mōhoor chief referred to by Māmūlanār, and

Identification of Palayan with the Mōhoor chieftain of Māmūlanār.

[1] Dr. Krishnaswami has unwittingly adopted the wrong reading of Kanakasabhai Pillai. The text merely reads as "பழையன்" and not as "பழையன் மாறன்"—*Vide The Tamils Eighteen Hundred Years Ago*, pp. 47 and 50.

[2] *Patirruppattu*, 44 and 49.

[3] *Patirruppattu* 5 and *Slappadikāram*, 27th Canto, II. 124 and 126.

whom the learned Professor considers to belong to the Mauryan period. In this matter of identification, we have to look for information in the poems composed not by one Sangam poet but by others as well. The following references in Sangam literature are specially to be noted in this connection.

> பறைபடப் பணிலம் ஆர்ப்ப இறைகொளத்
> தொன்மூ தாலத்து அரும்பணைப் பொதியில்
> நாலூர்க் கோசர் நன்மொழி போல
> வாயா கின்றே.
>
> (*Kurunthogai.* 15)

Here the poet, Perungadungō, says that the Kōsar true to their plighted word appeared at the place of assembly suddenly, with war-drums beating and conch resounding. This place of assembly was underneath the shade of an old and ancient banyan tree with magnificent branches.

Another poet Māmūlanār says :—

> கோசர்.—தொன்மூ தாலத் தரும்பணைப் பொதியில்
> இன்னிசை முரசங் கடிப்பிகுத் திரங்கத்
> தெம்முனை சிதைத்த ஞான்றை மோகூர்
> பணியா மையின். (*Aham.* 251)

Here the poet describes 'the place of assembly' practically in the same words but gives us the additional information that the truthful Kōsar came for purposes of war particularly against Mōhoor.

Who this Mōhoor chief was is clearly explained by another Sangam poet, a contemporary of Māmūlanār, *viz.*, Māngudi Marudanār.

"பழையன் மோகூர் அவயகம் விளங்க
நான்மொழிக் கோசர் தோன்றி யன்ன.

—*Mathuraikanchi.*

Thus further light is let in and we are told that the name of the Mōhoor chief who was attacked by the Kōsar was Palayan, in whose 'assembly place' the Kōsar appeared. Taking all these passages together and remembering that the poets who composed these verses were contemporaries, only one conclusion is possible, *viz.*, that all these refer to only one and the same individual, Palayan, who was defeated, as has already been stated, by Senguttuvan. The sameness of the language and the similarity of the ideas as regards the Kōsar and the place of assembly strongly tend to confirm our view. **Theory of Podiyil battle erroneous.**

In this connection it mustbe pointed out that the word "பொதியில்" occurring in the poems of Māmūlanār and others have been interpreted to mean "Podiyil hill" both by Professor S. Krishnaswami Ayyangar and Kanakasabhai Pillai. "தொன் மூதாலத்து அரும்பணைப் பொதியில்' simply means the Podiyil underneath the ancient and old banyan tree with its mighty branches. It is evident that this description of 'Podiyil' does not contain any attribute of a mountain. The poets would have undoubtedly chosen different epithets, if they had really intended to describe such a mountain as the Podiyil hill. But, as we have already seen, what they wanted to describe was 'the place of assembly,' where chiefs and ryots met frequently for purposes of common deliberation. In ancient India, nay, even in comparatively modern times, such places of assembly existed and they were invariably underneath the tall and shady banyan tree with its branches spread far and wide. It is such a place that is described by the poets. In Tamil, moreover, 'Podiyil' is always used to denote the vacant site underneath a tree. Hence the interpretation that the Mauryas with their advance guard, Kōsar, came as far as the Podiyil hill in the Tinnevelly district, seems to be untenable.

Identity of Palayan with Mōhoor chieftain and the contemporaneity of the poets with the incidents established.

It must be plain to those who have been following us so far that the Mōhoor chieftain who came in conflict with the Kōsar was Palayan, the contemporary of Senguttuvan. It is, therefore, more natural to suppose that Māmūlanār sang about a contemporary Mōhoor chief than to imagine, on insufficient grounds, that he referred to a chief of Mōhoor who perhaps flourished in dim ages past. While there existed during his life-time a Paḷayan of Mōhoor, of whose exploits other contemporary poets such as Paranar make laudable mention, why should Māmūlanār alone go out of the way and bring in for purposes of illustration another Mōhoor chieftain who, according to our learned Professor, Krishnaswami Ayyangar, was a contemporary of Chandragupta Maurya, the grandfather of Asoka. If Māmūlanār had really meant a different Mōhoor chief, he could be expected to employ different epithets in describing him but—that is the most astonishing thing—the description given by all the poets as regards the Kōsar and the 'Podiyil' is exactly similar.

The 'Red Chera' cannot be a contemporary of Chandragupta Maurya.

Having established the contemporaneity of Senguttuvan and the Mauryan invasion of the south, the next question is who these Mauryas are. If Senguttuvan, *ergo* the Sangam poets, flourished in the second century A.D., as has been conceived by some, what was the position of the Mauryas then? This period according to the best interpretation of North Indian history is the period of the rise of the Andhras and the Andhrabhrityas. It is impossible, therefore, to conceive of a Mauryan invasion of the distant south at this time of Mauryan decay. Consequently, the 'Mauryas' under reference must be some other *imperial* race that undertook a great South Indian invasion later on in history. Before discussing who these were, let us dispose of one objection that might be brought forward. It may be pointed out that even supposing that the South Indian invasion took place during the time of Senguttuvan, the latter might yet be a contemporary of Chandragupta Maurya. To suppose so would be to upset the entire chronology of South India. The Sangam literature is full of references to the spread of Jainism and Buddhism during the Senguttuvan era. The consequential inference is that at that time Buddhism was rampant in South India and Ceylon. But we know from history that it was Asoka that was responsible for the spread of Buddhism in the extreme south of India. If Senguttuvan was, therefore, a contemporary of Chandragupta Maurya who was a prominent Jain of the times, how can we account for the spread of Buddhism at this remote period? Yet another point. In *Manimēkalai*, canto 28, ll. 123–131, there is a reference to an ancestor of Kōvalan, who flourished nine generations previously having built a Buddhistic Chaitālaya at Vanchi (Karūr).[1] If, therefore, Senguttuvan was a contemporary of Chandragupta Maurya, how is it possible for a Buddhistic temple to have existed in the south, so early as 560 B.C. (290 plus 270)? Evidently it is absurd to make Senguttuvan a contemporary of Chandragupta Maurya.

'Vamba Moriar': its meaning.

Who were these 'Mauryas', then, who invaded South India during the time of Senguttuvan? Before answering this question, let us consider the various interpretations in regard to the expression 'Vamba Moriar.' It has been pointed out that the word 'Vambu' (வம்பு) is used by Tolkāppiyar in the sense of 'unstable' (நிலையின்மை). Some, therefore, have taken 'Vamba Moriar' to mean 'the unstable or nomadic Mauryas', evidently referring to the Mauryas who settled in the Konkan. It is argued that the passages of Māmūlanār have

[1] That 'Vanchi' is Karūr has been incontrovertibly established by Vidvan R. Raghava Ayyangar in his *Vanchi Mahānahar*. Mr. R. Rangachari, M.A., L.T., of the Christian College is of the same view, as can be seen from his article on 'Vanchi' in the 'Hindu' dated 30th August 1922.

reference to these Mauryas who must have flourished in the second century A.D. But important considerations militate against this view.

Were the 'Vamba Moriar' the Mauryas of the Konkan?

In the first place we know absolutely nothing about the movement and the early history of these Mauryas of the Konkan. Thus V. A. Smith[1]: "Petty Maurya dynasties, apparently connected in some unknown way with the imperial line, which ruled in the Konkan, between the Western Ghats and the sea and some other parts of Western India, during the sixth, seventh and eighth centuries, are frequently mentioned in Inscriptions." These inscriptions are very late in origin. The Aihōle inscription of Pulakēsin II (7th century A.D.) speaks of these Mauryas of the Konkan in a manner not very creditable either to their military valour or their power of resistance. They are further mentioned in the inscriptions along with other small tribes, such as the Nalas, and the Kadambas. And yet a close study of Māmūlanār's poems would indicate that the 'Vamba Moriar' were an *imperial* raco who undertook a great South Indian invasion. 'விண்பொரு நெடுங்குடையியறேர் மோரியர்.' This description of 'Vamba Moriar' is not in keeping at all with all that we know of the Mauryas of the Konkan.[2]

We are, therefore, not warranted in construing 'Vamba Moriar' [3] to mean 'unstable Mauryas'

[1] V. A. Smith, *Early History of India*, II Edition, p. 183.

[2] For an account of the Mauryas of the Konkan, see *The Bombay Gazetteer*, Vol. I, Part II, p. 282.

[3] The right meaning of the word 'Vamba' is therefore 'new'. Many examples might be quoted from classical poems to support this interpretation as hereunder:—

and then constructing, on imaginary grounds, a history and tradition for a people who had an obscure and a floating sort of existence for several centuries.

Were they then the forces of Samudragupta?

Perhaps the 'Vamba Moriar' of Māmūlanār were no other than the forces commanded by Samudragupta who is called by the late V. A. Smith 'the Indian Napoleon.'[1] The difficulty of identifying the Mauryas of Māmūlanār with the forces of Samudragupta is no doubt very great.

But the following points are urged in favour of such an identification. Historians are not

(1) வம்பு—புதுமை	(1) *Silap*: Canto 14, l. 175.
(2) ,, — ,,	(2) *Aham.*: Stanza 15.
(3) ,, — ,,	(3) *Puram*: ,, 3.
(4) ,, —புதிய்	(4) *Jīvakachintāmani*: poem 1068.
(5) வம்பமாக்கள்—புதியோர்	(5) *Silap.* Canto 5, l. iii.
(6) வம்பப்பரத்தை—புதியபரத்தை	(6) ,, ,, 16, l. 63
(7) வம்பவுரை—புதியவுரை	(7) *Purapporul. Venbamalai*, Ch. 12, Stanza 12.
(8) வம்பலர்—புதிய அலர் (மலர்)	(8) *Paripadal*, Stanza 10, l. 20.
(9) ,, —புதியவர்.	(9) *Pazhamozhi* 220.

[1] V. A. Smith, *Early History of India*, Third Edition, p. 283.

A few critics have pointed out that the orthodox estimate of Samudragupta's military achievements is grossly exaggerated and that the opinion of the French scholar, Dr. Jouveau Dubreuil's in regard to Samudragupta's invasion is much nearer the truth. We may remark that Dubreuil's is not the last word on the subject and even supposing it to be so, it does not materially affect our line of argument. Dubreuil does not say there has been no invasion of South India by Samudragupta. All that he says is that the Gupta emperor after defeating Vishnu Gōpa returned home by the way he came. It may be that small expeditions might have been sent by him to effect an entry into the Tamilakam. Perhaps it is these forces that came in conflict with Palayan of Mōhoor. At the same time, we may note that these minor incidents of warfare need find no place in the Pillar inscription, which is mainly concerned with major operations. What was undoubtedly a petty incident in the career of the conquering Guptas necessarily loomed large before the eyes of the Tamils whose land was about to be invaded, and hence the frequent mention of this incident by the Tamil bards who are either contemporary or nearly contemporary with the incidents narrated in their poems.

able to tell us anything about the origin of the Gupta dynasty. All that is known of it is that the founder of the dynasty was a petty local Zemindar at Pātaliputra, who contracted a lucky marriage, with the Lichchhavi princess, Kumaradevi, and thence rose to power and fortune. It is noteworthy that he assumed the same name as the grand-father of Asoka Maurya, the founder of Mauryan greatness, Chandragupta Maurya. What could be more natural for the people of the distant south than to connect the new Imperial power with the ancient Mauryas? Our point is that there has been a confusion in the mind of Māmūlanār himself in regard to Gupta ancestry. That such a confusion prevailed among the kings and princes of North India is evident from the remark of Dr. Fleet in his account of Gutta princes. Thus Dr. Fleet :—

Māmūlanār himself confused.

" The traditions embodied in the Gutta records involve some confusion. The mention of Pātaliputra shows distinctly that the Guttas supposed themselves to be descended ultimately from the great Maurya king, Chandragupta of Pātaliputra, the grand-father of Asoka."

And again :—

" It is plain, in fact, that the Gutta princes of Guttal claimed descent in reality from the early Gupta kings, of whose dominions, at any rate from the time of Kumāragupta I. onwards, Mālwa did form a part, and not from the Mauryas. From their use of the names Chandragupta and Vikramāditya, they seem to have really had some definite knowledge of the Early Guptas. But they mixed it up with matters which were probably more familiar to them. They evidently identified the Early Gupta king Chandragupta I., or his grandson of the same name, with the far more well known Maurya king, Chandragupta."[1] Thus it is plain that there was a strong tradition in the tenth century A.D. that the Guttas,[2] and therefore the Guptas, were connected in some manner with the ancient Mauryas. A similar tradition must have existed in a stronger form during the time of Senguttuvan and the Sangam poets. Hence, probably to distinguish 'the later Mauryas' from the ancient ones, Māmūlanār calls the Guptas, 'Vamba Moriar', *i.e.*, new Mauryar, as opposed to the old Mauryar.

An objection answered.

It has been pointed out that the Guptas themselves never thought that they were descended from the Mauryas. It is true that the Gupta records do not mention anything about their relationship with the Mauryas. It may also be a fact that the Guptas were not related to the Mauryas at all. It is enough for our purposes to note the existence of a tradition connecting theGuptas and the Mauryas, ill-founded though it be. Moreover in Asia, rulers of independent states always took pride in claiming descent from some ancient powerful sovereign, as that lent considerable prestige to their rulers. Thus Baber claimed descent from the great Timur and Chengizkhan.

[1] *Bombay Gazetteer*, Vol. I, Part II, pp. 579 and 580.

[2] According to Dr. Fleet, the word *Gutta* is a" well established corruption of *Gupta*."

Similarly it is in no way preposterous to suppose that the Guptas might have claimed in those days ancestry with the Mauryas. The fact that Samudragupta was the first imperial sovereign to inscribe his edicts underneath those of the Monk-Emperor Asoka in the famous Allahabad pillar, lends colour to our view of the whole question. Our want of knowledge as regards Gupta ancestry may not prevent us from accepting the commonsense view of the point in dispute. It may be that Māmūlanār himself gives us a bit of the history of the origin of the dynasty by calling the Guptas as the new Mauryas. If even in these days of scientific criticism and elaborate Indian Research, we are not able to know anything about the origin of the Guptas, why should we reject as unsound the view that Māmūlanār failing to distinguish clearly the Mauryas from the Guptas and relying on some such tradition as that of the Guptas of the 10th century A.D., wrote of the Guptas as new Mauryas ?

More light required in regard to Samudragupta's march.

We do not know enough details of Samudragupta's great march to South India to enable us to find corroboration of such incidents as are narrated by the Sangam poets in connection with the invasion, to wit, the coming in of the advance parties headed by Kōsar and Vadugar. As more materials are found to fill up the various gaps in the life of one of the greatest of India's sovereigns, Samudragupta, we will be able to realise more and more that the various points of historical interest mentioned by Māmūlanār do actually refer to the invasion of South India by the Gupta monarch.

It has already been stated that the southernmost point reached by the invading force was not Podiyil hill, as has been wrongly determined, but it has to be sought somewhere on the border of the Tamil land, from which entry into the heart of Tamilakam would be easy and convenient. It should either be Palghat or Mōhoor in South Arcot district. Not far from Mōhoor there is the famous Attur Pass through which Hyder Ali and his forces marched to reach South India.

S. K. Ayyangar's conclusions based on corrupt renderings of texts.

The second of Professor S. Krishnaswami Ayyangar's conclusions regarding the interpretation of Sangam poems next deserves our attention. According to him the Mauryas were in hostile occupation of forts in the northern border of the Tamil land extending from Pulikat[1] to Goa, and that these Aryans were beaten back by the Tamil chiefs at a period when the Mauryan power became feeble. There seems to be no

[1] Referring to Pulikat, the learned Professor says, "The Tamils marked out the limit of Tamil land at Pulikat, which is the Anglo-Indian corruption of Palavērkkādu (old forest of Vēl trees). This is referred to in Ancient Tamil literature as Vērkkādu, without the adjective for 'old' standing before the name." Page 83. *The Beginnings of South Indian History*. Here the Professor has adopted without examination, the wrong text of Pandit Rangaswami Ayyangar. The correct text is that given by Pandit Narayanaswami Ayyar. நற். முகவுரை 73. It should be 'பல்வேற்கட்டி நன்னாட் டும்பர்'. '*Katti*' (கட்டி) is here used in the sense of a race of Kshatriyas. Thus in *Silap*, we have 'பங்களர் கங்கர் பல்வேற் கட்டியர்', and also 'கட்டி கங்கன்' in *Aham*. According to Kanakasabhai Pillai the Kattiyar were the people who gave the name of Kattiwar to Guzarat. (Page 10. *The Tamils Eighteen Hundred Years Ago.*)

authority in Sangam literature for arriving at such a conclusion. The verses relied upon by him merely mention that the Mauryas came southwards. There is nothing to indicate that they stayed in the land in occupation of forts for any very length of time. Again all references in the Sangam poems to the defeat of Vada Ariyar or Northern Ariyar by Neduncheliyan, among others, indicate, perhaps, the attempt of the Tamil chiefs to prevent the Gupta forces from entering the Tamil country. The fact that Samudragupta did not care to penetrate into the Tamil land is a point in illustration. From the preceding discussion it is clear that the date of the Sangam cannot be the second century A.D.

A Resume.

An attempt has been made to show that the great Mauryan invasion of the south took place in the time of Senguttuvan. The Mauryas referred to were not the forces of Chandragupta Maurya who could not have been a contemporary of Senguttuvan. We are, therefore' forced to conclude that the invasion referred to by Māmūlanār was the one undertaken by Samudragupta, and that the date of the last Sangam is to be sought for at the end of the fourth or the beginning of the fifth century A.D.

Another criticsm.

We shall now proceed to consider another kind of criticism regarding the later origin of the third Sangam. It has been very often remarked that the Sangam should have existed centuries before the rise of the Pallava power on the ground that the Sangam literature did not contain any reference to the Pallavas or their activities. Let us consider the soundness of this argument.

The origin of Pallavas.

The origin of Pallavas is even to-day considered a mystery. It is one of the many unsolved problems of Indian history. The rise and progress of the Pallavas seem to be as astonishing as the various theories propounded regarding their origin. Certain facts, however, in their history are matters of common knowledge. In the seventh or the middle half of the seventh century A.D., they were predominant in South India and the various Tamil kingdoms were more or less subject to them. At the end of the fourth and the beginning of the fifth century A.D., their rule remained obscure : perhaps it was not widely known. The question now is when they assumed the name of Pallava. By what other name were they originally known ? Were they foreign or indigenous to India ? Unless these questions are satisfactorily answered, there can be no force in the argument that because Sangam literature makes no reference to them, the Sangam itself must have flourished long before their rule commenced. The Allahabad pillar inscription of Samudragupta merely speaks of Vishnu Gōpa as the ruler of Kāñchi. The name Pallava does not occur there. From this it is evident that in the fourth century A.D. the name Pallava was little used by them. Let us next see whether what is known as the Sangam literature yields us any clue as to the origin of the Pallavas, and whether references are made to them therein.

In Sangam literature the rulers of Kāñchi are spoken of as 'Tirayan and Tondaiman.' They are further said to have come from the sea. Mention is made in *Ahanānūru* that the Tirayar were Lords of Vēngadam. According to Nachchinārkkiniyar, these Tirayar were connected further with the Nāga princes. Again, in the age of Senguttuvan, the ruler of Kāñchi was the brother of a king who ruled at Kāvirippoompattinam. But he is not known as Tirayan. These would show that Kāñchi was ruled from time to time by kings belonging to the various races. Some called themselves 'Tirayar', others perhaps were mere fiefs of the Chola kings. Kāñchi, being near the border of the Tamil land, must have been the bone of contention between kings who belonged to different races. Vishnu Gōpa, therefore, who was ruling at Kāñchi at the time of Samudragupta's invasion, not being a Chola fief, must, therefore, be a Tirayan.

Pallavas and Sangam lietrature

One important information is furnished by Dubreuil in his *Antiquities of Pallavas.* According to him the Pallava rulers of Kāñchi had, as emblem on their coins, a ship with two masts. This explains their connection with the sea. The same author says that they were connected with the Nāga princes and there is every reason to believe that they came from the sea. Cannot therefore the Tirayar be identified with the Pallavas ?

The Tirayar were the Pallavas.

Absence of the word 'Pallavar' in Sangam literature explained.

The Tondaimandala Pattayam gives an account of the various branches of Tirayar. This has been noted by Kankasabhai Pillai, in his book "*Tamils Eighteen Hundred Years Ago.*" As one of the main branches of Tirayar, we have Pallava Tirayar, showing thereby the connection of Pallavar with Tirayar. It is therefore natural to suppose that the Pallavar were known to early Sangam literature by their group name of Tirayar; but, as their power and influence increased in the land, their branch name 'Pallava Tirayar' assumed greater importance. Hence the absence of the word 'Pallavar' in the 4th and 5th century literature, and the greater frequency with which this name 'Pallavar' occurs in later works, such as *Nandikkalambakam*. One other fact may be mentioned. The commentator of *Tolkāppiyam*, Nachinārk-kiniyar, quotes the following stanza by way of illustrating the 54th sutram of *Poruladikāram Ahattinai I-yal*.

"முலைமொழி திம்பான் மண்சேறு படுப்ப
மலர் தலையுலக மோம்பு மென்ப
பரிசிலைத் தொண்டைப் பல்லவஞணையின்
வெட்சித் தாயத்து வில்லே ருழவர்
பொருந்தா வடுகர் முனைச் சுரங்
கடந்து கொண்ட பல்லா நிரையே."

Reference to Chalukyas in Divākaram, a Sangam work.

We have here the words 'தொண்டைப்பல்லவன்.' It is an acknowledged fact that Nachchinārk-kiniyar always quotes from Sangam literature alone and the above stanza has the imprint of an old poem. For these reasons, it may be said, that Sangam literature has not omitted references to Pallavas who, in their earlier career, were known as Tirayar.

As one reads the Sangam works, one finds evidences that tend more and more to support the probability that the Sangam existed perhaps after the 4th or 5th century A.D. We shall examine one or two points. Throughout the Sangam literature, we have frequent references to a tribe called Vēlir. Who are these Vēlir ? Pundit Raghava Ayyangar in his book *Vēlir Varalāru* has stated that these Vēlir came from Belgaum and other places in the Bombay Presidency, and that they were the Chalukyas of Indian History. The literature of the Sangam period also makes mention of them. That the Vēlir were Chalukyas is known from the following passage in *Divākaram*[1]:— **Who are the Vēlir ?**

"வேள்புலவரசர் சளுக்குவேந்தர்"

What is the date of Divākarar ? The patron of Divākarar was Ambarkilan Aruvandai. Kallādanar, the well-known Sangam poet, sang in praise of this Aruvandai. At the end of one of the chapters, Divākarar says that his patron was also praised by Auvayār, the famous court poetess of Adihamān Elini. From this it is evident that Divākarar, Kallādar, Auvayār and Adihamān Elini are contemporaries. That they belonged **Divākarar: his date.**

[1] மக்கட் பெயர்த்தொகுதி.

to the Sangam age will be readily admitted by all scholars. Thus Divākarar, a Sangam poet, makes mention in his work of the Chalukyas of whom the earliest record is to be found only in the end of the 5th century A.D. It follows, therefore, that the poets of the third Academy must have flourished somewhere about that time. This view is further strengthened by the fact that the legendary account of the Vēlir, as given by Kapilar, a Sangam poet, is exactly the same as that traditionally attributed to the Chalukyas. It, therefore, seems highly improbable that Sangam should have flourished in the second century A.D.

The Gurjara difficulty.

Manimēkalai, one of the Sangam epics, has the following :—

"குச்சரக் குடிகை தன்னகம்புக்கு"

"குச்சரக் குடிகைக் குமரியை மரீஇ"

—18th Canto, ll. 145 and 152.

These are interpreted by Mahāmahōpādhyāya V. Swaminatha Ayyar to mean "The small temple built in Gurjara style of architecture." Here is, therefore, a clear reference to the Gurjaras. The late Mr. V. A. Smith[1] has pointed out that this reference to the Gurjaras in *Manimēkalai* is a great stumbling block for accepting the orthodox view regarding "The Sangam Age." No one has attempted to satisfactorily prove that the Gurjaras existed in the second

[1] See V. A. Smith's Introduction to S. Krishnaswami Ayyangar's *Ancient India*.

century A.D. and that they originated a style of architecture popular enough to be imitated in the extreme south of India. On the other hand, it is well known that the Gurjaras are not heard of in Indian History, before the middle of the fifth century A.D.[1]

In the course of the examination of the date of Senguttuvan, Pundit Raghava Ayyangar has shown actual reference to the probable age of Nakkīrar in a work reduced to writing in the eighth or the middle half of the eighth century. That point deserves mention here.

Date of Nakkīrar.

It is admitted by all that Nakkīrar, Senguttuvan and Chāttanar were all contemporaries, at any rate, that they lived in the Sangam age. This Nakkīrar is the author of a commentary on *Iraiyanar Kalaviyal.* This commentary, instead of being written then, was merely handed down orally from preceptor to student, for nearly ten generations. This information is furnished by the author who actually wrote down the commentary. The age of the latter is determined by his frequent mention of such titles as Arikēsari, Parāngusan and Nedumāran assumed by a Pandyan

[1] Thus Professor Macdonell (*Journal of the Royal Asiatic Society,* 1919 Vol, page 531):—
"The date C. 200 A.C. assigned to the *Silappadikāram* seems to be valueless, because in the companion romance mention is made of the Gurjaras, who do not seem to have entered India before C. 450 A.C."
Commenting on this Mr. K. G. Sesha Ayyar of Trivandrum writes (*The Quarterly Journal of the Mythic Society,* Vol. X, No. 2, page 186) that "the Gurjaras are of the same stock as the Sakas and came into India with them, and on the break up of the Mauryan empire they began to rule Gujarāt, Kathiawar and Mālwa where they had already settled." He further thinks that the expression Kuccarak-kutikai (குச்சரக்குடிகை) means a rock-cut shrine. This view, it is to be feared, has not found general acceptance.

king who is also spoken of as the victor of Nelvēli and Sangamangai. From the Vēlvikudi grants we can know that this Pandyan king was no other than the father of Jatila Varman Parāntakan who flourished in 770 A.D. It follows, therefore, that the compiler of the commentary must have existed before the 8th century A.D. Counting ten generations from him on the average of 30 years for each generation that preceded this king, the date of Nakkīrar falls in the 5th century A.D. (770 A.D. minus 10 × 30) which also may be the date of the Sangam.

Vēlvikudi grant.

This view is still further confirmed, if we carefully consider the circumstance under which the donee of the Vēlvikudi grant got back his village. We may briefly set them forth thus. One Narkorran complained to Jatila Varman Parāntakan that the village which was given to one of his ancestors by Mutukudumi Peruvaludi was taken possession of by the Kalabhras during their invasion of Madura and that, since then, it had remained as Government property. After satisfying that the proofs furnished by Narkorran were authentic, the king granted the village back to him. Now the question is, is it possible to conceive that the donee of the Vēlvikudi grant could have furnished proofs of his title to the village if the date of Mutukudumi Peruvaludi, that is, of the original grantor were to fall centuries before the birth of Christ. Evidently the interval between Mutukudumi Peruvaludi and the Kalabhra interregnum could not have been long. At best we can conceive that twelve generations had enjoyed the property from Mutukudumi. From Kadungōn to the donor of the Vēlvikudi grant, we have five or six generations of rulers. The remaining five or six generations of kings must therefore have flourished between the time of Mutukudumi and the Kalabhra interregnum and they were probably the Sangam kings. Counting back from Parāntakan (8th century A.D.) to Kadungōn in the usual way, we have nearly 200 years: in other words, Kadungōn was restored somewhere in the 6th century A.D. Counting from Kadungōn back to Mutukudumi, leaving, as has been pointed out, four or six generations of rulers, we arrive at the conclusion that the kings mentioned in Sangam literature must have flourished in the 5th or 4th century A.D.

Buddhism in Java and Sumatra.

Students of Ancient Indian History are aware of the close cultural contact between Peninsular India and the Eastern Archipelago in general, and Sumatra and Java in particular. The two latter are known in Tamil classical literature by the general name of Sāvakam, which is the Sanskrit Javadvīpa, the Subadīn of Ptolemy. Of this, writes Kanakasabhai Pillai: "Chāvaka or Chāivakadvīpa is the island of Sumātra. The king of Chāvaka appears to have ruled over also Java and the small islands adjacent to Sumātra." Apparently Dr. S. Krishnaswami Ayyangar agrees with this identification (see p. 24, *Mythic Society Journal*, Vol. XII, No. 1). This Sāvakam was visited by the famous Chinese pilgrim, Fa-hien, and he has left an impression of what he saw there. He found there " various forms of error and Brahminism flourishing." He also observes that much to his regret the "Buddhists in the locality were not worth speaking of." The famous Yūpa inscriptions of King Mūlavarman, ascribed by Dr. Vogel to the middle of the 4th century A.D., and which refer to the settlement of the Brahmins and their performance of *Yāgas* in the true orthodox fashion, also tend to support the observation of the Chinese Doctor in regard to the predominance of Brahminism in those regions. The main point to be observed, however, is that Buddhism was comparatively a negligible factor in the religious life of the communities in Sāvakam in the time of Fa-hien.

Observations of I-tsing.

A quite different condition of things existed in the last quarter of the 7th century A.D., when another Chinese traveller, I-tsing, visited the island. A great theologian and collector of manuscripts, this I-tsing was as precise and minute in his information as Fa-hien himself. According to him Sāvakam was essentially Buddhistic. " The change from just the beginnings of Buddhistic influence," says Dr. Krishnaswami Ayyangar, " in the age of Fā-hien to the dominance of Buddhism during I-tsing's stay in the island gives us clearly to understand that the intervening centuries, fifth, sixth and seventh centuries of the Christian era, constitute the period of Buddhistic outspread in this region." (*Mythic Society Journal*, Vol. XII, No. 1, page 38.) This description of the religious life in Sāvakam by I-tsing tallies with that given in *Manimēkalai*, Cantos 24 and 25. We may briefly set forth the story.

Evidence in *Manimēkalai*.

It is well known that Manimēkalai was implicated in the murder of Udaya Kumāran who passionately loved her. The Chola King, Killivalavan, ordered her imprisonment and she was subsequently released. Immediately after this, disgusted with her stay in the Chola country, she proceeded to Sāvakam whose king, Punnya Raja, was considered as an avatar of Buddha and to whom Manimēkalai desired to impart the secret of his former birth. The accounts of her meeting in that island a great Buddhistic sage, Dharma Sāvaka, the 'Preacher of the Law to the King,' and the subsequent interviews she had with Punnya Raja leave, no doubt, the impression that the whole island was swayed by the teachings of Buddhism. The personages mentioned in the two cantos may be mythical. One might even find in the whole account an echo of some of the Buddhistic *Jātaka Stories*. But there is absolutely no doubt that the whole story is based upon a substratum of facts and that is that Sāvakam in the time of Chāttanār, the author of *Manimēkalai*, was essentially Buddhistic. It is important to remember what has been stated before, that Fa-hien was disappointed to note the predominance of Braḥminism in those islands and the insignificant position which Buddhism occupied in the life of the people. The conclusion, therefore, is obvious that *Manimēkalai* was composed at a period when Buddhism was making rapid strides in Sāvakam and the neighbouring islands. This formative period, even according to Dr. Krishnaswami Ayyangar, is to be sought for in the time intervening the visits of Fa-hien and I-tsing and that is between the 5th and 7th centuries of the Christian era. If the date of *Manimēkalai* is to be sought in the 2nd century A.D., how can we account for the spread and predominance of Buddhism in Sumatra and Java in the time of Chāttanār? For, it should be noted, that even during the time of Fa-hien, Buddhism in that island was not worth speaking of.

Yet another piece of internal evidence.

Another piece of internal evidence may be pointed out here, which shows clearly that, whatever might be the date of the Sangam, *Manimēkalai* belongs to the sixth or seventh century A.D. In canto 12 of this work, Aravanavadigal thus speaks of the condition of Buddhism in South India then. "The Dharma has languished in this world, and forms of error are increasing. Yet I do not despair. I continue to preach the Law which few care to understand in the hope that the Dharma might be established to a little extent."[1] Thus the grey-haired monk laments the decline of Buddhism in the

[1] This is not a literal translation. Only the idea is sought to be conveyed here.

Tamil land. We know that Buddhism was flourishing in South India during the time of Fa-hien's visit (4th century A.D.). Since then, the decay of that religion was rapid and when Hiuen Tsang visited Kāñchi (640 A.D.), he heard that in Malakūta (Pandyan country) Buddhism was almost extinct, the ancient monasteries being mostly in ruins. This is the period that is probably referred to in *Manimēkalai.* Under the circumstance we are not wrong in concluding that *Manimēkalai* was composed after the time of Fa-hien.

Conclusion.

We have thus tried to make it clear that there are serious difficulties to be overcome before we can affirm that the date of the Sangam is the 2nd century A.D. The final statement of Dr. S. Krishnaswami Ayyangar in his *The Beginnings of South Indian History,* "And now that the necessary preliminary investigation has been carried to the degree of fulness to carry conviction, more work will be done to extract from the material all that may usefully be taken for the building up of the history of this part of the country and of that comparatively remote period," seems therefore to be premature. No doubt more work requires to be done, as he says, not so much for the purpose of building up a history on the foundation which scholars like him believe they have well and truly laid, as for laying the foundation itself.

[1] *The Beginnings of South Indian History,* p. 362.

NOTES.

Note 1.—The following note of Jacobi seems to be conclusive of the theory that Jainism was not an offshoot of Buddhism :—

" Notwithstanding the radical difference in their philosophical notions, Jainism and Buddhism, being originally both orders of monks outside the pale of Brahmanism, present some resemblance in outward appearance, so that even Indian writers occasionally, have confounded them. It is, therefore, not to be wondered at that some European scholars who became acquainted with Jainism through inadequate samples of Jain literature easily persuaded themselves that it was an offshoot of Buddhism. But it has since been proved beyond doubt that their theory is wrong and that Jainism is at least as old as Buddhism."

Hastings, *Cyclopaedia of Religion and Ethics,* p. 465.

Note 2.—The Jains give an altogether different version of Appar's life thus :—

" Appar was a Jain ascetic in his youth, a staunch Saiva in his middle age, and a repented follower of Jainism in his old age. On account of his reconversion to Jainism he was murdered by his Saivite followers lest he should undo what all he had done to glorify Saivism. His secret murder was concealed by popularising a mysterious story that he was devoured by a tiger which was only a manifestation of Siva." Certain Tamil hymns in praise of *Jina* or *Arhat* are attributed to Appar and are most popularly sung by the Jains even to-day. The hymns resemble the *Tēvāram* in many ways. Perhaps they were sung by Appar during the latter period of his life.

APPENDIX A.

GENEALOGICAL TABLE OF THE GANGA KINGS.

Of the Ikshvaku or Solar race, was
Dhananjaya
|
Harischandra
King of Ayodhyā
|
Padmanābha

- Dadiga
  - 2. Mādhava II, Kiriya Mādhava
    - 3. Harivarmma, ..247—266..
      - 4. Vishnugōpa. Prithivī—Ganga.
        - 5. Mādhava III, ..357—370 Tadangāla Mādhava, *m.* Kadamba princess
          - 6. Avinīta, 430—482
            - 7. Durvvinīta, 482—517 *m.* Punnād princess
              - 8. Mushkara, Mokkara *m.* Sindhu princess
                - 9. Srīvikrama
                  - 10. Bhūvikrama, Srīvallabha —670,
                  - 11. Śivamāra I, 670—713.. Nava Kāma, Śishta-priyah, Prithivī Kongani I
                    - ? Ereganga
                      - 12. Śrīpurusha, 726—776 Muttarasa.
- 1. Mādhava I, 103 Kongunivarmma.

- Saigotta
  - Mārasimha, 797
    Marasing—Ereyappa,
    Loka—Trinētra
  - Prithivīpati I, ? 815
    - Mārasimha
      - Prithivīpati II, Hastimalla, c. 910.

- Ranavikrama.
  - 14. Rājamalla Satyavākya I, [3]
    m. Pallava princess
    - 15. Nītimārgga I, [4]
      Ereyanga,
      Ranavikramayya
      - 16. Rājamalla Satya-vākya II, 870—907
      - Būtugēndra, 870
        Būtarasa,
        Gunaduttaranga
        m. Rāshṭrakūta princess
        - 17. Ereyappa, 886—913
          Ereganga,
          Nītimārgga II,
          Satyavākya
          Mahēndrāntaka
          - 18. Rāchamalla Satya-vākya III, 920,
            Kachcheya Ganga
          - 19. Būtuga, 938—953
            Būtayya,
            Nanniya Ganga
            Ganga Gāngēya,
            m. Rāshtrakūta princess
            - Marula Dēva
            - ? Sōmi Dēvi
              m. to Rāshṭrakūṭa prince
            - 20. Mārasimha, 961—974
              Guttiya Ganga
              Nolambakulāntaka
              - 21. Rāchamalla Satyavākya IV, 977
              - 22. Rakkasa Ganga, 984,
                Rāchamalla
                - 23. Nītimārgga III
                  Rāchamalla,
                  ? 989 or 992, 999.
              - Arumuli Dēva
                - Rāja Vidyādhara.

---

[1] This name is applied to all the kings to the end. The Tamil Chronicle says that he was ruling in 189 and reigned for fifty-one years.
[2] This title is used of all the subsequent kings, often alone, without any name.
[3] These names are used as titles by all the kings that came after.
[4] This name is used as a title by the kings that follow.

APPENDIX B.

REFERENCES.

'Indian Antiquary'—

Vol.	Page	Subjects.
II.	353	.. Statue of Karkala.
II.	14, 134, 354	.. Papers on the Jains.
II.	129	.. Sravana Belgola.
II.	193, 258	.. Lassen's Account of the Jains.
II.	265, 322	.. Jaina Inscriptions of Belgola.
III.	89	.. On the Oswal Jains.
III.	153	.. Legend of Bhadrabāhu.
VII.	28	.. Digambaras.
VIII.	30	.. Jainism.
IX.	158	.. Tirthankaras.
XI.	245	.. Historic Records of Jainism.
XII.	21	.. Date of Mahavira.
XIII.	191, 276, 280	.. Papers on Jainas.
XIV.	104	.. Palidhwaja.
XIV.	233, 292	.. A Jaina-Vaishnava Compact.
XVII.	279, 339	.. Sacred List of Jains.
XVIII.	181, 369	.. Do.
XIX.	233	.. Upakesa Gachchha.
XIX.	62	.. Sacred List of Jains.
XX.	341	.. Pattavalis of Sarasvati Gachchha of Digambara Jains.
XX.	18, 170, 365	.. Sacred List of Jains.
XXI.	..	.. Bhadrabāhu, Chandragupta & Sravana Belgola.
XXI.	57	.. Three further Pattavalis of Digambara Jains.
XXI.	14, 106, 177, 210, 293, 327 and 369	.. Sacred List of the Jains.

'Indian Antiquary'—

Vol.	Page.	Subjects.
XXIII.	352	.. Bulletin of the Religions.
XXIV.	33, 65	.. Do.
XXIV.	275	.. Katha Kosa.
XXV.	147	.. Some Modern Jain Sects.
XXV.	316	.. Modern Jain Antipathy to Brahmans.
XXVI.	196	.. Jaina account of the end of Vagheles of Gurjara.
XXVI.	57	.. Bulletin on the Religions of India.
XXVII.	358	.. Bühler on the Jainas.
XXVII.	49	.. Legend on the Jaina Stupa at Mathura.
XXX.	239, 288	.. The Satrunjaya Mahatmyam-history of Jains.
XXXI.	477	.. Sukrita Samkritam of Arisimha.
XXXII.	49	.. Digambara Jain iconography.
XXXIII.	330	.. Do.
XXXIII.	330	.. Do.
XXXIII.	196	.. Indian Sect of the Jains.
XXII.	240	.. Gadja Chudamani of Vadibha Simha.
XXXV.	96	.. Kshatra Chudamani of Vadibha Simha.
XXXV.	268	.. Champu-Jivandharu by Harischandra.
XXXIX.	257	.. The Kalpasutra—Disciplinary rules for Jains.
XXXIX.	288	.. Jaina Yasovijaya Grantha Mala.
XL.	46	.. Mallishena Mahapurana.

'Indian Antiquary'—

Vol.	Page.	Subjects.
XL.	125, 153	.. Jaina iconography.
XL.	209	.. Origin and decline of Buddhism and Jainism in S. India.
XLI.	195	.. Kumarapala and Arnoraja.
XLII.	220	.. Muktagire.
XLII.	148	.. Jains' version of the story of Solomon.
XLII.	307	.. Origin and decline of Buddhism and Jainism.
XLIII.	118, 125, 167	.. The date of Mahavira.
XLVI.	133	.. A Magazine of Jaina Literature.

'Journal of the Royal Asiatic Society.'.

Vol. 1917—		
„	122	.. Date of Mahavira.

'The New East' I—

Vol.	1-4	.. The spiritual heritage of the East.
..	1-4	.. Illogical Zen.

'Indian Philosophical Review' I—

Vol.	1	.. Under-currents of Jainism.

'Calcutta Review'—

Vol. CCLXCV. Jan. 1919	.. Jain Antiquties of S. India.

'Journal of the Asiatic Society of Bengal.'—

Vol. XV. 3	.. Influence of five heritical teachers on Buddhism and Jainism.

Travancore Archæological Series—

Vol. II. Part II	.. Jainism and Buddha Vestiges in Travancore.

APPENDIX C.

THE SO-CALLED SANGAM AGE.

Conflicting Theories.

Mr. R. Swaminatha Ayyar, B.A., writes[1] :—

"I have read with great interest the three lucid articles contributed to the 'Hindu' by Professor M. S. Ramaswami Ayyangar, M.A., of Vizianagram, in which while summarising the views of other scholars he makes valuable contributions of his own to the discussion. There are several conflicting theories on the subject and it is to be regretted that notwithstanding several decades of critical discussion there are still to be found, even among English-educated Indians, persons who still cling to theories based on mere legend about the existence of three Tamil Sangams each extending over several thousands of years which will take the beginnings of South Indian History and of Tamil culture to the last glacial period. The number belonging to this school is, however, rapidly diminishing.

Several conflicting theories

"Outside this school the only concession that is made to the antiquity of Tamil Literary culture is that prior to the time of the Tamil Vatteluttu inscriptions which begin in the Pandya and the Chēra country in the last quarter of the 8th century A.D., there was a period of great literary activity in Tamil which

Antiquity of Tamil Literary Culture.

[1] Reprinted with kind permission from the "Hindu" dated 6th May 1922.

has in later times come to be traditionally known as the Sangam (சங்கம்) age. The works composed by the poets of this period have come down to us arranged in eight collections or anthologies known as (1) அகநானூறு, (2) நற்றிணை, (3) கலித்தொகை, (4) குறுந் தொகை, (5) ஐங்குறுநூறு, (6) பரிபாடல், (7) பதிற்றுப்பத்து, (8) புறநானூறு. The poems comprised in each anthology are short nuconnected pieces dealing with various situations that may arise in the course of love, in married life, in war and in other affairs of life. There are, besides, தொல் காப்பியம் the grammar, of old Tamil, supposed to have been written by an author belonging to the second Sangam and இறையனார் அகப்பொருள், a short work on erotics, said to have been composed by God Parama Siva himself ; these two undoubtedly belong to the same archaic period as the Sangam anthologies. To this list must be added two epic poems சிலப்பதிகாரம் and மணிமேகலை, and a collection of ten long poems known as பத்துப்பாட்டு ; all of these are believed to have been composed by Sangam poets.

Sangam Works.

"The late Professor Seshagiri Sastri of the Presidency College appears to have been the first scholar to furnish materials for a rational discussion of the question of the age of the Sangam works. He drew attention to a statement in the last chapter of *Silappadhikāram* that king கயவாகு of Ceylon was present in

Gajabahu-Synchronism.

the Court of the Chēra King Senguttuvan at the time of inauguration of temple ceremonies for the goddess கண்ணகி and identifying கயவாகு with the earlier Gajabāhu of Ceylon history, he was able to fix the age of Senguttuvan and of the incidents related in *Silappadikāram* (not necessarily of the composition of the work in its present shape) as the 2nd century A.D. This Gajabāhu-synchronism was adopted by the late Kanakasabhai Pillai as the basis of his work 'The Tamils Eighteen Hundred Years Ago' and it forms the sheet anchor of Dr. S. Krishnaswami Ayyangar's theories elaborated in 'The Beginnings of South Indian History.' S. K. Ayyangar's view. In this book the learned Doctor places the Sangam poets in and about the time of the reign of the Chēra King Senguttuvan, and after making a detailed examination of all references made by the Sangam poets to contemporary and past events he arrives at the following conclusions :—

(1) That there was a great invasion of Southern India by the Mauryas who penetrated as far south as the பொதியில் mountain.

(2) That the invaders were in hostile occupation of forts on the northern borders of the Tamil land.

(3) That the Aryans were beaten back when the central Mauryan power became weak and that their dislodgment from the south must be referred to the period of Māmūlanār and other poets of the Sangam age.

Internal evidence showing a later date.

" Various eminent scholars have, however, pointed out from time to time that there is internal evidence in several works supposed to have been composed by prominent poets of the Sangam age which shows clearly that these compositions belong to a much later age than the second century A.D., and it is becoming more and more evident every day that the Sangam age should be put forward to the 5th or the 6th century A.D. It may be remarked in passing that the former of these is the estimate arrived at by Pundit M. Raghava Ayyangar of the Tamil Lexicon office and that the latter is the estimate arrived at by Mr. K. V. Subramania Ayyar of the Archæological Department.

" One of the foremost poets of the Sangam age was Sīttalai Chattanar (சீத்தலைச் சாத்தனுர்) who is believed to have composed மணிமேகலை referred to above, one of the five classical poems (பஞ்சகாவ்யம்) in Tamil.

(i) This work contains a reference to குச்சரக் குடிகை—' a small temple built in the Gurjara style '—and it has been pointed out that if this is a reference to Gurjaras the work could not be much earlier than the 6th century A.D. as the Gurjaras are not heard of in Indian History before the middle of the 5th century A.D.

(ii) In another place the month of Vaisakha is referred to in the work as இருது இளவேனில் எரிகதிர் இடபத்து, thus containing a clear reference to the second of the twelve Rasis by its Sanskrit name. Various scholars have pointed that the division of the year into solar months and the naming of these months by the corresponding Rasis did not begin in Northern India till after the 5th century and that the adoption of this system in Southern India in the Tamil country must certainly have been later than its adoption in the north.

(iii) Professor Ramaswami Ayyangar now brings forward a third piece of evidence in the picture given in the work of the prevalence of Buddhism in the Island of Java. He points out that when Fahian visited the island about 400 A.D. he found 'various forms of error and Brahminism flourishing' in the island and that 'the Buddhists in the locality were not worth speaking of'; while in the last quarter of the seventh century when the Chinese pilgrim I-tsing visited the island it was essentially Buddhistic. This latter description tallies with the picture one forms of the island from what is stated in cantos 24 and 25 of *Manimēkalai*. It is not an isolated word or phrase that is brought forward here but integral portions of the work. This new piece of evidence seems to be conclusive and we may now take it as proved that whatever may be the date of other works comprised in Sangam list, மணிமேகலை clearly belongs to the 6th or the 7th century A.D. The work is not of much literary merit and was probably put together by a monkish poetaster—a native apparently of Cholamandalam.

Prof. Ramaswami Ayyangar's evidence conclusive.

"One important argument greatly relied on by Dr. Krishnaswami Ayyangar and other believers in the Gajabāhu-synchronism is the

References to Pallavas.

entire absence or reference to Pallavas in the Sangam works. They point out that the Pallava kings of Kanchi were an important political factor in South Indian History from the 5th century onwards and that the absence of any reference to them in the Sangam works clearly indicates that these works belong to an earlier period. To this Professor Ramaswami Ayyangar replies that the Pallavas were known by their group name of 'Tirayars' in the Sangam works and that this name meant 'seafarers' or 'seamen.' *Drayah* and *darya* mean the 'sea' in Persian, and *tirayar* is apparently a Persian-derived name meaning 'seamen.' This fact is in entire consonance with the theory of Professor G. J. Dubreuil that the Pallavas are of Persian origin and with the fact noted by him that the emblem of the Pallavas was a ship with two masts.

Podiyil theory.

"There are several other points in which Professor Ramaswami Ayyangar has thrown light on what has till now remained obscure; I will mention only one of them here. He has clearly proved that the word பொதியில் in தொன்முதாலத்தரும் பணைப்பொதியில் does not refer to the பொதியில mountain as supposed by some but merely a meeting place in shade of a banyan tree; this takes away the basis of the theory that the Mauryas penetrated as far south as the பொதியில் hill."

APPENDIX D.

MISCONCEPTIONS ABOUT SANGAM CHRONOLOGY.

[*This was contributed by me to the Vizianagram Maharaja's College Magazine, 1922 July number, and with kind permission is now reprinted.*]

It is a great pity that in spite of several years of critical discussion, the date of the famous Tamil Sangam should still remain undetermined. On this account, the history of the Peninsular India up to the 9th century A.D. continues to be a tangled tale of brilliant guesses. The assertion of certain scholars, that they have incontrovertibly determined the age of the famous Madura Academy, is at best a pardonable boast. Under the title " The Sangam Age," the present writer has recently contributed to the " Hindu " three articles wherein the conflicting theories in connection with this vexed question had been examined in detail. The object of this note is to press as further evidence of the later origin of the Sangam two facts not mentioned before. Sangam Works: when were they written? What was the script employed?

The illustrious author of '*The Tamils: Eighteen Hundred years ago*' has mentioned that in Sangam Age yet undetermined.

what is known as the Sangam Age more than 25,000 lines of verse have been written by poets who flourished between the years 50 A.D. and 150 A.D. It is further assumed that many thousands more are lost owing, perhaps, to the ravages of insects. The first question that a scientific student of History will propose is when were they written and what was the script employed. For one thing it is certain that the poets of the Madura Academy could not have employed the modern Tamil character, which, as is well known, is the Grantha-Tamil introduced into the Pandyan Country by the Cholas at a period when their power was rapidly reviving after the fall of the Pallavas, *i.e.*, 9th and 10th centuries A.D. When later on the Cholas effected the conquest of the Pandya territory, the Grantha-Tamil which was essentially the Chola script was not only widely used but it gradually began to supplant the Pandyan character known to Palæographists as Vatteluttu. Writing many years before the discovery of the caverns and the Brāhmī inscriptions of South India, Burnell thought that the Vatteluttu and the South Asokan character were totally distinct importations and postulated a Semitic original in both the cases. The late Mr. T. A. Gopinath Rao in criticising the views of both Burnell and Bühler, has not only pointed out several points of similarity between Vatteluttu on the one hand and the other alphabets of South

India but has successfully established the fact that Vatteluttu is derived from the Brāhmī variety of the Asokan alphabet. We can therefore take it as proved that the most ancient Pandyan script Vatteluttu was derived from the Brāhmī inscriptions of the Madura, Ramnad and Tinnevelly districts. Epigraphists are inclined to assign the end of the 3rd or the beginning of the 2nd century B.C. for the date of the Brāhmī inscriptions. This furnishes us with the lower limit for the period of any Tamil literary activity. The upper limit may be said to be furnished by the Vatteluttu inscription of the Pandyan king Jatilavarman Parantakan (last quarter of the 8th century A.D.), the earliest known record yet discovered written in Vatteluttu. In between these two limits must be sought the period of literary activity known as the Sangam Age. According to the orthodox school of Tamil scholars the sage Agastya was responsible for the evolution of the Tamil language and one of his twelve disciples Tolkāppiyar wrote the famous treatise on grammar, Tolkāppiyam. This grammarian is also believed to have been a member of the first and second Academies each of which existed for hundreds of years. Then was founded the last or the third Academy in which time more than 25,000 lines had been composed. Divested of legend and myth we can reduce the traditional account to its proper limits thus. Long before Tolkāppiyar there was a

The period of Tamil literary activity: its limits.

period of literary activity, for there can be no grammar without literature. If it is true that Vatteluttu was the earliest Pandyan script and that, as has been remarked, it was derived from the Brāhmī inscriptions, we must allow at least three centuries for the development of a literature sufficiently wide to need a grammar. This would bring the date of Tolkāppiyar to the end of the 2nd century A.D. Allowing two more centuries for the first two Academies we may safely arrive at the conclusion that in all probability the third Academy was founded in the 5th or 6th century A.D., a period sufficiently near the epoch for which epigraphic records are available, when Vatteluttu was perfected and from which we have a continuous literary history.

Absence of inscription prior to 8th century.

It is well known that between the Brāhmī inscription of the South and the Vatteluttu inscription of the 8th century A.D. referred to above there is absolutely no inscription written in any character or any coin legend to enable us to fix with some certainty the chronology of the Pandyan kings. Scholars who in season and out of season sing the glories of the Sangam Age, its vast literature and spacious traditions have not cared to inquire why for a period of more than a thousand years there has absolutely been no inscription. A few who thought about the subject argue that notwithstanding the very early literary activity, the Tamils did not know or cultivate the habit of inscribing on stones and issuing copper-plate grants. This is too large an inference to be swallowed without critical examination. The early Tamils are said to be an intelligent and civilized race with a great deal of assimilating power. Not far off from their land the Pallavas were issuing copper-plate grants and in their own home they had the Brāhmī inscriptions. And they could have easily imitated the example of their contemporaries. The fact that they did not do so is due to want of a proper developed language of a uniform standard and not to their inability to understand the usefulness and value of inscription.

Tamil literary activity: its probable date.

It might be argued that even supposing that the Sangam works were reduced to writing in the period not far remote from the time of Jatilavarman Parantakan the Sangam scholars might still have handed down orally the innumerable verses. The Vedas, the Upanishads and the epics, one might say, were thus handed down from generation to generation by oral repetition. It is true that so far as religious poetry is concerned such a method might have been zealously adhered to. But most of the Sangam poems treat of love and war and are mostly panegyric in character and there is not much of religion in them. It is therefore hard to believe that the Sangam works intact would have been handed down to posterity in the manner of the Vedas. The conclusion of the whole matter is that such an intense literary activity as the one that has been ascribed to the legendary Sangam is to be sought for in the time approximating the century for which we have the earliest known Vatteluttu records.

A striking piece of internal evidence.

There is a striking piece of internal evidence in *Manimēkalai* which would open the eyes of those who hug to their bosom their pet theory of the early origin of the Sangam which however rests on the slender basis of the Gajabāhu-synchronism. Canto XII of *Manimēkalai* contains an account of an interview between Manimēkalai and a Buddhist Abbot of Kaviripoompattinam. In the course of a long sermon the grey-headed old monk Aravanavadigal says, " . . . . Buddha-Dharma is losing its hold in the mind of the people and as a result forms of error are increasing in the country. Yet do I not despair. I still continue to preach the law which few care to understand." Evidently the Abbot laments the rapid decay of Buddhism in the Tamil country. It is a well-known fact that Buddhism which was flourishing during the days of Fahien was in process of decay when Hieun-Tsang visited Conjeevaram (7th century A.D.). According to his testimony, in Malakuta or Malakota, the name by which the Pandya country was called by him, Buddhism was almost extinct, the ancient monasteries being mostly in ruins. " The inhabitants were reputed to care very little for learning and to be wholly immersed in commercial pursuits." Thus it requires no great ingenuity or verbal demonstration to show that Aravanavadigal's reference is to the period of Hieun-Tsang or better still to the century that immediately preceded the Doctor's visit.

BIBLIOGRAPHY.

Arunachalam, P.	..	'Sketches of Ceylon History.'
Barth	..	'Religions of India.'
Beal	..	'Life of Hiuen Tsang.'
Beauchamp	..	'Hindu Manners and Customs.'
Bhandarkar, Sir Ramakrishna	..	Report on the Search for Sanskrit MSS.
Buchanan	..	'Travels.'
Bühler	..	'The Indian Sect of the Jainas.'
		'Bōdhāyana Sūtras.'
Burnell, A. C., Dr.	..	'South Indian Paleography.'
Caldwell, Bishop	..	'Introduction to the Comparative Grammar of Dravidian Languages.'
Chakravarti, Prof.	..	'Panchastikaya.'
Colebrook	..	'Miscellaneous Essays.'
Cunningham	..	'Ancient Geography.'
Dubreuil Jouveau, Dr.		'Antiquities of Pallavas.'
....	..	'Epigraphia Indica.'
Fergusson	..	'Indian Architecture.'
Francis	..	Madras Census Report, 1901.
Frazer	..	'Literary History of India.'
Hastings	..	'Encyclopaedia of Religion and Ethics.'
Hunter, Sir William W.		'Non-Aryan Languages of India.'
....	..	'Imperial Gazetteer, Bombay Presidency.'
....	..	'Indian Antiquary.'
Jacobi	..	'Acharanga Sutras.'
		'Kalpa Sutras.'

BIBLIOGRAPHY.

.... ..	'Jaina Gazette', Madras.
.... ..	Journals of the Royal Asiatic Society and its branches.
Kanakasabhai Pillai, V.	'The Tamils Eighteen Hundred Years Ago.'
Kern, Prof. ..	'History of Buddhism.'
Krishnaswami Ayyangar, S., Dr. ..	'The Beginnings of South Indian History.'
	'Ancient India.'
MacDonnell, Prof. ..	'History of Sanskrit Literature.'
M'Crindle ..	'Fragments of Megasthenes.'
.... ..	'Madras Christian College Magazine.'
.... ..	'Madras Epigraphical Reports.'
Max Muller ..	'Hibbert Lectures.'
	'Sacred Books of the East.'
Nelson, J. H. ..	'Madura Country.'
Pope ..	'Kural.'
.... ..	'Quarterly Journal of the Mythic Society.'
Rice, E. P., Mr. ..	'History of Canarese Literature (Heritage of India Series).
Rice, Lewis, Mr. ..	'Mysore and Coorg from the Inscriptions.'
	'Epigraphia Carnatica.'
Seshagiri Sastriar, Prof.	'Essay on Tamil Literature.'
Smith, V. A. ..	'Early History of India.'
	'South Indian Inscriptions.'
Srinivasa Ayyangar, M.	'Tamil Studies.'
.... ..	'Tamilian Antiquary.'
Tennent ..	'History of Ceylon.'
Taylor ..	'History of India.'
Turner ..	'Mahavamsa.'

INDEX.

(References to pages.)

K—*contd.*

L

M

M—*contd.*

N

N—*contd.*

O

P

P—*contd.*

Q

R

R—*contd.*

S

S—*contd.*

T

PART II

ANDHRA KARNATA JAINISM

BY

B. SESHAGIRI RAO, M.A.,

Chief Lecturer in English, Maharaja's College, Vizianagram

AND

Sometime Reader in Dravidian Philology to the University of Madras.

INTRODUCTION.

This monograph on "Andhra-Karnāta Jainism" which forms the second part of the present volume of "Studies in South Indian Jainism" is the result of a vacation study undertaken in the summer recess of 1921 at the instance of the Trustee of the Vizianagram Raj and the Principal of the Maharajah's College.

It seeks to trace the influence of Jainism in the Andhra and Karnāta districts of the Madras Presidency. The traces of this influence are very largely obscured by the latterday Renaissance of Puranic Hinduism and afford an opportunity for extended exploration. This is the first attempt, so far as I know, to give any systematic account of them and none can be more conscious than myself of the want of more adequate information on the subject. In these circumstances, these studies cannot claim more value than can be given to the barest outlines of a subject which, for cultural reasons, demands more than a passing interest.

These studies serve to throw some light—however faint it may be—on the history of the Andhra Country from the Fall of the Satavahanas to the Rise of the Chalukyas. The views elaborated are my own, first formulated while working as a Reader in Dravidian Philology in the University of Madras (1914—1917); and I believe, the materials on which they are based are presented now for the first time in an ordered sequence.

South Indian History is yet a subject for research, and must continue to be so for at least a decade more. Andhra History is a comparatively more untrodden field. No opinions on these subjects can therefore be stated with an air of finality. I shall consider this labour of love amply rewarded if these essays provoke thought and constructive criticism. The period of history here treated requires elucidation from many points of view. I have endeavoured to suggest one line of elucidation.

My special thanks are due to the Telugu Librarian of the Oriental MSS. Library, Madras, for his invariable courtesy in facilitating my references and to M.R.Ry. M. Ramakrishnakavi Garu, M.A., for a loan of his rare Kannada works in print and MS. bearing intimately on the subjects of my investigation. The Index to this part is prepared by my colleague Mr. V. Visvanatha Sarma, Pandit, Maharajah's College and Mr. J. Venkataratnam of the fourth year University class.

I feel it my duty to state that these studies would not at all have been possible but for the noble enthusiasm and generous sympathy of the Trustee of the Vizianagram Raj and the Principal of the Maharajah's College for researches in the Indian Cultural Tradition.

MAHARAJAH'S COLLEGE,
VIZIANAGRAM,
July 1922.

B. SESHAGIRI RAO.

TABLE OF CONTENTS.

PART II.

ĀNDHRA KARNĀTA JAINISM.

CHAPTER I.

THE EVIDENCE OF TRADITION.

(*Local Records in the Madras Museum.*)

The fascination of the subject (*a*) Antiquity, (*b*) Disguise, (*c*) Represents struggle and achievement of a spiritual nature—Jaina and Upanishadic methods of spiritual culture—The Nandyāla tradition showing Jainism in relation to worldly realism, the progress of arts and sciences—Jaina fantasticism and neighbouring Vaidica Dharma—Kurimari and Pasapula tradition—Jaina village organisation (*a*) Pallis, (*b*) Bastis—Jaina bastis—Disguised Jaina foundations: Pedagadela, Tadinagarapupadu—Jaina liberalism in relation to Vaidica Dharma—Warrangal, Rāmathīrtham, Siddhavattam, Tenali—The beginnings of the decline of Jaina influence in the Andhra dēsa—Rāja Rāja Narēndra of Rajahmundry and his ancestors—The leaders of the Revival in the Andhra dēsa: The Kotas of Amaravati, The Parichchēdi-Pūsapātis of Bezwada and the Kakatiyas of Warrangal—The progress of revivalist antagonism to Jainism even in border districts of Āndhra-Karnāta dēsa like Warrangal—The kindlior treatment of Jainism in the Karnāta dēsa proper—The problem suggested—Materials for an answer.

Jainism in the Andhra-Karnāta dēsa is a fascinating subject of investigation. It has a fascination all its own. Chronologically, it helps to fill in the gap between the Fall of Satavahana power in the Deccan and the Rise of the Chalukyas, the Gangas, and the Parichchēdi-Pūsapātis of East Deccan definitely committed Antiquity.

to the revival of Vaidica Dharma. Its memorials come from well within the period of Buddhist influence under Asoka. Perhaps they are even earlier. Whether latterday Buddhism shaded off into Jainism, or whether both Buddhism and Jainism were parallel and contemporary protests against Sacrificial Hinduism, originating in the Upanishadic reflections of the Rationalistic period of Hindu thought or whether Jainism was an original primitive Indian faith, of the North Indian forest homes and tribes, modified, deepened and intellectualised largely by association with, and on the analogy of, the Aryan philosophical, ethical and sociological speculation and organisation,—these are matters of controversy amongst famous Indologists. The *view*, however, adopted as the *basis* of the present studies is that Jainism in the Andhra dēsa, at least, was probably pre-Mauryan, that its influence, humanising and cultural, was working in these lands before the Asokan version of the gospel of Buddha reached them and that the prevalence of its characteristic doctrine of *Ahimsa* prepared the Andhras and Kalingas in a way for the favourable reception of the Buddhist doctrine promulgated by the Asokan Edicts and propagandists. Herein may be found an explanation of the peculiar note of sadness characteristic of the Asokan Edict dealing with the conquest of Kalinga and Asoka's sudden conversion to Buddhism and the definite adoption by him of a policy of peace in preference to one of war and aggression. Recent interpretations of the Kharavēla inscription of Kalinga lend support to this view. The Bhadrabāhu inscriptions of Sravana Belgola are even earlier than the Kharavēla inscriptions, for the Karnāta country. This Bhadrabāhu tradition is the starting point of a *revival* of Jaina activity in South India.

" In Literature, the *Brihatkathākōsa*, a work by Harishēna, dated 931, says that Bhadrabāhu, the last of the Srutakēvalis, had the king Chandragupta as his disciple. A similar account is contained in the *Bhadrabāhu charita* by Ratnanandi of about 1450 ; as is repeated in the *Rajavalikatha* by Dēvachandra which is a modern compilation of about 1800." The points worthy of note in this summary of the Bhadrabāhu tradition in the Karnāta country are first, that the inscriptions know only of a Chandragupta-*muni*, the disciple of Bhadrabāhu, and secondly, that the Jaina literary tradition from the 10th century onwards knows of a *king* Chandragupta who was perhaps this disciple whom the inscriptions celebrate. Modern historical scholarship has sought to identify this Chandragupta, *king* and *muni*, with Chandragupta *Maurya*, the patron of Kautilya, the accredited author of the *Arthasastra*. The Kharavēla tradition makes the Nandas of Magadha the followers of the Jaina faith, for, it speaks of a Nanda Raja who led a conquering expedition into Kalinga and carried off (?) an image of Adi-Jina. (A passage in the Udayagiri inscription of Kharavēla seems to suggest that Kharavēla "made the king of Magadha bow down at the feet of the highest brought away by Nanda Raja." ? (*Cf.* పాదేవందా పయతి నందరాజానీతస అగజినస.)

Jarl Carpenter, PH.D., Upsala, says, "The agra-Jina may be Mahāvīra or Rishabha, but so much seems clear, that a Nanda king had taken away an idol of Jina during a raid into Kalinga, possibly about sixty years after the death of Mahāvīra." It is not clear whether "*Anītasa*" in the text can be rendered as "carried away" or "brought"; if the latter rendering be accepted, it would make Nanda Raja himself a ruler of Kalinga, perhaps a predecessor of Kharavēla. A Nanda Raja, no doubt seems to have ruled in Kalinga, for there are, for instance, villages in the populous parts of Ganjam, named after a Nanda Raja.[1] Of such names may be mentioned :—Nandagām (Berhampore Taluq), Nandarājapuram (Ichhapur Taluq).

This does not, however, affect adversely the argument of the antiquity of Kalinga Jainism. On the other hand, it takes us further a step back of the times of Kharavēla and makes it definitely *pre-Mauryan*.

While the Chandragupta of the Bhadrabāhu tradition is acknowledged to have been a Brahmanist before his conversion by Bhadrabāhu, an additional motive for his revolt against

[1] A version (Telugu) of *Markandeyapuranam* makes the *four* famous Kshatriya clans of the Andhra dēsa the descendants of a Nanda Raja of Kalinga.

the Nandas in combination with Kautilya is afforded by the evidence of the Kharavēla inscription noticed above as to the Jaina patronage of those kings. On Kautilya himself, the Jaina doctrine of *Ahimsa* made absolutely no impression. The point is proved by the fact that in the *Sūnadhyaksha*, a number of animals are exempted from slaughter (especially in the Abhayavanas) but meat diet was not tabooed. For otherwise, Kautilya would not give rules regarding the sale of meat.

Disguise. Aside from the fascination of this antiquity of Andhra-Karnāta Jainism, there is the added charm of its disguise. To the student of Indian Antiquities nothing comes beaming with so much inspiration as the disguise that covers in tradition many a monument of this immemorial past, rich with its message that man lives not for power and pelf alone, that in fact his high destiny lies more in the conquests of the spirit and its dominance over what is merely "of the earth, earthy." It is a message of struggle, of travail, of sacrifice, of devoted consecration, and concentration, of high and noble achievement for the freedom of the body and the soul.

The momentoes of this struggle and achievement, of this power of the spirit and its decay are obscured in the annals of the Andhra mandala, so completely obscured even in its literature, that, but for the records of the tradition collected by the late Col. Mackenzie and

C. P. Brown, all knowledge of them would have been lost to the modern world. These studies cannot therefore begin better than with salutations to those great souls that laboured in their own generation so earnestly that the world may think kindly and reverently of these whilom scenes of the conflicts of civilisations and systems of spiritual culture.

Jaina *vs.* Vaidica cultures.

The principal object or *pradhāna purushārtha* in life of a Jaina is meditation and self-purification for the attainment of arhathood ; indeed, it cannot be distinguished, except in the externalities of method, from the Upanishadic and Smarta ideal of life for a Brahmana desirous of the attainment of moksha, freedom, *viz.*, *Swādhyāya* and *Brahmacharya*, *i.e.*, study and self-control by concentration. In the later Jaina inscriptions which fall within the period of the present investigation, Jaina munis are often described as *yama-niyama-swādhyāya-dhyāna–dhārana–mounānushtāna- japa-samādhi-sīla-guna-sampannar* (యమ నియమ స్వాధ్యాయ ధ్యాన ధారణ మౌనానుష్ఠాన జప సమాధి శీల గుణ సంపన్నర్) and the followers of the Vaidica Dharma in similar terms as *yama-niyama-swādhyāya - dhyāna-dhārana-maunānushtāna - parāyana - japa - sīla-sampannar* (యమ నియమ స్వాధ్యాయ ధ్యాన ధారణ మౌనానుష్ఠాన పరాయణ జప శీల సంపన్నర్).

It is said in the Jaina Agamas that Mahāvīra was the first to insist on celibacy for the Jaina munis in addition to traditional *digambaratwa*, *i.e.*, nudity. A programme of life inspired by such high and difficult disciplines of yōga required for its successful cultivation a certain obscurity and considerable quiet. This determined the choice of the Jaina munis to carry wherever they went what Tagore would describe as "the message of the forest" characteristic of the freest period of Indian intellectual achievement. No wonder, then, that, in South India, the Jainas were in many cases the humanisers of forest glades and charming riversides, either long neglected by human life or quite untouched by it. That they had an eye for such picturesque spots in nature is obvious from the place—Katavapra—selected by Bhadrabāhu, the *Rejuvinator of the South Indian Jainism*, for his niryānam. The Sravana Belgola description detailing the event, perhaps the earliest inscription of Karnāta Jainas, has the following description of the *Katavapra* Hill :—

"అతః ఆచార్య ప్రభాచంద్రానాం అవనితలలలామభూతే థాస్మిన్ కటవప్రనామకోపలక్షితే వివిధతరువరకుసుమదళావళి వికచ నశబలవిపుల సజల జలదనివహ నీలోత్పల తలే వరాహద్వీపివ్యాఘ్ర ఋక్షతరక్షు వ్యాలమృగకులోపచితోపత్యక కందరదరిమహాగుహాగ నాభోగవతి సముత్తుంగశృంగే శిఖరిణి."

Translation (Lewis Rice) :—

"When they had reached a mountain with lofty peaks, whose name was Katavapra,—an ornament to the earth, the ground around which was variegated with the brilliant hues of the clusters of gay flowers fallen from the beautiful trees; the rocks on which were as dark as the great rainclouds filled with water; abounding with wild boars, panthers, tigers, bears, hyenas, serpents and deer; filled with caves, caverns, large ravines and forests."

Jainism and worldly realism.

The dwellers of such mountain regions, generally inaccessible to man or beast, however, became the fellers of the forest and the controllers of river-courses. These Jaina colonists coming down into South India in large groups, sometimes of 500 each, selected for their residence beautiful river banks and deep forest recesses redolent of the fragrance of creeper and flower and rich with the beauties of variegated landscape, so that they might imbibe their balm and assimilate themselves to the creative forces of nature as a first step to their gradual assimilation to the Arhats. Some such idea is discernible through the conventionalised description of the aspect of Kuntala dēsa, a famous resort of Jaina ascetics, occurring in an early Kannada inscription of S.S. 1130 from one of the present Andhra-Karnāta districts. The Brahmānda Purāna mentions the *Nirgranthas* among the early South Indian settlers known to the writers of Aryavarta. The forest recesses of the Andhra dēsa revealed to the illuminating gaze of these scholarly immigrants either virgin lands untouched by the feet of the unhallowed or ruins of former human habitation,—the traces of the achievement and decay of an earlier generation of Indian population. They no doubt dealt with these regions in the spirit of pioneers breaking new ground and planning out new foundations. Nandyāla otherwise called Dommara Nandyāla on the banks of the river Pinākini is one such colony. It lay in the neighbourhood of Hindu habitations, of people following Vaidica Dharma. The Jaina munis arrived there, cleared the jungle, marked out a plot of elevated ground for their *palli*, established their deity on it and settled down to their daily routine of study, meditation and sādhana. They seem to have tilled the soil (a point in which they assimilated themselves more to the followers of the Vaidica Dharma) and followed their ideals of life unmolested by their neighbours. Yet, it was definitely recorded in the tradition of Nandyāla that their faith was peculiar, as also their manners and general method of life. It is worthy of remark that these followers of the digambara tradition in Nandyāla covered themselves with leaves (which corresponded to *Nārachīralu* of the early Hindu settlers in the South Indian āsramas). This peace and quiet, this undisturbed concentration on the realisation of ideals, this atmosphere of pure study led to great intellectual power and achievement. The Jaina munis became masters of the arts and sciences, great scholars in medicine and magic, "conning" searchers of the heavens, the makers of logic, philosophy and literature. Such achievement characterises one of the early āchāryas of the Jaina tradition, *viz.*, Kundakunda who, according to tradition, lived and meditated in Konakundala in the Bellary District in the present Andhra-Karnāta country. Yet, scholarship so highly technical, self-centred and self-reflective, so much apart from the main currents of life round about, so insular and intensive, bred a certain type of arrogance which latterly came into violent collision with the propagandistic zeal of the followers of Sankara, Rāmānuja and Basava[1] and in the intellectual jousts that followed, the Jainas fell sorry and forlorn victims to what appears like self-sought destruction. Nandyāla fell into ruins like many an other such Jaina foundation and became for once nothing but a mound of high ground indicative of desolation and significantly known to later generations as Jaina-*pādu*. Many of the oddities of life and manners of the Jainas, some of which are noticed in the *Nandyāla Kaiphiyat*, are derivable directly from the doctrine of *Ahimsa* alleged to be characteristic of the Jaina and Bouddha protestant faiths. This doctrine is clearly stated in a work called *Ratna-Karanda* by Samantabhadraswami, one of the celebrated Achāryas of the Jaina pontifical heirarchy.

Jain fantasticism.

The Jaina munis had a clean shave to prevent the growth of lice and the possibility of their having to kill them. They swept the path with peacock feathers (barhipincham) wherever they walked, lest they should tread unawares on the tiniest insect. They became digambaras lest

[1] See *Basava Purana* (Telugu), Chapter 6.

the cloth they may wear should, by contact with their bodies, injure any microcosms that may alight on them. They did not eat after nightfall lest light should attract and kill the wandering insects of the air. Such life and manners no doubt appeared fantastic to the followers of Vaidica Dharma surrounding them, but they were tolerated by them as just a fantastic extravagance of precepts to which they themselves professed allegiance. For, as a writer in the American Oriental Society's Journal points out "that this non-injury rule was Buddhistic is contrary to evidence. Even the oldest Brahmanical law, which is at least as venerable as any Buddhist Literature, includes the general moral rule of doing as one would be done by in the matter of injuring, killing and eating one's brother-animal....Except for sacrifice, to kill no sentient thing and to eat no meat were absolutely priestly laws .... The later Brahmanic law, like that of the Jainas, was very particular in regard to these points." And yet, notwithstanding all this rigour, even fantastic rigour, of their *Ahimsa dharma*, such was the reaction of the surrounding Vaidica Dharma on their faith and life that these Jaina munis gradually assimilated their faith and practices to those of their neighbours and did not even scruple to offer *bloody sacrifices* for the satisfaction of their deities on the occasion of the foundation of their villages.

A very interesting account of such a *sacrifice by Jainas* is given in the *Kaiphiyat* of

Jaina Sacrifice.

a village called Jammalamadugu in the present Andhra-Karnāta country. The tradition is also borne witness to by an early Kannada inscription assigned by C. P. Brown to A.D. 1029 or 1089. The inscription states that a general of Sreeman Mahāmandalēsvara Trailōkyamalla Dēva called Chandra Dandanāyaka and his wife fell heroically fighting in a battle occasioned by a boundary-dispute between two villages called *Kurimari* and *Pasapula*. There is a Virkal describing this heroism in the former village fixed in the temple of *Tallakantisvarī* by whose favour king Trailōkyamalla had a son Bhīma Dēva and henceforward become devoted to her. Just as the inscription brings out the heroism of Indian manhood and womanhood trained under the hardy discipline of Jainism and its contempt for life in the service of Dharma or righteousness, so does the story of the foundation of the Jaina deity in Kurimari betray the influence, in Andhra-Karnāta Jainism, of the enveloping aspects of the more ancient Vaidica Dharma and even of the much earlier sacrificing faiths of the primitive forest tribes. A body of Jaina immigrants reached the heart of the forest near Jammalamadugu and discovered traces of human habitation there. They fixed a good day for the founding of a new village on that ancient site and first established their *Sakti*, on it, called Daitamma and wanted to offer a goat sacrifice. They went in search of a goat and finding near by a *golla* tending his sheep and goats, offered him anything he might ask as the price of a goat or *vēta*. He wanted to impress upon the munis the supreme lesson of sacrifice, *viz.*, that it is made at the birth of a new creation and that the sacrificed reincarnates in it and so agreed to give them a goat for a sacrifice on condition that they in turn agreed to call the village after the sacrificed animal. The munis consented, *made the sacrifice* and called the place *Kurimari* (goat sacrifice). The village flourished day by day. It became a great basti. Like this Daitamma, *Tallakantīsvari* was another deity latterly established at *Kurimari*. By the time of Trailōkyamalla Dēva, this deity had to be re-discovered and her temple renovated. During the time of Kākatiya Pratāparudra, the place came to be called *Dānavula-pādu*[1] (the ruined habitat of the dānavas or devils) probably by the followers of the Vaidica Dharma in their revivalist contempt for the Jainas or as a reminiscence of the tradition of *Daitamma* (the daityadānava goddess) the earliest Jaina deity ever established in that place.

Jaina Social Organisation.

The Jainas were not content to live an obscure and out-of-the-way kind of life in *pallis*. They developed *bastis*. A *palli* seems to be the Jaina unit of social and administrative organisation. A *basti* seems to correspond to a city or township formed out of a group of neighbouring villages. *Vanipenta* is an instance of such a

[1] For a description of the Jaina ruins of Dānavulapād, see *Madras Archæological Report*, 1903-04.

basti or township. It was originally a forest side cleared by the Jainas for a habitation. It latterly became a big *basti* under a Jaina king called Mallaraja with some villages (అముద్దిరెడ్డిపల్లి, అద్దిరెడ్డిపల్లి, మిట్టభూపనపల్లి, విశ్వనాధపురం) as its component parts. This happened during a Jaina interregnum between the Chola and Kākatiya suzereignties. The Reddis after whom the villages are named must have been powerful Jaina chiefs in the vicinity of Vanipenta.

Similar in status was *Kondrajupalem*, a Jaina *basti* in the Rētur paragana of Vinukonda Sarkar in the Andhra mandala. When it passed latterly into the hands of the Brahmanical revivalists, it was destroyed by them as a mark of the victory, under Mukkanti, of the Brahmans from Benares, over the Jaina gurus, in philosophical disputation.

To the isānya of *Chundūru* there used to be a similar Jaina foundation called *Peddintimma*. Jainism decayed there even before the rise of the Oddi, the Reddi and the Kākatiya Rajas to sovereign power. The villagers of Chundūru used the high level mound which represented it as their granary and the place came subsequently to be known as *Pedagādela* (gāde=grain-holder).

Similar again was Tādinagarapupādu (తాడినగరపుపాడు) to the west of the village now known as *Kollūru* in the Mrutyunjayanagar Taluq of Chintapalli Sarkar. In the early years of the Sālivāhana Saka, according to tradition, several

Jaina Rajas ruled here among whom the Kollūru Kaiphiyat mentions Jayasimha, Malla Dēva, Sōmidēva, Pērmādi Dēva, Singi Dēva and the Vengi king *Vishnuvardhana*. That a place is called basti at a more advanced stage of social development than palli is evidenced by the Kanaparru Kaiphiyat. The village Kanaparru was originally a Hindu foundation. Subsequently the Jainas came and occupied it. They developed the village, built several homesteads and jinālayas and " made the village into a basti." The word *basti* is also used in the Kaiphiyats in the sense of a Jaina shrine. It is derived from Sanskrit Vasati=a dwelling place (*Cf.* *nivēsanam*=house-site). Popular fancy treats it as a Hindustāni word but it can be traced in Jaina inscriptions quite earlier than the Muhammadan advent.

Such very early Jaina foundations of the Andhra-Karnāta dēsa are so subtlely disguised very often by the theological zeal and ingenuity of the latterday Hindu revivalists, that, while the fact illustrates the absorbing catholicity of the latter, it confuses all traces of historic continuity. For the glimmerings of such continuity almost the only source of material authoritative is the collection of Kaiphiyats in the Mackenzie manuscripts of the Oriental Library of the Madras Museum. It remains, for the South Indian epigraphist and archæologist, a sacred duty to follow up the suggestions offered by these glimmerings of ancient tradition and

Disguised Jainism.

unearth the actual traces of Rājāvalis and civilisations in the Andhra-Karnāta dēsa for *the period between the decay of the Satavahanas and the rise of the Chalukyas.* Much of this period is too readily supposed to be covered by the rule of the Pallavas, the tradition of whom is not as clear in the Andhra-Karnāta records and literature as in those of the Drāvida country.

Mutual tolerance. Instances of the liberalism of the Jainas and the followers of the Vaidica Dharma towards each other deserve particularly to be placed on record, for, they account largely for the great figure that Jainism could make even amidst adverse forces. The accounts of the foundation of Warrangal, so intimately associated with the Andhra dynasty of the Kākatiyas, record that Mādhavavarma, the founder of this dynasty, acquired the means of sovereign power by worshipping a goddess located in an underground temple near about the present site of Warrangal. Tradition as recorded in the Warrangal Kaiphiyat says that there was a hill called Hanumadgiri to the isānya of Hidimbāsrama in North Dandaka, the seat of dēvas and rishis. This was discovered by a person called *Ekāmbaranātha* (the muni with a single cloth). He founded near it a village called Hanumadgiri (Anumakonda) and established several deities in it—*Siddhēsvara* in the middle, Dēvi *Padmākshi* in the west, *Garga* sakti in the north, *Gōpālamūrti* in the south and

Bhadra Kāli in the east. The *Siddhēsvara* and *Padmākshi* may indeed be the later Saivite variants of the original Jaina deities of *Siddha* and *Padmāvati*. The rest of the deities may either be mistaken appropriations to an earlier time of a later day tradition of Hindu revival, or, if they really belong to the Jaina period, they may be illustrative of the catholicity of latterday Jainism in its assimilations to contemporary Hinduism. Anumakonda long continued, in literary tradition, to be a seat of *Avaidica* faiths. To such a period of Jaina catholicity would belong, for instance, the Rāma temple of Rāmathīrtham near Vizianagram in the Vizagapatam District. The fact is mentioned in the following excerpt from a Jaina inscription from the Vizagapatam District :—

> శాకాబ్దేనభఖేందుచంద్రగణితే శ్రీభోగపుర్యాంప్రభుః।
> శ్రీమన్మన్నమనాయకస్సుమతిమాన్ క్రీత్వాజినస్థాపనం।
> తస్యాగారమచీకరత్స్యవలనచ్ఛైలే...ధాభాసురం।
> రామోరామగిరౌయథాజినపదాబ్జాసక్తచిత్తస్స్వయం॥

That the Jaina kings who ruled the part of the country near Warrangal before the rise of the Kākatiya power practised such catholicity is shown by the *Siddhavattam Kaiphiyat* which distinctly says that they founded the temples of Siva and Kēsava in the east of that village. During the days of the Chola sovereignty, a Brahmana Agraharam of 360 homesteads was founded on the banks of the Pinākini within a radius of 5 kros from the village of Siddhavattam. To the east of that Agraharam, on a narrow strip of high level ground, the Jaina kings founded, subsequently, a Bhairavālaya. A similar instance of Jaina liberalism also occurs in the tradition of Tenali, a village in the Andhra mandala proper. The *Jaina Rajas* that ruled there were so devoted to the god *Ramalingaswami* of that place that they got their own devotee figures sculptured on the walls of that Saivite shrine. Such liberalism on both sides enabled Jainism to command a large following and influence in the Andhra-Karnāta mandala down to the time of the Eastern Chalukya king Rāja Rāja Narēndra of Rajahmundry and Mukkanti Pratāparudra Ganapati Dēva of Warrangal.

The *Warrangal Kaiphiyat* mentions a great Jaina patriarch called Vrishabhanādha Tīrtha of the time of Rāja Rāja Narēndra of Rajahmundry as having been very powerful about Warrangal. Why such a great religious teacher had left Rajahmundry, the capital of the Vengi Kingdom, for the border district of Warrangal in the Andhra-Karnāta dēsa is clear enough. Rāja Rāja Narēndra was perhaps the first of the Chalukyas of the Andhra country to begin definitely a seriously intellectual, and at the same time popular, campaign against Jainism or more properly, in favour of pauranic Hinduism.

Hindu aggression.

The *beginning of the decline* of the Jaina influence in the Andhra dēsa may be referred to the time of this Rāja Rāja Narēndra who ascended the throne at Rajahmundry in the year 1022 A.D. About the year 1053 A.D. he induced the Telugu rendering of Vyasa's Mahābhāratam by his courtier Nannayabhatta, as perhaps a rival to the Pampa Bhārata or Vikramārjuna Vijaya known to him in the Kannada language and setting forth ancient story and legend from a distinctly Jaina point of view. A critical and comparative examination of the Jaina and the Telugu Bhāratas does not fall within the range of the present investigation. Suffice it to say that later poets who attempted to appraise Nannaya's work regarded as "trashy worthless material," all the literature that preceded it in Telugu and delighted the hearts of the Andhras. This description may well indicate the attitude of the Pauranic Revivalists to Jaina literature even in the Telugu districts proper. Just a single verse may be quoted as an illustration of this type of appraisement of an old poet's work as a contribution to the progress of culture :—

భాసురభారతార్థములభంగులనిక్కమెఱుంగనేరమిన్ ।
గాసటబీసటేచదివిగాథలద్రవ్యతెనుంగువారికిన్ ।
వ్యాసమునిప్రణీతపరమార్థము తెల్లము జేసినట్టియా ।
జ్ఞానసకల్పులందలతు నాద్యులనన్నయతిక్కనార్యులన్ ॥

We say, the *beginnings* of the decline, advisedly, for a few years before A.D. 1022, during the time of Rāja Rāja's father Vimalāditya (Mummadi Bhīma), his guru visited Jaina decline.

Rāmathīrtham, near Vizianagram, then a great centre of Jaina culture. This fact is recorded thus in a Kannada inscription at Rāmathīrtham (that the language of the inscription is Kannada shows that that language was well understood in Rāmathīrtham, a place distinctly Andhra in foundation and tradition) :—

1. స్వస్తిసవ్వ౯లోకాశ్రయ శ్రీవిష్ణువద్ధ౯న మహారాజరాజ మాత్తా౯ణ్డ ముమ్మడి భీమనవారుగళ్. 2. శ్రీమద్దేసిగణాచాయ్య౯రుం సవ్వ౯ . . . . . రాజపూజితరుం మధ్యాహ్న సుభిక్ష . . . . 3. శ్రీ త్రికాళయోగిసిద్ధాన్తదేవర్। కన్ద।విమళాదిత్యన [గు] రుగళు . . .. 4. శ్రీత్రికాళయోగిమునీన్ద్రర్ క్రమమఱిదచ్చి౯సి [భక్తియొళమితం] శ్రీ రామకొణ్డమంబన్దిసిదర్ ॥

The ancestors of the Vimalāditya, Mummadi Bhīma, of the above excerpt, were themselves patrons of Jainism which perhaps was the original faith of the early members of the Chalukya family in West Deccan. The facts relevant to this point are thus summed up by the Epigraphist with the Government of Madras :—(*Cf. M. Ep. Rep.* 1917–18).

" Vishnuvardhana III of the Eastern Chalukya dynasty made a grant in S. 684 which registers evidently the renewal of an earlier grant of the village Musinikunda in Tōnka N [ā]ta-v[ā]di-vishaya to the [Jaina] teacher Kālibhadrāchārya. The queen of the King Kubjavishnuvardhana I influenced the grant of a village to a Jaina *Basti* at Bījavada. Amma II has made grants to Jaina temples and patronised the grant of a Jaina Srāvakī by lending his title to a charitable Jaina feeding house called Sarvalōkāsraya—Jinabhavana endowed by her."

Other Vaidica Revivalists.

Among the Andhra dynasties that played a great part in the revival of Vaidica Dharma by definitely ranging themselves heroically against Jainism and such other Avaidica faiths powerful in the Andhra country must be mentioned the *Kōtas* of Dhānya-Kataka, the Parichchēdi-Pūsapātis of Bezwada and the Kākatiya Ganapatis of Warrangal. These are all South Indian Rajaput clans. Tradition records their advent together to South India from their North Indian homes. Some Bardic verses bearing on this point may here be illustrated :—

అలఘువిక్రముఁడు కోసలజయాదిత్యుండు దక్షిణవిజిగీషఁ దాడి వెడలి।
నిగమాగమాంతపారగుఁడాజిభీష్ముండు శ్రీదేవవర్మ సైన్యాధిపతిగ।
నఖిలసీమలవిజయస్తంభములు నాటి దివి కేగను త్రిలింగదేశభూరి।
వాహినీపతి దేవవర్మప్రభుండయ్యె నద్ధూరిసీమ పేరాజిలోన।
వల్లభునోడించి వైభవంబులమించి సార్వభౌమపదంబు జగతిగాంచె।
అతని సుతుండు బుద్ధావనీశుఁడు రాచ తబిసియై గాంచెను ధర్మనృపుని।
తనయులాతనికి బుద్ధయ దేవవర్మలు బుద్ధరాజందుఁ బ్రసిద్ధుఁడయ్యె।
అతనితనూజుఁడాతతబలోన్నతుఁడు మాధవవర్మ ముత్తాతఁబోలె।
జనకునాజ్ఞను సత్తశతి సాంగముగ రామదేశికుచేనుపదేశమొంది।
కనకదుర్గాకటాక్షప్రాప్తవిభవుఁడై మళియసింగని బోర మ్రందజేసి।
చాబళిహస్తమల్లబలాధిపుని రక్తధార చేపరదేవతను భజించి।
వసుదిగింద్రియశకవత్సరంబుల జయవాటికాదుర్గవైభవము గాంచి।
గగనవాణీవాక్యగౌరవంబున పూసపాటి భూమిని పురీవరము గట్టి।
వాసిగాంచఁగ పూసపాటి వారనుయింటిపేరు గాంచిరి రాచపెద్దరికము।

This extract from a Sīsamālika composed by a member of the Pūsapāti family who calls himself Rājamārtānda Sri Rachiraj, son of Tammiraj, gives an account of the origin of the Pūsapāti family among the Andhra Rajaputs. According to this version Jayāditya of Kōsala came on a conquering expedition to the south of India. Along with him came his redoubted general *Dēvavarma*. Jayāditya conquered several lands and planted pillars of victory in various places and perhaps died in the return journey. His general *Dēvavarma* of the Trilinga command succeeded him in the Andhra country, defeated Vallabha in the severe contest at Addūr and became overlord. His son *Buddhavarma* was a saintly prince and he had two sons Buddhavarma and Dēvavarma, of whom the former became celebrated. His valiant son was Mādhavavarma who, like his great grandfather, obtained the Saptasati mantra along with its angas from Ramadēsika and attained status and wealth by the favour of Kanakadurga. He appeased Durga with the blood of Chauhattamalla Balādhipa and killed Maliyasinga in open warfare and became celebrated owing to Durga's favour in S.S. 548 (A.D. 626). He built a city on the site of Pūsapādu and henceforward his line of princes[1] like Amalraj became the leaders of the South Indian Kshatriya clans and were traditionally known as the Pūsapātis.

[1] According to Vishnubhakti Sudhākaram, Amal Raj was the first to call himself a Pūsapāti and the Rachiraj, author of the present Malika, must be Rachi I, son of Tammiraj, given in the "genealogy" of that work."

The following verses (bhat) refer with some enthusiasm to these successes of the Pūsapāti family from Mādhavavarma downwards which secured for them the leadership of the South Indian Rajaput clans :—

1. ఎనిమిదివేలపోరగల యేనుగులన్వడి నేలలోక్కలో
క్కనిదశలక్షవాజులును కవ్వడిబోలుననంతభృత్యులున్ ।
ఘనముగదుర్గ...ఖండధనంజయభీకరాంకుడై ।
మనుజవరేణ్యుడంబరగు మాధవవర్మకుగారవంబునన్ ।

2. కట్టెలగుండెపట్టు కైకట్టిధురంధర...తెచ్చియ ।
పృట్టునజంపచిత్రమని భల్లుని మెచ్చిసువర్ణవృష్టియ ।
పృట్టినభూమిలో గురువబంచెనుమాధవవర్మపాళిపెం ।
(పిట్టిద ?) యంచుయి...భభేరొక్కనిరిప్పురిదేవసంఘముల్ ॥

3. హేమాచలముదాక నేకచక్రంబుగాభువి నేలెమీతాతబుద్ధవర్మ ।
మీతాతగురియించిమెరసెమాధవవర్మ గరిమచే బెజవాడకనకవృష్టి ।
పాండ్యకేకయచోళపళవీరనృపతులతెగటార్చిమీతాతదేవవర్మ ।
పిడుగుముత్తునిచుగావడి నేసె మీతాతభీకరంబుగ-చిక్కభీమనృపతి ।

చండవిక్రమయినవంశజలధిచంద్ర ।
బాపు ! మగధీర ! రణరంగభైరవాంక ।
పోసగ నెవ్వరునీసాటిపూసపాటి ।
పగరకనుదింమ్మరాచభూధవునితిమ్మ ॥

(*From the MSS. of the late G. V. Apparao Pantulu.*)

These verses, the text of which is greatly corrupted by centuries of oral tradition in the mouths of family bards, testify in a general way to the incidents referred to in the above excerpt of a *Malika* composed by one of the members of the Pūsapāti family, who by the way, calls himself నరససాహిత్య సంగీత చక్రవర్తి (the master of fine poetry and music). They refer also darkly to conflicts with the followers of a *different faith.*

The Kōtas of Dhānyakataka were, like the Pūsapātis of Bezwada and Pūsapādu, the followers of a Saiva faith. These describe themselves in their inscriptions as follows :—

చతుస్సముద్రముద్రిత నిఖిలవసుంధరా పరిపాలక శ్రీమత్త్రినయన పల్లవ [ప్రసాద] . . . జ్ఞానదీదక్షిణాషట్సహస్రావనీవల్లభ . . . . . శ్రీమదమరేశ్వర దేవరదివ్యశ్రీపాద పద్మారాధక పరబలసాధక శ్రీధాన్యకటక పురవరాధీశ్వర ॥

The Amarēsvara of Dhānyakataka referred to in this description as the family deity of the Kōtas must originally have been a Buddhist or Jaina deity during the Satavahana period when Dhānyakataka was the primary capital of the Andhra Empire. By the time of the Kōtas this deity must have been metamorphosed into a Saivite one. The Kōtas of Dhānyakataka, the descendants of whom are still found among the Andhra Kshatriyas, had a special *birudagadya* of their own still recited on ceremonial occasions. The following extracts from it bear out the description of the dynasty quoted above from an inscription :—

స్వస్తిసమస్తపంచమహాశబ్దమహామండలేశ్వర । రాజపరమేశ్వర । యీశ్వరపదవీవిరాజమాన । విజయవినోద । . . . . మల్లచోళ సింహచోళ శార్దూల । మత్తమాతంగ । హరిరాయాస్థాన గజసింహ । బౌద్ధకండకుద్దాల । పాండియరాయమగ । ధనంజయగోత్ర పవిత్ర । . . . రాజుపేరు జగమెచ్చు గండండు । బంటుపేరు పగమెచ్చుగండండు । ఖడ్గంపేరు కాలమృత్యువు । శేవుపేరు పాపవినాశ

నంబు । నదిపేరు కృష్ణవేణి । దేవర పేరు అమరేశ్వరదేవుండు । పట్టణంబు పేరు ధరణాలకోట । వాటిపేరు ధాన్యవాటి । వీటి పేరు గండరగండవీడు। పడగ పేరు గండభేరుండ। . . . . . అంబ దేవర భూపాలుండు మొదలైన శ్రీకోటరాజుల అన్వయప్రశస్తి। విజయీభవ । దిగ్విజయీభవ ॥

Among the Andhra Rajaputs, there is a family called *Jampani's of Dhananjaya gōtra* who claim to be of the Kōta line.

The reference in this *prasasti* to the contests of the Kōtas with the Mallas, the Cholas and the Pāndyas must belong to the time when, as followers of the Kōsala king they came to South India under the leadership of Dēvavarma. There are dark suggestions in Drāvida Literature of a Mauryan expedition into the Deccan assisted by the Kōsars and Vadagus. The Vadagus or the Andhras referred to in these suggestions may possibly be the five clans of South Indian Rajaputs thus alleged to have followed the fortunes of Dēvavarma "of the Trilinga command" (త్రిలింగవాహినీ పతిదేవవర్మ). The Kōtas in this extract describe themselves as "the weapon by which the Buddha root is dug up" (బౌద్ధకంద్ద కుద్దాల), an expression very significant of the campaign they carried on against Avaidica faiths.

The Parichchēdi-Pūsapātis claim to have built Bezwada and resuscitated the worship of Durga therein at a time when the Chalukyas were founding Jaina shrines there. They professed to carry on their fight for Vaidica Dharma with the means of sovereignty secured by the worship of that ancient deity. The emergence of Mādhavavarma into sovereign power by the worship of Durga at Bezwada has already been illustrated. That this family who described themselves as an invincible race (దుర్జయకుల) were Saivas is also apparent from the following birudāvali occurring in one of their inscriptions dated S.S. 1188 :—

"స్వస్తిసమధిగతపంచమహాశబ్ద మహామండలేశ్వర కొల్లిపాక పురవరాధీశ్వర త్రిపురమాహేశ్వర దుర్జయకులాచలమృగేంద్ర శ్రీకృష్ణవేణ్యానదీదక్షిణ షట్సహస్రగ్రామావనీవల్లభ మల్లికావల్లభ ఎలదాయరక్కస పరబలకర్కశ గండధనంజయ ఆహవభీమ అరిబల (రామ) గండప్రచండమార్తాండ రణరంగభైరవ సహకారబాంధవ . . . కుంతకాంతేయచాళుక్యరాజ్యమూలస్తంభ."

This description agrees with the following birudāvali of the Pūsapāti family from *Sreekrishnavijayam* referred to in "*Vizianagram Treaty*" edited by the late illustrious Sree Sree Sree Sir Pūsupāti Anandagajapati Raz Maharaj, G.C.I.E., of Vizianagram :—

"స్వస్తిశ్రీ మన్మహామండలేశ్వర, మహీమండలరాయ, మన్నెసురత్రాణ, దర్భజకుల కలశరాకాశశాంక, హాసబిరుదగండ, ధారాపురీగహనదావధనంజయ, గండధనంజయ, మేదినీరాయమృగవేటకార, వీరకేదార, కృష్ణవేణీజలక్రీడా వినోదపరాయణ, ఖడ్గనారాయణ, దుర్జయకులకులాచాలకంఠీరవ, రణరంగభైరవ, మాళవరాజ మస్తకశూల, కర్ణాటరాజకంద్దకుద్దాల, వైరిరాజోరగవైనతేయ, శౌచగాంగేయ, వీరసేతుప్రతాపభాసుర, వామచురీధర, నెల్లూరెలమంచిలికంచి దేవగిరిచూరకార, ఆంధ్రకటకవజ్రప్రాకార, మానగోవింద, కుంతకాంతేయ, విజయవాటికాసింహాసనాధ్యక్షు మాధవవర్మాన్వయలలామ, ఘోరాహవభీమ, కనకదుర్గాప్రసాదలబ్ధవైభవ,

కొలిపాకపురీధవ, సహకారబాంధవ, దశలక్షహయాష్ట సహస్రగజ
వల్లభ, మల్లికావల్లభ, లాటభోటచోళగౌళాది రాజపురసర్వస్వాప
హార, పరిచ్ఛేదివంశాభరణ, బిరుదరాయరాహుత్తవేశ్యాభుజంగ,
కళ్యాణరాజదుర్మదవిభంగ, సేతుసీతాచలాస్తోదయాద్రిబిరుద శాసన
స్తంభవిరాజిత ..... చాళుక్యరాజ్యస్థాపనాచార్య .... ఎల
రాయరక్కసరాయ" ....

One thing is more than clear from these titles of the Pūsapāti family, *viz.*, that the Pūsapātis have all along claimed to belong to the *Parichchēdi-Pūsapāti* clan of Andhra Rajaputs. That these Parichchēdi-Pūsapātis professed to protect the Vaidica Varnāsrama Dharma down to the time of Sree Krishnadēvarāya, of the other Vizianagram, on the banks of the Tungabhadra river is evidenced by the following excerpt from an inscription dated in S.S. 1453 :—

"శ్రీవిజయనగర పట్టణాధీశ్వర యీశ్వరనాయకపౌత్ర నరస
నాయకపుత్ర శ్రీఅచ్యుతరాయ మహారాయ కృపాకటాక్షలబ్ధైశ్వర్య
ధుర్య సూర్యవంశోద్భవ వశిష్ఠగోత్రపవిత్ర బెజవాడ పురవరాధీశ్వర
మల్లికార్జునదేవర దివ్యశ్రీపాదపద్మారాధక మాధవవర్మకులప్రదీప
బెజవాడపాటిప్రతిష్ఠాపనాచార్య సేతుశీతాద్రిపర్యంత బిరుదరగండ
రణరంగభైరవ మన్నెభార్గవ ..... వర్ణాశ్రమధర్మప్రతిపాలక
కేవబ్రాహ్మణపూజాపరాయణ" ....

The more intolerant persecution of the Jainas by the Kākatiyas is very frequently described in the local records. **Persecution.**

One story goes that a Kākati king of Warrangal acquired a pair of charmed sandals with the help of which he used to visit Benares every morning without the queen and the people and return to his capital unnoticed when his morning ablutions were over. Once the queen happened to notice that the King was missing. She sent for her Jaina gurus who were proficient in Jyoutisham and asked them about his whereabouts. The Jaina gurus told the queen the truth of the matter. On the King's return she confronted him with the story of his " escapade " and only requested him to take her also to Benares for her own morning ablutions. The King came to know that the queen had the truth of the matter calculated by the Jainas and consented reluctantly to grant her wish. Later on, when once the King was in Benares with the queen, she happened to be in her " period " and the King found great difficulty in coming back to his capital. Henceforward the sandals lost their charm, the King felt mortified and took vengeance on the Jainas by persecuting them.

The worsting of the Jainas by Ganapati Dēva of Warrangal when they were defeated in disputation with Tikkana (the minister of Manumasiddhi of Nellore), the author of the Telugu Mahābhāratam, is more famous and the following extract from a manuscript poem in the Oriental Manuscripts Library of the Madras Museum has a clear reference to it :—

* * *

" అనుమకొండ నివాసులైనట్టిబౌద్ధ
జనులరావించివారిఁదిక్కనమనీషి।

తోడవాదింపజేసినతోడరివారి।
జాలుకగాసోమయాజులు గెలుచుటయును ॥

వ॥ అపుడు బౌద్ధదేవాలయంబులు గూలంద్రోయించి గణపతిదేవరాజు సోమయాజులపటువాక్యశక్తికిమెచ్చి॥" . . .

The Jainas are, no doubt confusedly, referred to as the Buddhas, for, a Jaina foundation by one Ekāmbaranātha is referred to in the traditions of Anumakonda.

Jainism had kindlier treatment in the Karnāta country just about this time when adverse forces were heading against it in the Andhra country proper and even in the border districts, like Warrangal, of the Andhra-Karnāta country. This may just be indicated from the traditions of the Karnāta country proper. In a grant dated in S.S. 1044, a Saivite king of Banavasi honours a Jaina foundation at Arapāku (ఆరపాకు) in the Pānugallu Taluq. The following excerpt from the *birudāvali* of that king makes his devotion to Saivism quite apparent : **Karnāta-Jainism.**

స్వస్తిసమస్తభువనాశ్రయం శ్రీపృథివీవల్లభ మహారాజాధిరాజ పరమేశ్వర పరమభట్టారక సత్యాశ్రయకులతిలక చాళుక్యాభరణ శ్రీమత్త్రిభువనమల్ల దేవర విజయరాజ్య ముత్తరోత్తరాభివృద్ధిప్రవర్ధమాన మాచంద్రార్కతారంబరం సల్లుత్తమిరె॥ తత్పాదపద్మోపజీవి॥ స్వస్తి సమధిగతపంచమహాశబ్ద మహామండలేశ్వరం బనవాసిపురవరాధీశ్వరం జయంతీమధుకేశ్వరలబ్ధవరప్రసాదం మృగమదామోదం। త్రియతుత్మాసంభవం। చతురాశీతి నగరాధిష్ఠితం లలాటలోచన చతుర్భుజం। జగద్విదితాష్టాదశాశ్వమేధ దీక్షాదీక్షితం। హిమవద్గిరీంద్ర రుంద్రశిఖరిశస్తి సంస్థాపిత స్ఫటికశిలాస్తంభబద్ధమదగజమహామహిమాభిరామం। మయూరవర్మ మహామహీపాలభూషణం। పేర్మాటి

తూర్యనిర్ఘోషణం । శాఖాచరేంద్రధ్వజవిరాజమానమానోత్తుంగ సింహలాంఛనం । దత్తార్థికాంచనం । సమరజయకారణం । కదంబరాభరణం । మారోర్కల్పరగండం । ప్రతాపమార్తాండం । మండలికగండ బంగారం ॥ . . . .

And yet, even in the Karnāta country, donors to Jaina shrines had to make special appeals to the liberality and generosity of the followers of the Vaidica tradition when it so happened that they had to grant Brahmana Agraharams to Jaina munis or the shrines at which they worshipped. Thus it was not the political influence and patronage that the Jaina munis commanded that secured their porperties to them but the generosity of the followers of the Vaidica tradition and the respect they had for genuine scholarship and character among the Jainas. In support of this view may be cited an inscription dated in A.D. 898 of the time of the Chalukya king Trailōkyamalla Dēva in which the donor makes a special appeal to the Brahmanas of a village that he was granting to a Jaina foundation. He addresses them thus:—" యమనియమస్వాధ్యాయధ్యానధారణామౌనానుష్ఠాన పరాయణజపశీలసంపన్నరుం । అతీతానాగతవర్తమాన కాలదూరశ్రవణ విజ్ఞానాదిగళోళతిపరిచితరుం । అనేక తర్కశాస్త్రవిద్యావిశారదరుం । ఆశ్రితజనాదరుం । ఏకవాక్యరుం । శ్వేతఛత్ర చామరాద్యనేకరాజచిహ్నోపలక్షితరుం । శ్రీవాసుదేవలబ్ధప్రసాదరుం ॥" and appeals to them to see that the enjoyment of the grant of their village to the Jaina scholar mentioned is maintained undisturbed. This scholar is described as " సమధిగతపంచ

మహాకల్యాణోష్ట మహాప్రాతిహార్య చతుస్త్రింశదతిశయవిరాజమాన భగవదర్హత్పరమేశ్వర పరమభట్టారకముఖకమల వినిర్గతసదసదాది సప్తభంగి సమాలింగితారాధ్యాంతాది సమస్తశాస్త్రపారావారగర్."

Thus the great feature that had won wide tolerance for the Jaina munis and Jaina foundations in the Andhra-Karnāta dēsa even during the bitterest periods of Hindu revivalist zeal was that that faith helped towards the formation of good and great character helpful to the progress of culture and humanity. The leading exponents of that faith continued to live such lives of hardy discipline and spiritual culture even during the days of discouragement, disfavour and antagonism from the patrons of religion and culture. A Jaina muni is thus described in an inscription dated in S.S. 1130 :—

క్షితిపరిపూజితపూర్వమజైన మహాంబుధివర్ధనవర్ణయా ।
న్వితరఖిళాగమార్థ పరిశుద్ధమహామతిగళ్నిరస్తదు ।
ప్రకృతరుపశాంతియుక్తరని పొందుపొగళ్తిగభానుకీర్తిస ।
గ్వ్రితిసుతమేఘచంద్ర మునిముఖ్యరయోగ్యరిళాతళాగ్రదోళ్ ॥

Hence the latterday persecutions of Jainism, like the persecutions of the Christians by Marcus Aurelius, are an extraordinary phenomenon deserving explanation on some hypothesis other than the *merely* revivalistic zeal of the followers of the *Vaidica*, which is for this period, the *Pauranica, Dharma*. But such persecutions paved the way for social reverses very often recorded in the traditions of the Andhra-Karnāta villages leading ultimately to the all but complete obscuration of all traces of Jainism in the Andhra-Karnāta country.

What credence do these traditions deserve, rich as they are in suggestiveness? This question must be faced as one turns from the curious pursuit of these glimmering lights of South Indian antiquity. Sufficient cumulative evidence has been let in from other sources not wholly traditional to enable one to arrive at a decision. It must however be acknowledged that a possible answer is offered by the recent progress made by South Indian Epigraphical Research. A similar answer, not perhaps so complete, yet equally authoritative and suggestive, is found in the progress of research in South Indian Archæology and Literature.

APPENDIX A.

The following account of Jaina Dharma is from a kaiphiyat from the Chingleput District (*vide J.A.S.B.* Vol. 7, p. 108):—

(*a*) *Yati Dharma* (1) *Ardhyavam* to follow the right way and teach it to others, (2) *Mardhava* to behave with reverence to superiors and carefully to instruct disciples, (3) *Satyam* invariably to speak the truth, (4) *Sasiyan* mentally to renounce hatred, affection or passion and evil desire and outwardly to act with purity, (5) *Tyagam* to renounce all bad conduct, (6) *Kshama* to bear patiently like the earth in time of trouble, (7) *Tapasu* outward and inward self-mortification, (8) *Brahmacharyan* to relinquish all sexual attachment in word and thought, (9) *Aginchanam* to renounce the darkness of error and follow the light of truth, (10) *Samayam* duly to celebrate all specied periods, festivals or the like.

(*b*) *The Sravana Dharma* (1) *Tarisinigen* one who relinquished certain unclean kinds of food; (2) *Vritiken* one who eats not at night, is faithful to his teacher, to his family and to his religion; he is self-restrained and keeps silence and zealously renounces the use of all pleasant vegetables; (3) *Samathiken* one who with foregoing qualifications, renders homage to the Divine being three times a day, morning, noon and evening: (4) *Proshopavasen* one who fasts on certain days so appointed to be observed; (5) *Sachitan-Vrithen* one who with the foregoing dispositions renounces certain kinds of food; (6) *Rattiribhaktan* one who observes mortification (?) during the day only; (7) *Brahmacharya* one always occupied in the contemplation of God; (8) *Anarampan* one who quits cultivation and all other secular occupations; (9) *Aparigrapam* one who renounces all kinds of earthly gain: (10) *Amemati-pinda-Vriten* one who forbears to eat even that which he has prepared; (11) *Utishtu-pinda-Vriten* one who relinquishes dress, except for mere decency. He carried a pot and lives in the wilderness.

(*c*) *The Purva Karma and Apara Karma.* Birth Samskaras and Death Samskaras (obsequies).

CHAPTER II.

EPIGRAPHIA JAINICA.

Progress in the discovery of Andhra-Karnāta Jaina epigraphs—Bearing of the progress of epigraphy on the materials of the last chapter—Places at which Jaina epigraphs have been found—Main indication—Difference between the Andhra and the Andhra-Karnāta epigraphs—More numerous in the Andhra-Karnāta than in the Andhra districts—Scope for further enquiries—Regions in the Andhra dēsa awaiting exploration—Difference between the Hindu Revival in the Andhra and the Andhra-Karnāta districts in its bearing on the fortunes of Jainism—Tabulation (classified) of Andhra-Karnāta Jaina epigraphs and a few points of further interest brought out—Jainism and its antiquity in the Andhra-Kalinga country.

Epigraphic Research in the South Indian Presidency is still in a state of continuous progress. Yet, so far as it has succeeded in interpreting the memorial epigraphs of the past, it has proved in a considerable measure the validity of the traditions of the Local Records relied upon as the chief materials for the foregoing survey, in outline, of the meaning and message of the social tradition of the Jainas in the Andhra and Karnāta mandalas. The District Manuals and Gazetteers largely trusted to the guidance of these local traditions in the conduct of further enquiries and their light never proved illusory. In and about the centres of Jainism mentioned in these records, the officers of the Epigraphist department have discovered traces of Jaina epigraphs taking us back to the times when Jainism played a predominant and significant part in South India. These epigraphs still await publication. At Penukonda, Tādpatri, Kottasivarām, Pātasivarām, Amarapuram, Tammadahalli, Agali and Kotipi in the Anantapur District; at Nandapērur, Chippigiri, Kogali, Sogi, Bagali, Vijayanagar, Rayadurg in the Bellary District; at Dānavulapādu in Cuddapah District; at Amaravati in the Guntur District; at Masulipatam, Kalachumbarru in the Krishna District; at Srīsailam in Kurnool District; in the Madras Central Museum; at Kanupartipādu, in the Nellore District; at Vallimalai in the North Arcot District; at Basrur, Kōtēsvara, Mulki, Mudabidire, Venur, Karkala, Kadaba, in the South Kanara District; at Bhōgapuram, Lakkumavarapukōta and Rāmathīrtham in the Vizagapatam District, have been discovered Jaina epigraphs.

Find spots of Jaina Antiquities.

Extermination or toleration.

These, for one thing, indicate the large vogue that Jainism once had in the Andhra and Karnāta mandalas. The epigraph from Srīsailam is interesting in that it shows the kind of persecution to which Jainism in these lands had finally to succumb. The epigraph in question is indeed a Saiva one. It records in Sanskrit, " on the right and left pillars of the eastern porch of the Mukhamantapa of the

Mallikharjuna temple, in S. 1433, Prajōtpatti, Magha, ba. di. 14, Monday, a lengthy account of the gifts made to the temple of Sreesailam by a certain chief Linga, the son of Santa, who was evidently a Vīrasaiva, one of his pious acts being the beheading of the Svetambara Jainas. " This record is important in two ways. It shows how the Saivite opposition gathering force in the Andhra dēsa against Jainism about the first quarter of the eleventh century A.D. developed into an *exterminating persecution* by the first quarter of the sixteenth century A.D. and how the *Svētāmbaras* also are represented in South Indian Jainism as a class deserving the expurgatory attention of the Saiva fanatics.

In this respect the records from the Andhra-Karnāta districts tell a different tale justifying the remark made in the former chapter about the kindlier treatment of Jainism in the Andhra-Karnāta, and Karnāta districts proper. A few grants to Jaina foundations by *non-Jainas* about the year S. 1433 and following deserve notice in this context.

The smaller Venkataramana temple at Chippigiri in the Bellary District records a grant in S. 1528 to a Jaina foundation by Sri Krishnadēvarāya of Vijayanagar.

At Kurugodu in the same district, a record of the time of Vīrapratāpa Sadāsivadēvarāya Mahārāya of Vijayanagar, on the south wall of a ruined temple, mentions in S. 1467, Visvavasu, a gift of land to a Jaina temple by Ramarajaiya, elder brother of Aliya-Lingarajaiya and grandson of Ramaraja Odeya, for the merit of his father Mallaraja Odeya. The important fact to be noticed is that these *Jaina* grants *are allowed to be recorded in non-Jaina shrines.*

Similarly, in the Karnāta dēsa, in the S. Kanara district, at Kōtēsvara, in the local pagoda of Kōtēsvara there is a record dated in S. 1468, Prabhava, in the reign of Sadāsivarāya, stating that Echappa Udayar gave 50 gadyanams of land to that deity. Echappa was the same as the Jaina chief of Garisappa who married a daughter of the last Karkal king. If Kōtēsvara is a Jaina deity, there is nothing very remarkable in this grant. But it solves a very interesting problem regarding the foundation of Chicacole (Srikakulam) in the Ganjam District with its temple of Kōtēsvara, *viz.*, its early Jaina associations. Otherwise, a grant by a Jaina to a Saiva shrine in the Karnāta country, about the time when Vīra-Saiva persecution of Jainism was rampant in the Andhra dēsa throws a flood of light on the great religious toleration of the Karnātas, to which Jainism owed its continued life and prosperity on the West Coast of the South Indian Presidency.

Distribution. This circumstance accounts for the fact that among the discovered epigraphs relating to Jainism, the more numerous ones occur in the Andhra-Karnāta and Karnāta mandalas. Still, it must be observed that further research is bound to be fruitful in discoveries in the history of Jainism in the Andhra mandala which fill the large gap between the fall of the Satavahana power and the beginning of the decline of the Jaina influence about the 11th century A.D. A few considerations based on the discoveries already made are urged here below as indicating such a hope of further Archæological exploration.

Openings for *Archæological* exploration.

The Tādpatri inscription from the Anantapur District dated in S. 1120 (1130 ?) expired, Kalayukta, is suggested by Dr. Hultzsch to indicate the presence of a Jaina shrine in that place. The inscription itself refers to "Chandranātha-Parusvanātha-dēvara Anādiyāsthāna," *i.e.*, to an ancient shrine of Chandranātha Parsvanātha. This shrine is *yet to be discovered.*

The Bagali inscription from the Bellary District refers to the gifts of the Western Chalukya King Tribhuvanamalla to a Brahma Jinālaya there. This is *yet to be identified.*

The Amaravati inscription of Chula-Aira and of the nun Nanda Nandā speaks of the gifts of a pillar. The Jaina shrine to which this gift is supposed to have been made remains *yet to be unearthed.*

A copper-plate grant of Amma II Vijayāditya (945-70) of the Eastern Chalukya dynasty records gifts to *two* Jaina temples which have not *yet been discovered.*[1] Perhaps their traces are completely lost on account of the steady persecution of the Jainas and powerful propaganda against them started in the district by the Kōtas of Dhānyakataka and the Parichchēdi-Pūsapātis of Bezwada.

The Kalachumbarru grant of the same king, Amma II, refers to grants to a Sarvalōkāsraya Jina Bhavana in that village. This temple is *yet to be found out.*

The Kanupartipādu inscription from the Nellore District refers to the "pallichchandum" of a Jinālaya named after Karikālachōda, the traces of which are *yet to be recognised.*

The Bhōgapuram inscription from the Vizagapatam District refers to a Jina foundation of that place called Rāja Rāja Jinālaya, the location of which *remains to be marked out.*

The inscription in the Anjaneyaswami temple in Nandi-pēruru in the Bellary District registers gifts for the worship of Jina. The Jaina shrine to which this inscribed slab from the Anjaneya temple must have belonged is *yet to be identified.*

Unbroken ground.

Nor is this all. There are yet regions in the Andhra and Karnāta mandalas, supposed to contain Jaina relics, which still await exploration by scholars official or otherwise interested in Indian Antiquities. Some of these deserve mention for the additional evidence they offer

[1] Mr. K. V. Lakshmana Rao, M.A., says that the traces of a temple are newly discovered near the Bezwada Railway Station. It may turn out to be Jaina or Bauddha. (4th June 1922.)

as to the early vogue of Jainism in the Andhra and Karnāta lands.

Jaina relics are said to be found in Ariyavattam in Cocanada taluq, Nēduluru, Atreyapuram in the Amalapuram taluq, Kazuluru, Yendamuru, Sila in Cocanada taluq, Pittapuram and Jalluru in the Pittapuram division, in Tatipaka in Nagaram taluq and Draksharamam in the Ramachendrapuram taluq of the Godavari District.

At Jayati in the Vizagapatam District, a small village eight miles north-west of Gajapatinagaram, there are two odd little deserted Jaina shrines.

At Nandapuram, in the Pottangi taluq, of the present Agency division, about three miles along the track to, Sembliguda is a very ancient and curious Jaina relic, *viz.*, a small shrine in which are three stone images of nude individuals sitting cross-legged which appear to belong to Jaina times. This takes us very far back into times of the Nanda Rajas when Jainism was a dominant faith in the Kalinga country. In fact, as regards much of Epigraphical and Archæological exploration, the Kalinga districts are still a largely unbroken field.

The village of Ariyavattam in Cocanada Taluq in the Godavari District is also called " Jaina Pādu " and contains several large but rude images of figures sitting cross-legged in the traditional attitude of contemplation. Images of a like kind are worshipped in the streets of Pittapuram by Hindus under the name of Sanyāsi Dēvulu (ascetic gods). Pittapuram = Skt. Pishtapuri Skt. = Pristapuri is so called after the Jaina goddess *Pristapuri Dēvi.* The Jalluru Kaiphiyat shows how it once was a flourishing Jaina city. Many large rivetted wells in the Nagaram and Amalapuram taluqs are still known as "Jaina Wells."

Ratnagiri and Kambaduru in the Anantapur District, Lachmēsvara, Nayakallu and Yachavaram in Kurnool District, Kurugodu, Pedda Tumbalam and Chinna Tumbalam in Bellary District also contain traces of Jainism *not yet adequately explored.*

Another interesting fact brought out by these epigraphs is that in the Andhra-Karnāta districts in which the Hindu Revival was so powerfully organised by Sāyana-Mādhava, the real founder of the city of Vijayanagar, Jainism fared better under the Vijayanagara Kings than at the hands of the Revivalists in the Andhra districts proper. The point is interesting in that it shows that the influence of a Hindu Revival strictly based on the Vaidica and Upanishadic tradition is bound to be more catholic and tolerant of differences of religious opinion than religious sects starting from a narrower point of view. In support of these observations may be noticed a few grants of the early Vijayanagar Kings to professedly Jain foundations.

A Sanskrit record of Dēvarāya II, dated S. 1348, Prabhava, at Vijayanagar, mentions the building of a Chaityālaya to Parsvanātha in the Pansupari street.

At Mudabidire, on the north wall of the Gaddigimantapa in the Hosa basti, right of entrance, there is a record of the Vijayanagara King Vīra-Dēvarāya IV in S. 1351, Saumya, which refers to the building of a basadi.

On a slab set up in the Gurugala basadi of the same place, there is another epigraph of the Vijayanagara King Vīra-Bukkarāya II (1399—1406), son of Harihararāya II (1377—1402), in S. 1329, Vyaya, which mentions a gift of land.

At Basrur, a record of Dēvarāya II (1422—49) in S. 1353 relates the gift of one Kolaga of paddy on every bullock load coming from other places to Basrur, for the benefit of Jain basadi by the Chettis of Basrur.

A classified tabulation of these Jaina epigraphs will easily display other points of interest bearing on the progress and decay of Jainism in the Andhra and Karnāta districts. The epigraphs are therefore classed here below as (1) Memorial, (2) Architectural, (3) Votive, (4) Iconographic, (5) Votive and Commendatory, (6) Commendatory. Epigraphs classified

A.—MEMORIAL.

Anantapur District.

Penukonda (k) On a slab placed by the side of the well in the Parsvanātha temple. Records that it is the tomb stone of Nagaya, the lay disciple of Jinabhushana Bhattaraka Dēva.

Amarapuram (k) On a stone in the village. The Nisidi (tomb) of Sambisetti, son Berisetti Sarvari, Asvija, Su. di. 15, Friday.

(k) On a stone lying in the tank to the south of the same temple. This is the tomb (Nisidi) of Bommisettiyara Bachaiya, a lay disciple of Prabhachandra Bhattaraka of Ingalēsvara, who belonged to the Mūla Sangha, etc.

(k) On a second stone in the same place. This is the tomb of Bhavasena Traividya Chakravarti who was a terror to disputants and belonged to Mūla Sangha and Sēnagana.

(k) On a third stone in the same place. This is the tomb of Virupaya and Maraya, the lay disciples of Balēndu Maladhari Dēva of the Mūla Sangha, Dēsigana.

(k) On a fourth slab in the same place. This is the Nisidi of Potoja and Sayabi-Maraya, father and son.

(k) On a fifth stone. This is the Nisidi of Kommasetti, a lay disciple of Prabhachandra Dēva.

Tamada-halli On a stone lying on a platform in the courtyard of the Anjaneyaswami temple. This is the Nisidi of Chandraka Bhattaraka, pupil of Charukīrti Bhattaraka of the Mūla Sangha, Dēsigana.

Agali (k) On a stone lying in the courtyard of a Jaina basadi in the village. This is the Nisidi of Krishnisetti, son of Bettisetti, a lay disciple of Dēvachandra Dēva of Mūla Sangha and the Dēsiyagana.

Kotipi (k) On a boulder in a field below the tank bund in the same village. Bears the sentence "Hail! the speech of the blessed Mandachari has proved true." On another part of the stone are three lines of writing not quite legible. The first line seems to contain the name Charurasi Bhanditar for Charurasi Panditar, the title of a particular order of Jain monks.

Bellary District.

Raya-durg. (k) On a pedestal of the Rasasiddha images in the same village. Records in Pramādi, Magha, Su. di. 1, Monday, that a Nisidi was constructed on this day. In eight different sections of the stone are given the names of eight persons whom perhaps the images represent. Some of these were Chandrabhuti of Mūla Sangha, Chandrendya, Badayya and Timmanna of Apaniya (Yapaniya) Sangha.

Cuddapah District.

Danavulapādu. (k) On a slab set up in the Jain temple recently discovered. Records the Nisidi of a merchant of Penugonda whose preceptor was the Jain teacher Kanakakīrti Dēva.

(k) On a third pillar set up in the same place. Records the Nisidi of a Jain teacher.

South Kanara District.

Mudabidire. (k) On a broken slab in front of the Nayi basti. Records the death of a Jain teacher named Chandrakīrti and the building of the mantapa (*i.e.*, Nayi basti) in his memory.

(k) On stones built into the Jain tombs in the same village.

Vizagapatam District.

Lakkavarapukōta. (Hindia Nagari) On the pedestal of a mutilated Jaina image preserved in the Vīrabhadra temple in the same village. A damaged record. Refers the image of Bhattaraka Jina-Chandra of Mūla Sangha.

B.—Architectural.

Anantapur District.

Tād-patri. (k) In the north-west corner of the Prakara of the Ramesvaraswami temple, first stone. A Jain record of Udayāditya, son of Sōmidēva and Kānchaladēvi in S.1130 expired, Kalayukti. The donor resided at Tatipara, Tādpatri.

Kotta-siva-rām. (k) On a pillar in the same place. Registers that this basadi was built by Dēvanandi Achārya, pupil of Pushpanandi Maladhari Dēva of Kanurgana, Kondakundānvaya.

Amara-puram. (k) On a pedestal lying in the court-yard of the same temple. This is the basadi caused to be made by a pupil of Balēndu Maladhari Dēva, a disciple of Tribhuvanakīrti-Ravula of Ingalēsvara, belonging to Mūla Sangha, Dēsiyagana, Kondakundānvaya and Pustakagachcha.

North Arcot District.

Vallimalai. Rock inscription in a Jain cave on the hill. A record of the Ganga King Rachamalla I, the son of

Ranavikrama, grandson of Sreepurusha (726—733) Rajamalla, was the excavator of the cave.

(k) (In grantha) On a rock. Records the founding of a Jaina shrine by the Ganga King Rajamalla.

Bellary District.

Kogali. (k) On a slab in the Jain basti. Mentions Durvinita as the builder of the basadi.

Vijayanagar. (Skt.) On a lamp pillar in front of the Gangisetti temple. A record of Harihara II, son of Bukka I, S. 1307, Krodhana, Phalguna, Krishnapaksha dvitiya, Friday (February 16, A.D. 1386), saying that Iruga, the son of Dandanāyaka Chaicha, one of Harihara's Ministers, caused a Chaityālaya of Kundu Jinanatha to be built at Vijayanagara which belonged to Kuntala Vishaya in the Karnāta country. The donor is the author of Nanartha Ratnamāla. A Jain teacher Simhanandi and his apostolic pedigree are given in the inscription.

(Skt.) A record of Dēvarāya II, dated S. 1348, Prabhava. Records the building of a Chaityālaya to Parsvanātha in the Pansupari street.

Guntur District.

Amaravati. (Pkt.) On a stone gift of a pillar by Chula-Aira, the pupil of the greater elder Ayira-Bhuta-Rakhita who lives at Rayasela and by the nun Nanda Nandā, the pupil of Arhat Ayira-Budha-Rakhita.

South Kanara District.

Muda-bidire. (k) On the north wall of the Gaddi-gimantapa in the Hosa basadi, right of entrance. A record of the Vijaya-nagar King Vīra-Dēvarāya II in S. 1351, Saumya. Refers to Perumal Dēva-Dandanāyaka and to Dēvarāja Odeya of Nāgamangala who was ruling the Mangalura-Rajya, and to the building of a basti.

(k) On the same wall. A record of the Vijayanagara King Praudha Dēvarāya II in S. 1373 Prajōtpatti. Mentions Ganapanna Odeya and refers to the building of a Mukhaman-tapa of the basti called *Bhairadēvi Mantapa.*

(k) In the same place, left of the entrance. A record of the Vijaya-nagara King Dēvarāya II in S. 1351 Saumya. Mentions the building of the basti.

(k) In the same place, left of entrance. Records a list of merchants who built the second story of the basti.

(k) Do. names of the merchants who built the second story of the basti.

(k) On a pillar in the Gaddigimantapa of the Gurugala basti. A record of S. 1460 mentioning the building of the mantapa.

Venur (k) On the Nandi pillar in front of the Mahālingēsvara temple. Records that a merchant set up the Mānasthambha, a big monolythic column set up in front of the bastis. From the fact that almost all of them are known as *Settara bastis* it is inferred that the Jain merchants constructed them.

(k) On a pillar in the verandah in front of the Ammanavara basti at Hirigangadi near the same village, left of entrance. Records in S. 1397, Manmatha, the building of the Mukhamantapa in front of the Tirthankara basti by several merchants. The teacher Lalitakīrti Bhattaraka Dēva Maladhari is mentioned.

Nellore District.

Kanupartipādu. (Tam). In field No. 383 to the east of the village. Records that in the thirty-seventh year of the reign of the Emperor Rāja Rāja Dēva, one Pramaladēvi had the steps leading to the shrine (Pallichchandum) of the Jaina temple (called after) Karikālachōda built on behalf of Matisāgara Dēva.

Vizagapatam District.

Bhōga-puram. (Telugu and Sanskrit) On a slab lying in the middle of the village. Records in S. 1109, eleventh year of the Eastern Ganga King Anantavarma Dēva, that the merchant Kannamanāyaka constructed the Jaina temple called Rāja Rāja Jinālaya at Bhōgapura.

C.—VOTIVE.

Anantapur District.

Kottasi-varām. (k) On a pillar of a dilapidated mantapa at the entrance into the village. Alpadēvi, the queen of Irungola and a lay disciple the fo Kānūrgana of Kondakundānvaya, protected this Jaina charity while it was in a ruined condition.

Amara-puram. (k) On a pillar set up in the courtyard of a Jain temple in the same place of the time of Mahāmandalēsvara Tribhuvanamalla Nissankapratāpa Chakravarti Vīradēva Navamurari Irungondadēva Chola, Maharajah of the Chola race ruling at the capital town of Nidungallu. S. 1200 Isvara, Āshadha, Su. di. Panchami, Monday. Registers that Mallisetti, son of Sangayana Bommisetti and Melavve and the favourite lay disciple of Balēndu Maladhari Dēva who was the senior pupil of Tribhuvana Chakravarti Rāvula of Ingalēsvar of Mūla Sangha, Ḍēsiyagana, Kondakundānvaya and Pustakagachcha, gave at Tammadihalli the 2,000 areca trees which belonged to his share to Hasanna-Pārsvadēva of the Basadi of Tailangere known as Brahma Jinālaya. The priest of this temple was Challapille, a Jaina-Brahmana of Bhuvalōkanāthanallur of Bhuvalōkanātha Vishaya, a sub-division of Ponnamaravatisīme, north of Dakshina Mathura in the Southern Pāndya country.

Bellary District.

Chippigiri. (k) In the smaller Venkataramana Temple.

(3) Dated in S. 1528. Records a grant by King Krishnadēvarāya of Vijayanagar.

(k) On a slab set up in the Bhōgēsvara Temple.

(4) In archaic characters. Records gifts of 50 Mattar of land for a flower garden. Date lost. Mentions Vijayāditya Satyāṣraya Sree Prithvivallabha Maharajah also Bhavadharma Bhattaraka Nera Boya.

Kuru- (k) On the south wall of the ruined
godu. (5) temple. Dated in the reign of the Vijayanagara King Vīrapratāpa Sadāsivarāya Mahārāja. Records in S. 1467, Visvavasu, gift of land (4 vokkals) to the Jaina temple by Ramarajaiya, elder brother of Alia-Lingarajaiya Odeya, for the benefit of his father Mallaraja Odeya.

Kogali (k) On the base of a pillar in the
(6) Rangamantapa of the Jaina basti. Records gift of money by different persons for the daily bathing of the images in the temple.

(k) On another slab set up in the
(7) same place. The Western Chalukya King Trailōkyamalla (Sōmēsvara I, 1042-68) records in S. 977, Manmatha, a gift by the Jaina teacher Indrakīrti.

Sogi. (k) On a fragment, lying before Vīrappa's house.

(8) The Hoysala King Vishnuvardhana Vīra Bhallala seems to record in Kartika Su. di. 5, Thursday, a gift of land to a Jaina institution.

Bagali. (k) On the fourteenth slab set upon
(9) the south side of the Kallēsvara temple. The Western Chalukya King Tribhuvanamalla records in Chalukya Vikrama year 39, Jaya, gifts to the

Kālidēvaswami temple, the big tank, and the Brahma Jinālaya.

South Kanara District.

(k) (10) A. C. P. Records a grant of a land by a prince named Kanniyabhūpāla for the purpose of maintaining the worship in a Jaina temple, S. 1513.

Basrur. (k) (11) A record of Dēvarāya II (1422-49) in S. 1353 relating to a gift of one Kolaga of paddy on every bullock load coming from other places to Basrur for the benefit of Jaina Basti by the Chettis of Basrur.

Kōtēsvara. (k) (12) In the local pagoda of Kōtēsvara. Records that Echappa Udayar gave in S. 1468, Prabhava, in the reign of Sadāsivarāya, 50 gadyanam of land to that deity. (Echappa was the same as the Jaina chief of Gairappa who married a daughter of the last Karkal King.)

Mudabidire. (k) (13) On the north wall of the Gaddigi-mantapa in the Hosa basti, right of entrance. Records in the reign of the Vijayanagara King Virūpāksa in S. 1394, Khara, a gift of land in the time of Vittarasa.

(k) (14) On a slab leaning against the south wall of the inner enclosure of the Hosa basti. Records in S. 1493,

Prajōtpatti, a gift of land, and mentions the Chanta family which had its seat at Mudabidire.

(k) On a slab set up in the Gurugala
(15) basti at the same village. An epigraph of the Vijayanagara King Vīra Bukkarāya II (1397-1406), son of Harihararāya II (1377-1402), in S. 1329 in Vyaya. Mentions Bāchappa Odeya and gift of land.

(k) In a field one mile south-east of
(16) the travellers' bunglow. Records in the reign of the Vijayanagara King Vīra Harihara II, in S. 1312 Sukla, a gift of land to the Gurugala basti at Bidire. Mentions Mangarasa Odeya of Mangalura Rajya.

(k) On a slab set up close to the east
(17) wall of the Tirthankarabasi within the Sāntīsvara basti at the same village. Records in S. 1544, Durmati, the gift of land to the basti by Ramanatharasa, while Mathurakadēvi was ruling over the Punjalikēya Rajya.

Karkala. On a slab set up close to the west
(Skt. & K) wall of the Chaturmukha basti. Re-
(18) cords in S. 1508, Vyaya, the building of the basti and gift of land and money by Immadi Bhairarasa Odeya of Pattipombuchcha.

(k) On a slab set up in the north-
(19) east corner of the same basti. Records in S. 1501, Pramādi, gift of money by Srāvakas for the study of the Sastras. Lalitakīrti is to be the *Vichārakarta* (supervisor) of the charities.

(k) On another slab set up in the
(20) same place. A record dated in S. 1379, Isvara, mentioning Abhinava Pāndya Dēva Odeya of Pattipombuchcha who belonged to the family of Jinadatta and the gift of paddy by merchant. Lalitakīrti is said to have belonged to Kondakundānvaya and the Kālōgragana—probably a local branch of dēsigana.

(k) On a slab set up close to the Guru-
(21) gala basti near the same village. A record dated in S. 1256, Bhava, a gift of land to the Sāntinātha basti which was built in that year.

Kadaba. A. C. P. grant of the Rāshtrakūta
(22) King Prabhūtavarsha (Govinda III) made at the request of Ganga chief Chāgiraja to a Jaina sage Arakīrti, disciple of Vijayakīrti (who was a disciple of Kuliyachārya), for having removed the evil influence of Saturn from the Chāgiraja's sister's son Vimalāditya. Issued from Mayurakhandi.

Krishna District.

Masulipatam

(Skt.) (23) A. C. P. grant of Amma II (945-70) or Vijayāditya. Records a gift by the king to two Jaina temples at Vijayavātika (Bezwada). He is said to have had for his enemy Rājamārtānda and Mallapa (probably Yuddhamalla II).

Kalachumbarru

(Skt.) (24) A. C. P. grant of Amma II, called also Vijayāditya VI. It is undated and records the grant of the village Kalachumbarru in the Attilinādu province to a Jaina teacher named Arhanandin of the Valaharigana and Addakalingachcha for repairing the dining hall of a Jaina temple Sarvalōkāsraya Jina Bhavana. The grant was made at the instance of Chamakāmba of the Pattavardhani lineage, a pupil of Arhanandin.

Vizagapatam District.

Bhōgapuram

(Skt. & Tel.) On a slab lying in the middle of (25) the village. Records in S. 1109, eleventh year of the Eastern Ganga King Anantavarma Dēva, that the merchant Kannamanāyaka constructed the Jaina temple called Rāja Rāja Jinālaya at Bhōgapura and gave two puttis of land to that temple with the consent of Dēsi-Rattadhu.

(Tel.) (26) On a third slab lying in the same village. A partly damaged record of the Eastern Ganga King Anantavarma Dēva (1076-1146) dated S. 1027, thirty-first year. Records gift of land measured by Lokanikkasetti, who seems to have purchased it from Dēsi-Rattadhu.

Madras (Museum) (Skt.) (27) A.C. P. grant of Eastern Chalukya Vishnuvardhana III, S. 684. Registers evidently the renewal of a grant of the village of Musinikonda in Tōnka-Nātavādi Vishaya to the Jaina teacher Kālibhadrāchārya. Ayyana or Ayyana-Mahādēvi, Queen of Kubjavishnuvardhana, was the Ajñāpati of the grant and the charter was marked with the seal of Kubjavishnuvardhana.

D.—Iconographic.

North Arcot District.

Vallimalai (k) (Grantha) (28) The record of a Bana King. Records the setting up of the image of Dēvasēna, the pupil of Bhavanandin and the spiritual preceptor of the king.

(29) (k) On the same rock. Setting up of the image by the Jaina preceptor Aryanandin.

Bellary District.

Kogali (k) (30) On the pedestal of a smaller Jaina image in the Jaina basti. Registers in Paridhāvi, Chaitra, Su. di. Chaurdasi, Sunday, the construction of the image by a certain Obeyamasetti, a lay pupil of Anantavīryadēva.

Rayadurg (k) (Skt.) (31) On a pedestal of a Jaina image kept in the Taluq Office. A damaged record of the Vijayanagara King Harihara I, dated S. 1277, Manmatha, Margasira, Purnima. Records that a Jaina merchant named Bhōgarāja consecrated the image of Sāntināthа Jinēsvara. The merchant is stated to have been a pupil of Maghanandi-Vratin. the disciple of Amarakīrti-Achārya of Kondakundānvaya, Sarasvatigachcha, Balatkāragana, Mūla Sangha.

South Kanara District.

Venur (Skt.) (32) On the right side of the colossal statue of Gummata on the hill. Records in S. 1525, Sobhakrit, the setting up of the image of Bhujabali by Timmaraja of the family of Chamunda at the instance of Charukīsti, the family teacher.

(k) On a slab set up in the south-east corner of the mantapa in front of the Sāntīsvara basti. Records in S. 1459, Hemalambin, the consecration of the 24 Tirthankaras in the basti.

Karkala (Skt.) (33)	On the right side of the colossal statue of Gummata at the same village. Records in S.1353, Virodhikrit, the setting up of the image of Bahubalin by Vīra Pāndya, the son of Bhairava of the lunar race, at the instance of the teacher Lalitakīrti of Panasoka and of the Dēsigaṇa who was also evidently the guru of the Karkala chiefs.
(k) (34)	On the left side of the same statue. Records in verse the same fact but gives the name of the image as Gummata-Jinapati.
Madras (Museum) (k) (35)	On the base of a Jaina image. Records that King Sālva Dēva, a great lover of Sahitya, got an image of Santi-Jina made *according to rule* and set it up.

Vizagapatam District.

Rāmathīrtham (Tel.) (36)	On the pedestal of a broken Jaina image on the Gurubhaktakonda hill. Seems to state that the image was set up by Prammisetti of Chanudavōlu in the Ongēru Mārga.

E.—VOTIVE AND COMMENDATORY.

South Kanara District.

Mudabidire (k)	On the north wall of the Guddigi-mantapa in the Hosa basti, right of entrance. A record of the Vijayanagara King Vīra Dēvarāya II, in S. 1351, Saumya. Refers to

Perumal Dēva Dandanāyaka and to Dēvarāja Odeya of Nāgamangala who was ruling the Mangalur Rajya.

(k) On a slab built into the wall of the Kshētrapāla shrine in the Hosa basti. An inscription of the Vijayanagara King Virūpāksharāya II (1465-86) in S. 1398, Durmukhi. Mentions Singappa Dandanāyaka and Vittarasa Odeya.

Venur ..(k) On a slab set up to the right of the entrance of the mantapa in front of the Sāntīsvara basti. A record dated in S. 1411, Saumya, mentioning a chief of Punjalingaraja.

(k) On a slab set up close to the west wall of the Gurugala basti near the same village. The inscription opens with a long list of birudas of Lokanātha Dēvarasa (son of Bommidēvarasa and Siddhaladēvi).

F.—Commendatory.

Vizagapatam District.

Rāmathīrtham (k) On the back wall of the Durgapancha. A much damaged record of the Eastern Chalukya King Sarvalōkāsraya Vishnuvardhan Maharajah Rājamārtānda Mummadi Bhīma.

South Kanara District.

Mulki .. (k) On the south face of the Mānasthamba in front of the Jaina basti.

Records 5 verses arranged in twenty-five squares and praising the Tirthankara.

Mudabidire (k) On the east, north and west faces of a pillar in the Bhairavi mantapa. A record in praise of Mahāmandalēsvara Sālvamalla.

(k) On another pillar in the same mantapa. Records 5 verses in praise of Tirthankaras arranged in 25 octagons.

(k) On a slab built into the wall of the Kshētrapāla shrine in the Hosa basti. An inscription of the Vijayanagara King Virūpāksharāya II (1465-88 A.D.) in S. 1398, Durmukhi. Mentions Singappa Dandanāyaka and Vittarasa Odeya.

Details about Jaina āchāryas.

From these epigraphs we learn some details about the great ascetics and āchāryas who spread the gospel of Jainism in the Andhra-Karnāta dēsa. They were not only the leaders of lay and ascetic disciples, but of royal dynasties of warrior clans that held the destinies of the peoples of these lands in their hands. Since some glimpses of the lines on which they influenced the administration of these lands by their warrior pupils are presently to be described in the sequel the details regarding them as given in the epigraphs noticed above may be remembered :—

No.	Teacher-Ascetics.	Pupil-Ascetics.	Sangha.	Gana.	Remarks.
1	Jinabhūshana Bhattaraka.				
2	Prabhachandra Bhattaraka.	....	Mūla.		
3	Bhavasēna Traividya Chakravarti.	....	Mūla ..	Sēna ..	Terror to disputant.
4	Balēndu Maladhari Dēva.	....	Mūla ..	Dēsi.	
5	Charukīrti Bhattaraka ..	Chandrānka Bhattaraka.	Mūla ..	Dēsi.	
6	Dēvachandra	....	Mūla ..	Dēsiya.	
7	Chandrabhūti	....	Mūla.		
8	Chandrēndra	....	Yapaniya		
9	Kanakakīrti Dēva ..				
10	Chandrakīrti ..				
11	Bhattaraka Jinachandra ..	....	Mūla.		
12	Pushpanandi Maladhari Dēva.	Devanandi Achārya.		Karanurgana, Kondakundānvaya.	
13	Tribhuvanakīrti Rāvula ..	Balēndu Maladhari Dēva.	Mūla ..	Dēsigana, Kondakundānvaya.	Pustakagaçhcha.

No.	Teacher-Ascetics.	Pupil-Ascetics.	Sangha.	Gana.	Remarks.
14	Simhanandi.				
15	Ayira-Bhuta Rakhita ..	Chula Ayira.			
16	Lalitakīrti Bhattaraka Dēva Maladhari.	....	..	Kālōgragana (of Dēsigana).	Konda-kundānvaya.
17	Bhavadharma Bhattaraka.				
18	Indrakīrti.				
19	Vijayakīrti	(Arkakīrti).			
20	Kaligachārya	(Vijayakīrti).			
21	Arhanandi	....	..	Valaharigana ..	Addakali-gachcha.
22	Kalibhadra Achārya.				
23	Bhavanandi	....	..	..	Preceptor of Bava king.
24	Anantaviraya Dēva.				
25	Amarakīrti Achārya ..	Maghanandi ..	Mūla ..	Balatkāragana.	Konda-kundānvaya, Sarasvatigachcha.

Kalinga Jainism.

[1] This Jaina period of Andhra-Karnāta history and culture started under the auspices of the North Indian Immigrant Members of Ascetic and Warrior Clans, begins, as indicated by these epigraphs well within or even earlier than the Buddhist period. The Kharavēla inscription of Kalinga is the earliest of such known Jaina epigraphs. The date of this inscription is yet in doubt. Nevertheless, its Jaina character, and the antiquity of the references therein to Andhra-Jainism are beyond all doubt. This interpretation of the Kharavēla inscription gives very high antiquity to Jainism in the Kalinga dēsa which is sometimes conterminous but always contiguous with the Andhra mandala. Thus, what may be called "The Jaina Period" of Andhra History and Culture starts quite early in history and well within or even earlier than the Buddhist(or Satavahana) period. Jaina religious life on its ceremonial side and Jaina mythology on its imaginative side are so much like Puranic Brahmanism, that Jaina influence working through the Buddhist period formed an easy and imperceptible transition to Brahmanism, at any rate in the Andhra country. The " Amaravati Marbles " dating back to the Satavahana period, closely studied towards the latter part of the last century, contain among them, as noticed by Dr. Burgess in 1888, (*a*) " the upper part of a round topped

[1] In this section I have mostly reproduced my articles already published in the *Jaina Gazette* of Madras.

slab, with head and halo of an image. It has curly hair and might possibly be Buddhist.... but there seems a probability that this is the head of a Jaina image" and (*b*) "The right portion of a slab with the left half of the panel is perhaps Jaina." In 1892 Mr. Rea, the Superintendent of Archæological Survey, Madras, discovered, in the Krishna District, a fine Jaina image at Gudivada and a very curious Jaina column sculptured with four images at Bezwada, both places noted in the Telugu country for their importance in the Buddhist period.

The Telugu people use the formula "Om Namah Sivāya Siddham Namah" at the beginning of their *varna māla* ; the latter part of the formula is distinctly Buddhist. While, their neighbours, the Oriyas of Kalinga, so far as I know, use the formula "Siddhir Astu." This formula, I find, closes a Jaina grant.

The history of the Kalinga provinces of the Telugu country which is yet an unbroken field,[1] shows traces of the political influence of Jainism, dating from the times of Kharavēla, the Chetiya King. "The Kols and Khonds of Kalinga have a traditional notion that they displaced an earlier people vaguely called Jainas

[1] Of the Andhra scholars engaged for sometime in clearing it up may be mentioned the *late* Mr. G. V. Apparao Pantulu of Vizianagram, Rao Saheb G. V. Ramamurti Pantulu of Parlakimedi, G. V. Ramdas Pantulu of Jeypur, Ch. Narayana Rao, M.A., of Rajahmundry (all old boys of the Maharajah's College)—I hope to edit for the College a *Sanskrit* champu work called "*Gangavamsanucharitam*" dealing with Kalinga History.

and Bhuyas." Bhūja and Jaina villages, judging by names, are frequent in the Kalinga Māliyās. The "Jainas," I take it, are the Kadambas who seem to have had considerable political influence in the part of the country now inhabited by Kols and Khonds, as well as in parts from which they had been ousted during historic times.[1] Certain *place-names* in the Ganjam District bear traces of this Kadamba occupation. "Brihat Paralur" is the name of a Kadamba village from an early Kadamba grant of the Bombay Presidency. In Telugu it may stand as "Pedda Parlapuram" which is an equivalent of Oriya "Bodo (Parla)-Khimedi" the seat of a Zamindari in the Ganjam District. A "Paralur" is mentioned in another Kadamba grant by a Rēvisarma of Maudgalya gotra and archæologists have identified it with the modern Harlapur five miles to the North of Addūr in Dharwar District. Harlapur by the interchange of P and H very common between Old and Modern Canarese becomes Parlapur or Parlapuri, the capital of the Parlakimedi Zamindari, and the seat of an ancient line of kings of the Ganga dynasty. Tekkali, another place in the Ganjam District, corresponds to an early Kadamba town known as Tēkal.[2] (These must have been Kadamba cities before they came under the Gangas.)

These Kadambas, a line of Brahma-Kshatris, were Jains, and their capital was Palasika

[1] These are called Rudraputras in Kalinga Inscriptions.

[2] I owe this suggestion to Rao Saheb G. V. Ramamurti Pantulu.

the modern Halsi. To this Palasika corresponds *Palasa* in the Ganjam District, which must once have been a flourishing capital of the Kadamba line of Kalinga whom perhaps the Gangas of Kalinganagara succeeded as Trikalingadhipatis. But we have the modern city of Banavasi or Vaijayanti as residence of one of the Kadamba kings called Mrigēsa. Corresponding to this Banavasi or Vaijayanti, we have in Kalinga, a Jayantīpura ; and a Jayanti family of Telugu Brahmans. Either this Jayantīpura of Kalinga was the capital of a collateral line of Kadambas who adopted Saivism or Vaishnavism or it was made capital in succession to Palasa when the Jaina Kadambas adopted Puranic Brahmanism as their state religion. A family of Kadambas, however, tracing their descent from Mayuravarma state that they acquired sovereignty through the favour of Jayanti-Madhukēsvara (Banavasi being otherwise called Jayantīpura). There is a temple of Madhukēsvara in Banavasi and Madhulinga occurs as the name of a Brahman priest thereof. The village called Mukhalingam in the Ganjam District owned by the Zamindar of Parlakimedi is called Jayantīpura in the Sthalapurana relating to it. Rao Sahib G. V. Ramamurti Pantulu Garu, B.A., my revered teacher, identified this village many years back as the Kalinganagara mentioned by the Eastern Ganga Kings of Kalinga in their copper-plate grants and stone inscriptions. This place contains a temple dedicated to Madhukēsvara. But Madhukēsvara was never the family deity of the Gangas who were unswerving worshippers of Gokarnēsvara of Mahēndra. Clearly therefore this Madhukēsvara and this Jayantīpura were established by the Kadamba line whom the Gangas must have displaced. Madhulinga in its modified form as " Moholingo " occurs as a personal name even to this day among the Oriya people of that part of the country.

A family of Telugu Brahmans called the Jayantis have long been settled in Sreekurmam, a village near Chicacole in the Ganjam District. They must originally have hailed from Jayantīpura (Mukhalingam) when it was a Kadamba capital.

Kadamba Chronology

By the time of the late Rao Bahadur V. Venkaiya, Epigraphist with the Government of India, the chronology of the Kadambas was not settled. I do not see that it has made any considerable advance towards a settlement even to-day. Venkaiya however refers to a Kadamba grant of Jayavarma which Dr. Hultzsch thought to belong to the *Second Century A.D.* Some fresh evidence is available to strengthen this suggestion. In the Annual Report on Archæology for 1914-15 just to hand some inscriptions belonging to the Satavahana period are given (pp. 120-121) in which the name *Hariti* appears. Now, the Kadambas were the earliest South Indian Ruling dynasty to style themselves " Mānavyasa gotra, Haritiputra." *Hariti* is a Buddhist goddess and *Hariti*, a Buddhist personal name from Buddhist votive offerings. The adoption of *Haritiputra* by the Kadambas as a family title indicates the way in which *later Buddhism* shaded off into Jainism. The people who availed themselves and made capital out of such cultural fusion must originally have belonged to the later period of Satavahana decline, *i.e.*, to *the early Centuries of the Christian Era*. From about this period comes the grant of Kadamba Jayavarma. A little later, we hear of a Vishnukundi-Kadamba-Satakarni from Mysore Inscriptions (*vide* Carmichael Professorship Lectures on Indian History by Prof. Bandharkar).

If on the basis of such data we can start with the *hypothesis* of an early Jaina Kadamba immigration into South India in the early centuries of the Christian era, I think there is clear enough evidence to indicate the route of their immigration along the East Coast through Kōsala and Kalinga.

Taylor's Catalogue of Oriental MSS. (Vol. III, p. 60) contains references to a *Kannada* work speaking about a line of Kadamba kings who ruled in Magadha. If from Magadha, they wished to migrate to South India, they had to pass through Kōsala and Kalinga. Such would be the most natural route for a migration. On pp. 704-5 in the same volume, there are references to a *Marathi* work containing accounts of a later Kadamba King Mayuravarma (of Southern Karnāta branch) from which the only valid inference that can be drawn is that he was an immigrant from North India, with a strong partiality for North Indian culture and those that cultivated it. Thus a migration from North India and along Magadha, Kōsala, Kalinga and the East Coast line, of a North Indian family of Kadambas, is preserved in *literature* as an immemorial tradition.

If these early Kadambas were Jainas, as I suspect they are, they must leave behind in the several places they touched and colonised, some clear and definite traces of their occupation of such places. The '*Satrunjaya Mahātmya*' is an important Jaina work. It is not later than the *Eighth Century A.D.* It may be conceded that it is a fairly reliable collection of Jaina traditions current among the Jainas about the period of its composition. Among the sacred hills of the Jainas mentioned in it occurs a hill called Kadambagiri. The Kadamba line of Brahma-Kshatris who adopted the Kadamba as a totem must have been Jainas to whom Kadambagiri was particularly sacred. The Chalukyas, following perhaps the tradition of the Kadambas, say, in their grants, that their ancestors secured royal power by the worship of the family deities on Chalukyagiri (*vide* Nandamapudi grant E. Chalukya Rāja Rāja Narēndra). This tradition of the Chalukyas, who adopted the Kadamba style of Mānavyasa gotra, Haritiputra, is evidence of the sacredness of 'Kadambagiri' to the early Kadambas, and incidentally, of their being

Jainas. I venture to regard the appearance of *Kadambagiri* or *Kadambasingi* or their varients among place-names as a sure indication of those places having been originally so described by a Kadamba line of kings or their admiring officials or subjects. They indicate Kadamba colonization near about and a type of civilisation nourished by them.

Evidence of such place-names is fairly well establishable for the agency tracts of Ganjam and Vizagapatam the newly constituted '*Agency-Division*' in the North-East Coast of the Madras Presidency.

Kadamba Place-names indicative of Jaina culture.

The Parlakimedi Agency of the Ganjam District has places called *Kadamasingi* (Kadambastringi) and *Muni-Singi* suggesting a sacred hill (sacred to Jaina) and a colony of Jaina munis near about it. The place-names are significant and suggestive of religious culture. At a later date, it was in this taluq, that the Kadambas built their capital Vaijayantipura in the plains. Similarly, in the Aska taluq of the Ganjam District there is a village called Jaya-Singi, possibly named after Jayavarma, the early Kadamba king of 2nd century A.D.(?) or a Kōsala "Jayāditya" preserved in the traditions of the present-day Andhra-Kshatriyas.

In the Bissamcuttack [Visvambhara (dēva) Kataka] Agency of the Vizagapatam District there are two villages called *Kadambaguda* and *Kakadamba*. "Guda" is the same word as "Gūdem", possibly derived from the Dravidian root Kūd=to gather together. Hence Guda= collection. It may mean a collection of Kadamba trees or Kadamba people. The existence of this place along with *Munisingi* (Munisringa)points to Jaina colonies of Kshatriyas and ascetics, as in the case of Parlakimedi Agency. It is also interesting to notice as a piece of cumulative evidence, the existence in this division, of place-names ending in *bhatta*, probably formed after the names of scholars who had considerable fame and influence. As instances may be noted *Katchangibhatta*, *Kuddubhatta*, *Kumbibhatta*, *Lakkabhatta*, *Pedabhattuguda*, *Ranibhatta*, *Sukulabhatta*. Who these Bhattas were (they must have been famous scholars, possibly Jains) and what part they played in the cultural life of the period remains to be unveiled by patient research and exploration in these forest glades oblivious of "the madding crowd." Jayapura, Jayanagaram in the Jeypur Agency must have derived their names from sovereigns of the Kadamba line called *Jayavarma*; Jayantigiri reminds one of the Vaijayanti of later Kadambas linking up the later line with the earlier one. Kadamaguda occurs eight times as a place-name in the Jeypur Agency. I regard this as an indication of a long occupation of these tracts by a Kadamba line of kings. Place-names in *bhatta* are also frequent in this division. For instance; *Amalabhatta*, *Bannabhattiguda*, *Bhattiguda*, *Dalubhatta*, *Mavulibhatta*. Other places are sometimes named in this division, after

Rani, *Ravutu*, *Pradhani*, *Vahanapati*, *Pujari*, which shows the nature of civic life brought into these parts by the Kadamba immigrants.

In the Koraput Agency of the Vizagapatam District, *Kadamba guda* occurs twice as a place-name, while, there is but one village name in bhatta, *viz.*, *Vuskabhatta*.

In the Malkanagiri Agency, Kadambaguda and its varients occur thrice and Jayantigiri occurs once. *Amalabhatta*, *Kosarabhatta* occur as place-names. Village names in *Sanyāsi*, *Pujari*, *Patra*, *Pragada*, *Pradhani*, *Mantri*, *Nayaka*, *Dalapati*, *Dandusena* occur and they indicate a high state of political organisation after the manner of Kautilya and other early authorities on Arthasastra. This familiar and significant place-name *Kadambaguda* also occurs in the Navarangapur Agency. Quite a large enough number of place-names in *bhatta* also occur, *e.g.*, *Amalabhatta*, *Bhattikota*, *Daibhatta*, *Kodubhatta*, *Mohabhatta*, *Movulibhatta*, *Posakabhatta*, *Pulobhatta*, *Sindibhatta*, *Sorsubhatta*. Place-names in *Turangi*, *Raja*, *Rani*, *Nayaka*, *Pradhani*, *Mantri*, *Adhikari*, *Pujari*, *Pandita* indicate the arts and institutions of civic life.

The Raigada Agency of the Vizagapatam District has a village called *Kadambariguda*, named perhaps after a chieftain who conquered the Kadamba sovereign of these parts and adopted it as his style like the title *Sakari* adopted by the Andhra king who destroyed the Saka ascendency.

These agency tracts of Ganjam and Vizagapatam of the ancient Kalinga kingdom are to-day regarded by the generality of people as the haunts of the wolf, the bear and the tiger and of men equally barbarous and ferocious. Little do we regard, in our ignorance, how they were once teeming with organised communities of highly civilised men and women, well established principalities, flourishing towns, pandit *parishads*, ascetic *viharas*, moving armies and civil and military officers of all grades and ranks. In the building up of this early civilisation in these battle-grounds for the colonisation of northern and southern peoples, the Jaina Kadambas of the early centuries of the Christian era must have had a no mean share.

The inscription published by J. F. Fleet (in the *Journal of the Bombay Branch of the Royal Asiatic Society*, Vol. IX, No. XXVII) probably speaks of a Western Deccan branch of this line of Jaina Kadambas. He says " they belong to some epoch when the great kings of the south, the Chalukyas, were not in possession of such power as they attained to in later times. The Chalukya dynasty..................in earlier times." Palasika was their capital in the Western Deccan, and it is not extravagant to suppose that Palasa in the Ganjam District was founded by a branch of this line of Jaina Kadambas. A more difficult question to solve is which foundation is the earlier,—the Kalinga one or the Western Deccan one.

The Andhras of Kalinga.

The Andhras of the Talevāha river (referred to in the Jataka stories of the sixth century B.C.), the contemporaries of Kharavēla, must likewise have been Jainas, as also the Nāgas in alliance with them and the Sēndraka-Nāgas in alliance with the Kadambas. Very little is known about these Andhras of the Talevāha river, except that their South Indian colony is as old as the *Aitereya Brahmana*; that they were immigrants into the lands inhabited by the Kalingas and the Telingas (howsoever the latter may have during historic times been fused into them) is clearly shown by villages named after them existing side by side with those named after the Telingas, the Kalingas, the Munds and the Sabaras. Whether they belonged to the Satavahana clan or not is difficult to determine. But there seems to be little doubt that along with the Kadambas they contributed to the progress of arts and culture. Bühler is of opinion that it was the Kadamba script that latterly developed into the Telugu-Canarese or Andhra-Karnāta variety of South Indian Alphabets. This opinion lends colour to the suggestion that the Andhras and Kadambas together contributed to the earliest growth of the fine arts and culture in the Andhra and Karnāta Provinces. The evidence of place-names from the Kalinga part of the Telugu country may here be pertinently summarised :–

Andhavaram (Andhravaram) beside Oddepādu in Chicacole taluq, Ondhrokōta in Gumsur taluq, Ondhorigam (Andhragrama) in Balliguda Agency, Ondhari-gumma or Andhragumma in the Parlakimedi Agency, Ondhrasingi in Ramagiri Agency, Ondaribondo in Surada Agency, Ondirigudo beside Oddunāju in Udayagiri Agency (nāju in Khond=country),—all these are from the Ganjam District. The occurrence of the larger number of these names in the agency tracts is the more important part of this evidence. In the Vizagapatam District, Ondhorulimma in Bissamcuttack Agency, Andhrododdi in Golgonda Agency, Ondroguda in Gunupur Agency, Andromunda in Jeypur Agency, Andhraguda in Navarangapur Agency, —all again from the agency tracts, indicate the find spots of the Andhra colonies of East Deccan in the prehistoric times spoken of in the Buddhist *Jatakas*. From these traces it is possible to infer that a branch, possibly, the Dhānyakataka branch, of "the Andhra-Satavahanas of History" were immigrants into the Krishna District through the Kalinga and the N.E. Coast of the Madras Presidency. Their capital Dhānyakataka must have been founded after their earlier capital Dhannupuro in the Jeypur Agency of the Vizagapatam District. There is also an Amaravati in the Sompeta taluq of the Ganjam District. The Kalingas call the Andhras 'Westerners' (పడమటివాండ్లు). In Kharavēla's time these Andhras were to the West of Kalinga (plains).

The early years of the fourth century A.D. saw the break-up of the Satavahana power and empire. Did it involve a break-up of civilisation and culture? Did it involve the throwing of the empire of the Satavahanas in the Deccan into a chaos of warring forces which destroyed all elements of culture in the land?

Continuity of Andhra Culture. One result of this break-up which must have occurred about the year 302 A.D.—for there is a coin of a Satavahana king bearing that date,—was to give a chance to some of the local dynasties to come into power and use it for the protection of culture and the maintenance of its continuity under new auspices. Of such dynasties that emerged into power and established local sovereignties and spheres of influence may be mentioned the Abhiras or Kalachuris or Haihayas, the Rāshtrakūtas and the Kadambas on the ruins of whose power the Chalukyas claim to have built up their empire in the Deccan. That the particular dynasty by subduing whom the Chalukyas came to sovereign power were the Kadambas is manifest from the style of "Mānavyasa gotra Haritiputra, etc.," which they have adopted from their Kadamba predecessors, for, so far as can be gathered from inscriptions, the Kadambas were the earliest South Indian dynasty to adopt this style.

The problem, therefore, arises,—'are the Chalukyas a North Indian race or warrior clan who immigrated to the Deccan and profited by the break-up of the Satavahana power and the conflicts of local dynasties in power and influence, or are they, like the Rāshtrakūtas, a Deccani clan who emerged into power after the downfall of the Satavahanas ?' The former hypothesis leads to that of the naturalness of the bias of the family towards a North Indian culture, and equally to that of a natural tendency to patronise attempts to engraft it on a South Indian one ; the other hypothesis leads to that of a natural tendency of the family to the strengthening or modification of South Indian culture in an atmosphere of North Indian civilisation.

The evidence from inscriptions and literature is not uniform as regards the origin of the Chalukyas. The earlier inscriptions do not give the family a puranic genealogy, although they contain elements out of which a puranic genealogy was worked out for the family about the eleventh century A.D. It has been noticed how the style of 'Mānavyasa gotra Haritiputra' was adopted from the Kadambas. Yet these sources of information seem to contain darkly a family tradition that the Chalukyas originally hailed from Ayodhya. Pampa's *Vikramarjunavijaya*, Nannaya's *Mahābhārata*, Bilhana's *Vikramankadēvacharita* and Peddiraja's *Kavyalankara*, among other works composed under the patronage of the later Chalukyas, regard the Chalukya family as immigrants from the North. They also affiliate them to the lunar race of

Rajputs. In this respect these works bear out the evidence of the inscriptions. But this view of the inscriptions and literary works requires to be controlled by some important considerations.

The Rajaputs of North India who do not belong to the recognised vedic or puranic dynasties and *gotras* generally describe themselves as belonging to the *gotra* of Manu or Mānavyas. There is a tradition among the Andhra or Deccani Kshatriyas to this day that North Indian Rajaput clans belonging to five specific *gotras* (Vasistha, Dhananjaya, Koundinya, Bharadwaja, Kasyapa) originally immigrated to the south ; but the *Mānavyasa gotris* are not mentioned among them. There are no Mānavyasa gotris among Kshatriyas in the Andhra dēsa of to-day. One Chēdi inscription, however, refers the Chalukyas to the *Bharadwaja gotra*, but the Chalukyas of historic times must have, somehow, forgotten this earlier tradition (see sequel).

Secondly, those Deccani Rajaput clans that claim to have immigrated from Ayodhya describe themselves as belonging to the solar and not the lunar race[1] ; and there is no evidence of a lunar dynasty having, ever before fifth century A.D., ruled in Ayodhya. Thus the description of the Chalukyas as belonging to the lunar race seems to be inconsistent with the idea of their

[1] A North Indian clan of Rajaputs of the *Ikshvāku* race seems to have settled in the Krishna District in very early times (Insns. Madras Pcy.).

immigration from Ayodhya. Possibly this Ayodhya tradition must have been appropriated by the Chalukyas from the Satavahanas, as the Mānavyasa gotra tradition was adopted from the Kadambas.

Thirdly, the name Chulika, Chalukya or Chālukya is suggested to be a Sanscritised form of some South Indian vernacular name.

Fourthly, it remains to be seen whether there is any present-day Rajaput family in the North which traces descent from the Chalukyas as there are families tracing their descent from the Satavahanas.

These considerations, among others, throw a strong suspicion against the hypothesis of a North Indian origin for the Chalukya family. The literary movement that the dynasty patronised from time to time seems to strengthen this bias. Culturally, therefore, the significance of the Chalukyas seems to be in their use of their political sovereignty for the strengthening of South Indian culture with North Indian elements and the re-shaping of North Indian culture in the light and after the methods of South Indian culture. Thus under the Chālukyas, *South Indian culture came to its own,* while under the previous imperial dynasty of the Satavahanas, North Indian culture absorbed into it the elements of South Indian culture. The transition from the Satavahana type of cultural fusion to one with a South Indian basis and in a South Indian atmosphere was effected by the movement of culture which the Kadambas and the Rāshtrakūtas used their political power to patronise and extend. Thus, through the rise and fall of the warrior clans in power and influence, the continuity of culture and civilisation goes on undisturbed along the lines of cultural affiliation and fusion.

The formula which expresses Satavahana culture best is "Siddham namah"; the formula that expresses Chalukya culture best is "Om namah Sivāya Siddham Namah" or "Om namo *Nārāyanāya.*" Saivism and Narayanism are said to be particularly of South Indian origin, while Buddhism represented by "Siddham Namah" is Mauryan and North Indian.

A word, in passing, about the Kadamba, the early Kalachuria and Rāshtrakūta services to the progress of scholarship may be necessary to facilitate later the appreciation of the Chalukya contribution to the development of South Indian culture.

II

The Cultural Transition from the Satavahana to the Chalukya Period.

It has been urged above that the Chalukyas consolidated their political power by a process of social and cultural fusion and the appeal to a new literary interest in which the local languages of their dominions came in for a larger recognition and patronage. This process of political consolidation they seem to have inherited from the local dynasties which were powerful in the Deccan immediately before them. This point will become clear by a consideration of the family histories of the Kalachuris, the Rāshtrakūtas and the Kadambas.

Kalachuri Culture.

The Kalachuris belong to the Chēdi country in the Central Provinces. They are supposed to be a race of Abhiras. Cunningham gives A.D. 249 as the starting point of the Chēdi era in which the Kalachuris date their grants. They emerge into history about the time of Mangalēsa Chalukya, for, from his grants we learn that they must have been a powerful dynasty in his time. Some of their grants show that in early times they must have patronised Buddhism and Jainism. During times later than that of Mangalēsa, we find the same sovereign, now being described as Saiva and again as Vaishnava. That shows a catholicity of faith on their part, an attempt at cultural fusion as a bulwark of political power. Their grants in later times show a marked literary development in Sanskrit poetic style under the influence of South Indian culture. Very few references can be found in North Indian Sanskrit Kavyas proper (either monumental or literary) to preliminary lists of "ishtadēvata stutis." This tradition the poetic bards of the Kalachuri courts must have developed as a sort of reflection of the religious catholicity and cultural fusion which the dynasty was trying to adopt. In South Indian Karnāta Literature this tendency becomes marked during

Chalukya times and there are glimpses of it in the Telugu *Mahābhārata* of Nannaya and the *Kumāra Sambhava* of Nanna Choda who seems to have followed the Kannada tradition, and the *Dasakumāra Charita* of Ketana who seems to have followed the Andhra-Chalukyan tradition of Nannaya.

The Satavahanas, before the Kalachuris, must have attempted a social fusion with dynasties whom they conquered or who were becoming powerful in their time. This they must have done to safeguard their political power. Evidence of this is found in Vishnukundi-Kadamba-Satakarni who must have been a prince born of the Satakarni and Kadamba union. Similar relations the Satavahanas are said to have contracted with the Pallavas and the Nāgas. This earlier tradition of social fusion for the consolidation of political power must have been followed by the Kalachuris, for their grants indicate such marital relations with the powerful dynasties of the time. A few instances may be noticed in passing. The Bilhari inscription of the Haihalya-Kalachuris of Chēdi is one of their earliest inscriptions which gives the names of Kokalla, Mugdhatunga, Keyuravarsha, etc. *Tunga* or *Varsha* occur familiarly in the personal names of the Rāshṭrakūtas. Whether the latter adopted them from their relations, the Kalachuris, or whether the Kalachuris adopted them from the Rāshtra-kūtas, is difficult to determine, but it must be from social relationship by marriage that such a tradition regarding personal names could develop. During the time of Keyuravarsha, the Kalachuris are said in this inscription to have contracted marriages with the Chalukyas, the descendants of Bharadwaja.[1] The Chalukya queen of the Kalachuriya chief Keyuravarsha was an ardent devotee of Siva. Of the marriages between Rāshtrakūtas and Kalachuris in historic times, Cunningham gives the following references :—

(1) In one Rāshtrakūta inscription Krishna Raja is said to have married Mahādēvi, the daughter of K. Kokalla, Raja of Chēdi.

(2) In another R. K. inscription King Jagatrudra, son of Krishna, is stated to have married the two daughters of Sankaragana, Raja of Chēdi and son of Kokalla I.

(3) In a third Rāshtrakūta inscription Indra Raja is said to have married Divijāmba, the great-grand-daughter of Kokalla I.

(4) Amōghavarsha, the Rāshtrakūta Raja who was himself the great-grandson of Kokalla I, through his mother Gōvindāmba, married the princess Kandakadēvi,

[1] Are the Chalukyas, then, a *branch* of the *Pallavas* who affiliate themselves to the Bharadwaja gotra ? Could they have concealed this identity owing to clannist conflicts ? Such things do occur even to-day in Hindu society.

daughter of a Chēdi King called Yuvaraja.

From these references it would appear that the Kalachuris and Rāshtrakūtas in their intermarriages follow the Andhra principle(enunciated by Apastamba) of marrying maternal uncles' daughters. At any rate it is a principle of South Indian social tradition by which they are governed. From the last evidence of Amōghavarsha Rāshtrakūta it appears as if the *varsha* personal name is adopted by the Rāshtrakūtas from their Kalachuri grandfathers on the maternal side.

These Kalachuris call themselves Trikalingadhipatis. They thus connect themselves with a branch of Andhra history.. Kharavēla of Kalinga is said to be a Chetiya, *i.e.*, a Chēdiya. Their influence in Kalinga remains still open to research. The Kadambas are another South Indian power whom the Chalukyas had to subdue before they could get into power in the Deccan. The Kadamba plates of Goa give a good deal of valuable information as regards their contribution to South Indian culture.

Kadamba Culture.

The Kadambas must, from the reference to Vishnukundi-Kadamba-Satakarni, be referred to the last years of the Satavahana rule in the Deccan. The Talgund inscription referring to a Satakarni or the Satakarnis may also be used to fix this point. However, it is suggested that there were two or three synchronously reigning branches of this family in the Deccan, *e.g.*, the Kadambas of Banavasi and the Kadambas of Goa. The significance of the early Kadambas whom the Chalukyas overpowered lies in their association with the later Satavahanas and their patronage of Jaina culture. Although these Kadambas describe themselves as " Mānavyasa gotra Haritiputras and Swami Mahāsēna Padanudhyāyis ", yet their leanings lay definitely towards Jainism. Their poets were Jains ; their ministers were Jains ; some of their personal names were Jaina ; the donees of their grants were Jain—the type of literature as evidenced by the Goa copper-plates was of the Jaina Kavya kind. This they handed down to the Chalukyas. Thus, their conquerors became captives in turn to the scholarship and culture which the Kadambas promoted. Among the Goa Kadambas occur personal names in *Kēsi ;* such words are familiar among the Chalukyas. Possibly there is some relationship between the Chalukyas who rose to power in W. Deccan and the Kadambas of Goa as there is traced between the Kalachuris and Rāshtrakūtas. Any way the Chalukya inscriptions make it clear that they adopted the Kadamba style of family insignia.

Jaina Scholarship.

It has already been pointed out how the Jaina Achāryas secured grants from kings for their foundations through the respect they inspired in them for their character and learning. Pūjyapādaswami was one of such early Achāryas.

like Kundakunda, who, in the 5th century A.D., spread the Gospel of Jainism throughout the Andhra and Karnāta mandalas. Jaina literary tradition has preserved a story about him that he toured through the Andhra dēsa for literary disputations and royal patronage.[1] In a work called *Pūjyapāda-charita* the various kinds of arts and sciences that he mastered are enumerated. The list stands thus :—Prajñapti (ప్రజ్ఞప్తి), Kāmarūpini (కామరూపిణి), Agnisthambhini (అగ్ని స్తంభిని), Udasthambhini (ఉద స్తంభిని), Visvapravēsini (విశ్వప్రవేశిని), Aprathishtāthagāmini (అప్రతిష్టాతగామిని), Akasāgamini (ఆకాశగామిని), Urvātini (ఉర్వాటిని), Vasikarini (వశీకరిణి), Avēsini (ఆవేశిని), Sthāpini (స్థాపిని), Pramōhini (ప్రమోహిని), Prāhirini (ప్రాహిరిని), Samkramini (సంక్రమిని), Avarthini (ఆవర్తిని), Prarōdani (ప్రరోదని), Prahāvaṇi (ప్రహావణి), Prabhāvasa (ప్రభావస), Pratāpini (ప్రతాపిని), Vikshēpanī (విక్షేపని), Sāmbhari (శాంభరి), Chāndāli (చాండాలి), Mātari (మాతరి), Gauri (గౌరి), Bhattāngi (భట్టాంగి), Mudgi (ముద్గి), Kamkasamkuli (కంకసంకులి), Kumchānidi (కుంచానిడి), Vīradalavēgi (వీరదళవేగి), Karnalatki (కర్ణలట్కి), Laghukari (లఘుకరి), Vēgavati (వేగవతి), Sētavētāli (శేతవేతాళి), Sarvavidyābhēdini (సర్వవిద్యాభేదిని), Yuddhavīrya (యుద్ధవీర్యా), Bandhavēlāchini (బంధవేలాచిని), Praharnāvarni (ప్రహార్ణావర్ణి). These are mostly names to us, men of the modern generation in India, their tradition being hopelessly buried in the mantra and yoga

[1] Rice's *Karnātaka-Kavicharitre.*

sastras. But when they were practised by achāryas like Pūjapādaswami, they had a meaning and a potency which humbled the most arrogant of early Hindu rulers. This is the proper place to sum up the leading facts regarding the patronage of the Jaina achāryas and colleges by South Indian rulers. The earliest of such South Indian sovereigns was Kharavēla Kalinga. He does homage in the Jaina form, *i.e.*, నమో అర్హంతానాం, నమో నవసిధానాం. In the 12th year of his reign he constructed a statue of అగ్రజన, *i.e.*, Adīsvara or Vrishabha. He honoured the Jainas of Kalinga (అర్హంతపసాదానాం కాలింగానాం సమనానాం). Of the Kadambas of Banavasi, Kākusthavarma (Halsi) allowed his general Srutakīriti to donate land to the Jainas. Mrigēsavarma, son of Sāntivarma and grandson of Kākusthavarma, gave land grants to Jainas at Vaijayanti. In these grants several Jaina achāryas like Dāmakīrti, Jayakīrti, Bandhusēna and Kumāradatta are mentioned. Harivarma, son of Ravivarma, son of Mrigēsavarma, donated at Halsi a village to Chandrakshanta of the college of Vīrasēnachārya.

Patronage of Jain Scholars.

The Gangas of South India, a collateral branch of the Gangas of Kalinga, acknowledge that they established their kingdom in the South through the help of the Jaina Achārya, Simhanandi of Nandigana.

Mādhava II (Mādhavavarma Ganga) made a donation to Vīradēvāchārya in favour of a

Digambara temple. Avanitakonganivarma in the first year of his reign made a donation to his preceptor Vijayākīrti in A.D. 466 and also to Vandananandi of Dēsigana. This grant mentions other achāryas of Dēsigana, Kondakundānvaya, like Gunachandra, Abhayanandi, Silabhadra, Jñanānandi and Gunanandi. Sreepurusha in A.D. 776 gave a donation to Govapaiya in favour of the temple of Sripura and mentions the Achāryas Vimalachandra, Kīrtinandi, Kumāranandi, Chandranandi.

Of the Chalukyas the ancestors of the Eastern Chalukya line of Rāja Rāja Narēndra of Rajahmundry,

Pulakēsi I in S.S. 411 made a donation in favour of a temple constructed by his feudatory Sāmiyārya and mentions Siddhanandi, Jinanandi and Nāgadēva.

Kīrtivarma I gave a donation to Prabhachandra, disciple of Vinayanandi of Paraluru.

Vinayāditya S. 608 gave a donation to Dēvagana of Mūla Sangha.

Vijayāditya 651 gave a grant to a temple at Puligire which mentions Udayadēvapandita, disciple of Pūjyapāda of Alaktapura.

It must be observed that the *Chetiyakula* mentioned in the Kharavēla grants, the earliest, perhaps, of South Indian Jainism, is a branch of the Jainas which has not spread itself in South India. It perhaps represents one of the Jaina Sakhas of North Indian origin which flourished before the great schism in the time of Bhadrabāhu and Chandragupta. Possibly this branch belonged to Chēdi Kingdom. These Sakhas may be noted in passing, especially because no trace of them is yet discoverable in South India :—

A. Uddēhikiyagana. (a) Parihasakakula-Pūrnapatrika Sakha.
(b) Nāgabhutikiyakula.

B. Vēgavatikagana .. Mehikakula.

C. Varanagana ..(a) Hatikiyakula-Vajranagari Sakha.
(b) Aiyabhishtakula-Samkasika Sakha.
(c) (Chetikiya) kula-Haritamalakari Sakha.
(d) Petivamikakula.
(e) Nadikakula.

D. Kōtikagana (a) Sthaniyakula-Vajri Sakha.
(b) Brahmadasikakula-Uchchanagari Sakha.
(c) Prasnavahanakakula-Madhyama Sakha.
(d) Vatsaviyakula.
(e) Vidyadhari Sakha.

One may be curious to know what kind of **Jaina Polity.** influence it was that these achāryas of the various ganas and Sakhas exercised over their disciples who were rulers of provinces. Some light is thrown on this point by a Jaina work in the Madras Oriental MSS. Library called

Nītivākyamritam. Hindu authorities on Polity have always urged that the primary duty of the king is the securing of the happiness of the people. They go a step further. They say that the king should protect his people, with the same care with which a pregnant woman protects her child even at the sacrifice of her own special tastes, *Cf. Vaisampayana Nīti* :—

లోకరంజనమేవాఽత్రరాజ్ఞోధర్మః సనాతనః ।
యథాహిగర్భిణీహిత్వా స్వంప్రియంమనసోఽనుగం ।
గర్భస్యహితమాధత్తే తథాకుర్యాత్ప్రజాహితం ॥

Jaina Polity. *Nītivākyamrita*, the Jaina work on Polity, goes still further and makes the king a servant of the state. Its theory evidently is that the king is for the state and not the state for the king. Hence it begins with a salutation to the state as follows :—

Atha Dharmārtha Kāma phalāya *rājyam namah.*

(అధ ధర్మార్థ కామ ఫలాయ రాజ్యం నమః.)

From the following colophon of this work it is clear that it was composed by the Jaina Achārya Sōmadēvasuri who wielded large influence at a royal court in South India :—

" ఇతిసకలతార్కికచక్రచూడామణి చుంబితచరణస్య, రమణీయ పంచపంచాశన్మహావాదివిజయోపార్జితకీర్తి మందాకినీ పవిత్రితత్రిభువనస్య, పరతపశ్చరణ రత్నోదన్వంతః శ్రీనేమిదేవభగవతః ప్రియశిష్యేణ, వాదీంద్రకాలానలశ్రీమన్మహేంద్రదేవభట్టారకానుజేన। స్యాద్వాదాచలసింహతార్కికచక్రవాదీభ పంచాననవాక్కల్లోల పయోనిధి కవికులరాజకుంజర ప్రభృతిప్రశస్తిప్రసాదాలంకారేణ, షణ్ణవతి

ప్రకరణాయుక్తిచింతామణి త్రివర్గమహేంద్ర మాతలిసంజల్పయశోధరమహారాజచరిత మహాశాస్త్రవేధసా । శ్రీమత్సోమదేవసూరిణావిరచితం నీతివాక్యామృతం నామరాజనీతిశాస్త్రం సంపూర్ణం."

This work has 30 chapters :—1. Dharmasamuddesah (ధర్మసముద్దేశః), 2. Arthasamuddesah (అర్థసముద్దేశః), 3. Kāmasamuddesah (కామసముద్దేశః), 4. Arishadvargasamuddesah (అరిషడ్వర్గసముద్దేశః), 5. Vidyasamuddesah (విద్యాసముద్దేశః), 6. Anvikshisamuddesah (అన్వీక్షీసముద్దేశః), 7. Trayisamuddesah (త్రయీసముద్దేశః), 8. Vartasamuddesah (వార్తాసముద్దేశః), 9. Dandasamuddesah (దండసముద్దేశః), 10.Mantrasamuddesah (మంత్రసముద్దేశః), 11.Purohitasamuddesah (పురోహితసముద్దేశః), 12. Sēnapatisamuddesah (సేనాపతిసముద్దేశః), 13. Dūta-Sa.. (దూత-స), 14. Chāra-Sa. (చార-స), 15. Vichāra-Sa. (విచార-స), 16. Vyasana-Sa. (వ్యసన-స), 17. Svāmi-Sa. (స్వామి-స), 18. Amātya-Sa. (అమాత్య-స), 19. Janapada-Sa. (జనపద-స), 20. Durga-Sa. (దుర్గ-స), 21. Kosa-Sa. (కోశ-స), 22. Bala-Sa. (బల-స), 23. Mitra-Sa. (మిత్ర-స), 24. Rajarakshita-Sa. (రాజరక్షిత-స), 25. Divasanushtana-Sa. (దివసనుష్ఠాన-స), 26. Sadāchara-Sa. (సదాచార-స), 27. Vivāda-Sa. (వివాద-స), 29. Shādgunya-Sa. (షాడ్గుణ్య-స), 30. Vivāha-Sa. (వివాహ-స).

From this enumeration of its contents, it will be clear that it is an exhaustive work on polity after the manner of the Arthasastras of Kautilya or Sukra. The training that the Jaina gurus prescribe for their royal pupils and the *Dandanīti* which they taught them are points of interest to a modern reader, for it is from them that the value of their influence over their pupils can be safely judged.

The following is a summary of such views : (*a*) " He is an intelligent prince whose mind is disciplined by education. Long-standing happiness does not fall to a person who, like the lion, always rests his claim for respect solely on his prowess. He that is not cultivated by the sastras, becomes, like an unarmed hero, a target for all, his capabilities notwithstanding. In the realisation of what transcends the naked eye, the sastra is like a third eye. A person in possession of sight is as good as a blind man if he has not made himself acquainted with the sastras (sciences). *It is better for a kingdom to be in anarchy rather than to be under an ignorant and pig-headed person.* A king's son, though high born, like an unpolished diamond does not deserve leadership or sovereignty, if uncultivated.............. The qualities that make a prince intelligent and capable are discipleship, hearing, comprehension, memory, criticism, imagination, inference and the appreciation of the nature and tendency of things."

" A king who does not cultivate the company of the highly educated is sure to be ruined like the uncontrolled elephant let loose. Though he is not well learned, he acquires a good deal of knowledge by the association with learned persons of character. Pupils generally follow the character of their gurus. Hence he that may be guru to a prince should be 'well-born', 'well charactered,' 'well-learned'".

"(b) Danda is, like medicine, the agency that cures the distempers of the state. The objective of *Dandanīti* is the securing of the welfare of the people. It is never to be used for the acquisition of wealth. The king should not be on the look out for faults in his people, like the quack doctor who makes a living by the exploitation of diseases in his neighbours. If *Danda* is misused under the inspiration of ignorance or a lust for wealth or revenge it alienates the subjects. The whole state (bounded by the sea) is the family of the king. His wives are just the means of perpetuating his race.......... One man does not slave for another except for wealth. Among all kinds of wealth, education is the chiefest, for it can never be stolen. Since its quality is to spread itself, it can easily be secured by a king though in the possession of a lowly person. He to whom such learning becomes propitious possesses insight into everything in the world. Those persons only can be called well learned (and capable), who can teach others what they know (and inspire them with their own enthusiasm)."

CHAPTER III.

JAINISM IN ANDHRA-KARNATA LITERARY TRADITION.

A conspectus of Andhra-Karnāta Jaina Literature in manuscript—Some notable Jain works—Tendency of Jain versions of Hindu Puranic and Itihasa material—Karnāta Jaina literary contribution to Andhra culture—Jaina Karnāta influence in the earliest extant work in Andhra Literature—Jaina Karnāta literary types also extant in Andhra Literature—The makers of Jaina Andhra-Karnāta Literature—A Jain *Achārya Birudavali :* Islamic patronage of Jain scholarship.

Here below is a conspectus of the Jaina contribution to literature and knowledge as represented by the Sanskrit and Kannada Manuscripts of the Oriental Library in the Madras Museum :—

S.—Sanskrit. K.—Kannada.

A. *Jaina Agama* :—

S.

1. Jina Devata Pūja Vidhana.
2. Jina Samhita.
3. Jinēndrālaya Vishaya.

K

1. Ananta Katha.
2. Abhishēka *Sandhi.*
3. Karma Nirjhara.

4. Karmaparashtamiya *Nompi.*
5. Chandradarsana *Nompi.*
6. Tirthēsapūja *Sandhi.*
7. Navanidhi Khandarada *Nompi.*
8. Nāgakumara Panchamiya *Nompi.*
9. Nāgapanchami.
10. Pālana *Sandhi.*
11. Bhavyananda *Nompi.*
12. Migaya *Nompi.*
13. Savajyotiya Katha.
14. Siddhana *Nompi.*

B. *Jaina Purana.*

K. 1. Anjana charitra.
2. Kamanakatha.
3. Gurudatta charitravu.
4. Jinakatha.
5. Jinadattarāyana charitra.
6. Jinavachanamrita Saradhi.
7. Jivadhara charitra.
8. Trishashti lakshanapurana.
9. Dharmamritapurana.
10. Nāgakumarana charitra.
11. Padmavatiya charitra.
12. Prabhanjana charitra.
13. Pushpadantapurana.
14. Pūjapādacharitra.
15. Bharatēsvara charitra.
16. Varaganripa charitra.
17. Vardhamānabhattaraka Purana.
18. Sanatkūmaranakatha.
19. Bijalarāya charitra.

C. *Jaina Mata and Siddhanta.*

S.

1. Atmanusāsana.
2. Upasakāchāra.
3. Karmaprakriti.
4. Gomathasara.
5. Jaina Gayatrimantra.
6. Jaina Pūjahoma.
7. Jainōpasanamantra.
8. Dravyasangraha.
9. Dravyasamgraha sutra vritti.
10. Panchaparameshti prameya-nirūpana.
11. Parikshamukha laguvritti.
12. Ratnakaranda.
13. Saptabhangi tarangini.

K.

1. Jivahitratha.
2. Jainavarnāsrama.
3. Dwādasanuprēksha.
4. Dharmapariksha.
5. Rayanasārasutravritti.
6. Vakyāvali.
7. Haribhaktiprāmukhya.
8. Samyaktvakaumudi.

S.

C. *Jaina Kavya.*

S.

1. Chandraprabhajinagadyamālika.
2. Jinastuti.
3. Jainadēvatastotra.

4. Dharmasarmabhyudaya.
5. Neminirvana Kavya.
6. Samādhisataka.
7. Sinduraprakara Subhashitakosa (Anthology).

K. 1. Aparajitesvarasataka.
2. Jagannādhavijaya.
3. Jainakadamba.
4. Jainabirudavali.
5. Sringaralilavati.
6. Nemichandra charitra.

D. *Jaina Rhetoric and Grammar.*

S. Jainendravyakarana.

K. 1. Kavirajamärga.
2. Chamdombudhi.
3. Rasaratnakara.

E. *Jaina Logic.*

1. Prameyakamthika.
2. Prameyaratnamāla.
3. Nyayamanidipika.

F. *Jaina Ethics and Politics.*

S. Nītivākyāmrita.

K. 1. Chinmayachintāmani.
2. Jinamunitanayasataka.
3. Trailōkyarakshamanisataka.
4. Ratnakaradhīsvarasataka.
5. Haradanīti.

G. *Geography.*

K.

1. Lōkasvarūpa.
2. Trilōkasataka.

H. *Arithemetic.*

K. 1. Ganitasutra.

2. Jaina Ganitasutragalu.

I. *Music.*

K. Ratnakarajangala Padajati.

Jaina Literary types in Andhra-Karnāta Languages.

This is, though considerable, yet, a speck in the ocean of Jaina literature. The list is given here just to indicate the variety and standard of Jaina literature, mostly in the Vernacular. How close a relation it bears to Sanskrit culture may be quite clear from even a glance at these lists or the names of their authors. Jaina Karnāta literature stands for the attempt of the South Indian genius *to reinterpret and express after its own fashion* some of the leading themes and ideas of North Indian culture. In this attempt it has evolved for once, some new types of literature, *e.g.*, the Champu, Sandhi Nompi and Katha (Yakshagāna). The *Champu* and *Yakshagāna* types are common to Kannada and Telugu literatures. In fact they must originally have come into vogue in Telugu literature through the influence of Kannada. The *Champu* had developed in Kannada a curious fusion of Sanskrit and Vernacular which is known as Manipravāla style, and its respectability and patronage in the Vengi mandala of the Andhra dēsa (*vide* Pampa's *Adi Purana*) a century before Nannaya, must have largely influenced the formation of the Telugu literary dialect which Nannaya had used as the vehicle of the Telugu *Mahābhārata.* The *Yakshagāna* type of Kannada literature is interesting as representing the Andhra-Karnāta variety of the Dravidian drama. *Vijaya Kumarana katha* is an example of such a type. It is an ancient work. The manuscript in the Oriental MSS. Library, Madras (No. 18-417), is copied by Padmaraja Pandita of Mysore. It is in *desi* metres, prose and song as in Telugu Yakshagāna works.

It begins as follows :—

శ్రీపరమేశజినేశపాపనాశ । రవికోటిసంకాశ ।
కందర్పమదదహన భవమోహభంజన ।
గంధర్వాధిపతివందితపాద । దివ్యభాషావినోద ।
మంగళాకారసచ్చరితహార । శృంగారదూరసద్వక్త్రమందార ।
మూలోకసుగుణముక్త్యంగనారమణ ।
లీలావిలాస శ్రీ శాంతితీర్థేశ ॥

అజ్ఞానమంకొట్టి ప్రియదిందలెన్న । అజ్ఞానమ . . . . కలెదు సల
హిందుముత్తిన ॥

Of the *Sataka* type with the same last line or part of line repeated in each verse and called *Makuta*, a type which has had a very respectable vogue in Telugu devotional, and ethical and satirical literature, there is an early Kannada example in *Jinamunitanaya Sataka*. Of similar type and tendency are the Telugu *Satakas* that go by the names of *Vema* and *Sumati*. The following is an excerpt from it :—

వరణింద్రనభోగంగళు ।
సురరాజనసుఖమనరేంద్రన సంపత్తుం ।
వరధర్మదింద ఆదుదో ।
పరమశ్రీధర్మదింద జినమునితనయ ॥

The existence of this type acquires value for Telugu Literary History when it is observed that Nannaya in the Telugu *Mahābhārata* seems to work out its method into his Champu *Bhārata* as suggested by the following verses :—Adiparva, First Asvasa, 104–107 (verses).

(*N.B.*—The Sataka method is herein used for panegyric.)

Jaina Karnāta influences that shaped early Telugu literature.

In the wake of the Chalukya conquest of the Vengi Kingdom and consequent on the establishment of the E. Chalukya dynasty in Vengi, there must have taken place a considerable migration of a Canarese-Maharatta population of the 'governing' and 'co-operative' type, the members of which must have brought with them into the Andhra Kingdom, their traditional love of Karnāta literature and possibly, of Jaina culture. It is, at any rate, a significant fact that two of "the three gems" of Karnāta poetry, *viz.*, Pampa and Ponna, were pandit poets of the Vengi mandala, and that both of them flourished before Nannayabhatta the earliest known poet of the Andhra mandala. The celebrity which these authors attained in their time and the fact of their having belonged to "the governing and co-operative class" in the country is further of interest as indicating one of the important influences under which the literary movement was developing in the Vengi mandala before Nannaya's time.

Nannaya, himself, was the fellow pupil of a great Karnāta poet and scholar, *viz.*, Narayanabhatta and it is not extravagant to suppose that he himself was acquainted with Karnāta literature.

Though Nannaya professes to follow Vyasa's Sanskrit *Bhāratam*, his method may be called the Champu method, but it is not the Champu method of, say, Bhoja Champu.

Rice, in his introduction to Bhattakalanka's *Sabdanusasanam* says "the leading characteristic of the earlier Jaina works (Karnāta) is that they are Champu Kavyas or poems in a variety of composite metres, interspersed with paragraphs in prose." This description applies to Pampa's *Vikramārjuna Vijaya*, otherwise known as Pampa *Bhārata*, and an analysis of that portion of it which corresponds to the three *parvas* of Nannaya's Telugu *Bhāratam* shows that the author used most frequently (is it in deference to the Nripatunga [*vide* Kaviraja Mārga] school of Karnāta Rhetoricians) the Kanda, Campaka, Utpala, Mattēbha types of verse, and his prose pieces outnumber his verses. Out of 772 verses in all, distributed over about 7½ chapters, we find 372 Kandams, 190 Campakams, 101 Mattēbhams, and 70 Utpalams. This type of Champu prabandham with a predominance of prose and Kandam, and, with Campakams, Utpalams, Mattēbhams from the Sanskrit Chandas, must have become the predominant Kavya type before the time of

Nannaya in the Vengi Kingdom, and in adopting it as a vehicle of literary expression, Nannaya was perhaps attempting to combat the Jainas of the Andhra mandala with one of their own weapons. In Pampa *Bhārata,* done in the Kannada before his time and celebrated in the Vengi country, Nannaya and Narayanabhatta, had before them a Jaina presentation of the *Bhārata* story in the Champu method. In presenting their Brahmanic representation of the same story, and anticipating even a greater celebrity for it, they seem to have chosen wisely in accepting the very kavya method by which the Jainas made their ideas popular. An elaboration, in some detail, of the Kannada influence on the Telugu literary dialect of Nannaya may be in point in this context.

Traces of Canarese influence in Nannaya's Telugu Literary Dialect.

One of the most fascinating problems of Dravidian philology is " the rise of the literary dialects " in the various cultivated Dravidian languages. No doubt, the relative antiquity of Tamil or Karnāta can in a way be established, as has been attempted to be done, by the discovery of words from these languages in foreign records the antiquity of which has been fairly settled. But such discovery relates mostly to the spoken variety of these languages, unless it be that such words can be shown to have become literary by the time at which they were imported into or to have been quoted from literary works in which they can now be identified or the authenticity of which can now be established beyond doubt. A few such Telugu or Andhra-Karnāta (for they are common to both these languages) words have been identified by me in *Gatha Sapta Sati*, a collection of verses in an old Maharashtri dialect, the compilation of which is attributed to Hala, a prince who belongs to the line of Satavahana (Andhra) kings who ruled over a vast empire (in second century B.C.) including the later Andhra and Karnāta kingdoms. At about the same time, the Andhras (among whom I include the Karnātas also, for the latter were not distinguished as such) had developed special forms of dress and ornamentation which marked them out from other communities of South India and began to distinguish members of other South Indian communities, at least the Tamils, as Dravidas. Evidence of these facts has been traced by me on the sculptures and in the inscriptions on the Amaravati and Jaggayapeta Stupas. As is evident from a comparison of word-forms from these inscriptions and *Gatha Sapta Sati* with forms of *Tadbhava* words in Acca Telugu Nighantus, the Telugu and Karnāta peoples were in the early centuries of the Christian era under the influence of Prakrit and Pali Literature. Small wonder, then, that similar forms of Tadbhavas had filtered down into the later literary dialects of both these languages. Here below is a specimen table of such words.

Kaviraja-Mārga K.-R.-M.	Pampa-Bhārata P. B.	Adi Purana A. Pu.	Nannaya's Bhārata Bh.
Kabbam I. 27, 32, 34, 45, 49, 136.	I. 7, 9, 13 ..	....	....
....	Konti II. 2; III. 7p.	....	Goniti I. V. 21, 23, 61, 72, 132. VI. 19, 128, III. III. 3, 10. I. VIII. 54, 222.
....	Jauvana I. 17.	Jauvana II. 35.	....
....	Javvana I. 75, II. 39p.	Javvana III. 10.	Javvanambu III. III. 184, I. I. 38; III. 95, 96, 190, 192, 195, 202.
Dhāruni-tala 139	....	Dharini IV. 29.	Dhāruni I. 1–89, 11–58, 128, 130, 136, 223. IV. 25. V. 85. 113. VI. 67. VII. 34, 128, VIII. 63. II. 1. 41, 84, 99, 196, 207, 271, 275. II. 12, 182, 249. III. 1. 155. 11. 47, 171, 270. 285.
Nikkuva I. 41, 115, 116. III. 63.	....	....	Nikkuvambu I. III. 72; VI. III. 1, 229. (218, I. VII. 283. II. 1. 115.
....	VI. 2p, 2p ..	....	Rakkasal, VI. 199, 135, 200, 203, 206, 211, 212, 260, 264, 270, 273, 275, 287, 289, 295, 303, 304. III. I. 106, 107, 116.
V, 25, 26, 69, 70, 73, 74, 77.	I. 55, II. 9, 19, 39p, 49, 53p, III. 58p, IV. 53p, VII. 8, 50.	VIII. 39, VI. 52.	Mogambu I. 11, 220, V. 18, 11. 1. 4, 11, 198. n 1. V. 224, 111. 111. 58.
....	III. 8, IV. 43p, 78, 92p, VI. 33p.	VII. 109 ..	Santasamu I. VIII. 181, 226, VIII. 16, 11. I. 152; II. 119, 152.
....	I. 50; Kambham III. 39p.	....	Kambamu II. I. 11. 79.
....	Kanneya I. 67, 77, III. 67; IV. 16. V. 25.	....	....
....	Kanne IV. 16p, 40, 55.	....	Kanniya I. I. 46, VII. 208.
I. 99	Desa IV, 49.	V. 26, V. 8, 18, VI. 21p; VIII. 26p, VIII. 69.	Desu I. II. 25; VI. 281; VII. 172, 304.
....	Gujju III. 80p. V. 17p.	V. 22; VI. 21p.	Gujju.

The paucity of scholars interested in academic studies as such is so great, and, the enthusiasm for seeking out the historical origins of things so rare in South India that as yet it has not been possible to discover any literature earlier than the 8th century in Kannada, or earlier than the 11th century in Andhra (Telugu). Nanne Coda, the author of a Kavyam called "*Kumārasambhavam*", on a plan other than that of Kālidāsa, says definitely "that the cultivation of Telugu poetry was first encouraged by the Chalukyas from Satyāsraya in the Andhra country." Though I cannot agree with the learned editor of this work in claiming it to be earlier than Nannaya's Mahābhārata (for reasons a full statement of which had best be reserved for the present), I take it, that the reference to Satyāsraya quoted above is to Pulakēsi II whose conquest of the Andhra country, among others, is celebrated in the Aihole Inscription of *Ravikīrti*, a Jaina poet who claims to have equalled the fame of Bharavi and Kālidāsa.[1] This inscription is dated S. S. 556 (described as the year 3735 since the Bharta War), *i.e.*, 23rd July A.D. 613. Rāja Rāja Narēndra, the patron of the Telugu Mahābhāratam of Nannayabhatta, traces his descent from the brother of this Pulakēsi II, called *Vishama Siddhi* or *Kubjavishnuvardhana* who was left as the sovereign of the newly conquered Andhra kingdom and founded the Eastern Chalukya line of Vengi. This Rāja Rāja Narēndra was crowned King in

[1] This reading however is doubtful.

S. S. 944, *i.e.*, A.D. 1022, and reigned till about 1062 or 1063 A.D. Thus, from the first quarter of the 7th century A.D. to the third quarter of the 11th century for about *four centuries* the Telugu country was under the benevolent sway of the Chalukyas, a line of rulers whom Fleet very appropriately calls a *Canarese dynasty*. According to both Andhra and Karnāta accounts, these rulers were great patrons of literature. The kind of poetry cultivated under their patronage was of the courtly type and character, as evidence of which may be mentioned Andhra and Karnāta Kavyas and Inscriptions (Panegyric poetry). It has been said above that back of 8th century A.D. in Karnāta and of 11th century A.D. in Andhra (Telugu), no Kavyas in these languages have yet been discovered, although there are references in Kavyas referable to these centuries and subsequent thereto, to the existence of literary tradition contemporaneous with or earlier than such works. But a few inscriptions back of 8th century A.D. in Kannada or Sanskrit and Kannada, and of 11th century A.D. in Telugu or Sanskrit and Telugu, have been discovered and support the claims of the scholars of that day in Andhra and Karnāta countries to *Ubhaya Bhasha Panditya* (proficiency in both the languages). *In the cultivation of panegyrical poetry by scholarly officers at court, we find the first parallelism between early Karnāta and early Andhra literary efforts, a parallelism which has been, surely, at work in fashioning the literary dialects of both these languages on same or similar models.* Such influence of *Canarese taste* in literary matters has, I think, been only accelerated by the conquest of the Vengi kingdom by the Chalukyas, for about 5th century A.D., a Jaina scholar and grammarian, Pūjyapāda, is said to have visited the Andhra mandala, evidently on a tour for patronage. This presupposes high cultivation of Kannada in the Andhra mandala at the date and also a regard for Jainism. It is not therefore extravagant to suppose that about that period, Jainism had favour in the Andhra and Karnāta mandalas and Jaina Karnāta literature was known in the Andhra mandala. From the century following, for *four* centuries together, the Andhra mandala came under the influence of a Canarese dynasty of kings with their courtly retinue of Canarese officials, scholars, poets and generals but they found themselves at the head of a movement of Brahmanic revival which fought successfully against Jainism and Buddhism in the Telugu country with their own weapons,—the establishment of seats of learning, the securing of royal patronage for the places of worship, the reinterpretation of old puranic materials derived from earlier Sanskrit literature, the development of literary types in the vernaculars. To such a movement of Brahmanic revival, with all the fully developed literary resources of early Jaina Karnāta literature at its service, I find reasons to attribute the rendering of *Mahābhāratam* in Telugu or Andhram by Nannaya Bhatta under the patronage of the Eastern Chalukya Rāja Rāja Narēndra of Rajahmundry.

Of specimens of Kannada and Tẹlugu earlier than Kannada Kaviraja Mārga or Andhra Mahābhārata, I give below a summary of select references available in epigraphical publications :—

Traces of the Canarese Language in Inscriptions earlier than S. 736.	Traces of Telugu Inscriptions earlier than S. 944.
W. Gangas.—	
S. 169.—Sanskrit and Canarese Tanjore Plates of Arivarma (Ind. Ant. VIII).	S. 890.—Sannamuru grant of Bana Aggaparaju (Nellore Ins.)
S. 188.—Sanskrit and Canarese Plates of Harivarma (Ep. Car. III).	Aṅadanakaram Plates (Sanskrit and Telugu) of Eastern Chalukyas Mahārāja Vishnuvardhana.
S. 261.—Kalchavi Sanskrit and Canarese Jaina Insn. of Kambharasa (Ind. Ant. XVIII).	(Kalivishnu vardhana) (Ind. Ant. Vol. XVIII).
S. 588.—Sanskrit and Canarese Plates of Avinita (Coorg Insns. No. 1).	Ranastipudi Plates of the eighth year of Vimalāditya Vishnuvarddhana S. 933. (Ep. In. VI).

Traces of the Canarese Language in Inscriptions earlier than S. 736.

W. Chalukyas.—

About S. 520 Badami and Canarese rock Ins. of Maṅgalēsa (Ind. Ant. V).

S. 621.—Badami Sanskrit and Canarese Ins. of the reign of Vijayāditya Satyāsraya.

S. 631.—Aihole Canarese Ins. of the 3rd month of the 8th year of the reign of W. Chalukya Mahārājādhirāja Vijayāditya Satya-narayan (Ind. Ant. VIII, XIX).

About S. 651—Badami (Manapata) Canarese Ins. of Vinapoti, the heart's darling of Mahārājādhirāja Vijayāditya (Ind. Ant. X).

S. 651 Ḥ.—Pathadakal Canarese Ins. of Vijayāditya (and his son) Vikramāditya II.

S. 654-676.—

(1) Aihole Canarese Ins. of the reign of Vikarmāditya II (Ind. Ant. VIII).

(2) Conjeevaram Canarese Ins. of Vikramāditya II (Ep. Ind. III).

(3) Pathadakal Canarese Ins. of Lōkamahādēvi, queen of Vikramāditya II (Ind. Ant. X).

(4) Pathadakal Canarese Ins. mentioning the same lady (Ind. Ant. X).

(5) Pathadakal Canarese Ins. mentioning the same lady.

(5) Pathadakal Canarese Ins. mentioning the same lady (Ind. Ant. X).

(6) Pathadakal Canarese Ins. mentioning the same lady (Ind. Ant. X).

Rāshtrakūtas.—

S. 687.—Hatti Matlur Canarese memorial tablet—of the reign of Akalavarsha (Krishna I) (Ep. Ind. VI).

S. 796.—Canarese Plates of Rāshtrakūta Govindaraja III Prabhutavarsha (Ind. Ant. XI).

Anything like a thorough discussion of the features of phonology, grammar and syntax of these inscriptions in either of the languages in comparison with those of either Kaviraja Mārga or Mahābhāratam, however interesting and important for the historical study of the Karnāta and Andhra literary dialects, falls outside the scope of the present studies. What is urged by this table of parallelisms is just the fact of panegyrical poetry having been cultivated on similar lines in both the Karnāta and Andhra countries, particularly under Chalukya patronage. A further feature which is important from the point of view of the make-up of the literary dialects of Karnāta and Andhra, brought out by these inscriptions is the gradual development of a highly sonorous literary style by the intimate association of Sanskrit and the vernacular languages, leading to an importation of Sanskrit words into vernacular compositions and the fashioning of the syntax according to the models of Sanskrit prose celebrated during those times for euphony and grandeur.

Karnāta influence in Kalinga.

While literary styles have thus been fashioned in the Andhra and Karnāta mandalas, a similar process of development was going on in the Kalinga mandala, the other great strong hold of the Telugu peoples. The Kingdom of Kalinga is probably more ancient than any of the Andhra or Karnāta kingdoms. At a time when the latter were yet undifferentiated parts of the Andhra Empire of the Satavahanas, the Kalinga kingdom was so celebrated that it attracted an expedition from Asoka which proved a turning point in his spiritual history. Even by the time of Asoka's conquest, Kalinga was a seat of learning and under his immediate successors, it became in a larger measure the seat, particularly, of Buddhist learning. But the history of Kalinga, social, political and cultural is yet so much of an unbroken field (notwithstanding the few Kalinga grants yet published), that nothing can be stated with an air of finality in matters affecting the chronology of its kings. But until the political history of that Ancient kingdom is attempted in some satisfactory measure, its cultural history in relation to the history of the Telugu literary dialect cannot be undertaken with any measure of confidence. But yet, I shall urge in this chapter just the tendency of some facts connected with its interesting dynasty of rulers called by epigraphists, "the Eastern Gangas of Kalinga", to indicate the possibility of the Kalinga kingdom also having been under the influence of a Canarese dynasty at about the same time that the neighbouring Vengi kingdom (with its capital at Rajahmundry) was enjoying the benefits of the benevolent rule of the Eastern Chalukyas.

The Kallurgudda stone Insn. (sh. 4 *Ep. Car.*) S.S. 112–A.D. 1190 describes *Ganganvayavataranam* and the following is a summary of it (*Ep. Car.* Vol. VII, Part (1). *Intn.* p. 14) :—" In Ayōdyapura was born the head-jewel of the Ikshvāku race, Harischandra (according to sh. 10, the son of Dhananjaya, Capturer of Kanyakubja and Gandhari Dēvi) who ruled in peace for a long time. His son was Bharata, whose wife was Vijaya Maha Dēvi. When the longing of pregnancy arose in her, she went to bathe in the Ganges and recovered her brightness. In due time she bore a son, who from the above circumstance was named Ganga Datta. He in turn had a Bharata, whose son was again Ganga Datta, whose son was Harischandra. His son was another Bharata, whose son was also Ganga Datta. While the Ganga line was thus continuing, there arose in it a king named Vishnugupta who gained an Empire and ruled from

Ahichchatrapura, where he performed the Aindradhvajapūja and Dēvēndra being pleased thereat gave him *airavata* (his elephant, regent elephant of the east). To Vishnugupta and his wife Prithvīmati were born the sons Bhagadatta and Srīdaṭta. To the former (*Bhagadatta*) *the father gave Kalinga* which he ruled in peace as *Kalinga Ganga*."[1] Thus the Kalinga and Maisur Gangas seem to have been connected in a common progenitor Vishnugopa of Ahichchatrapura, thus :—

Vishnugopa of Ahichchatrapura
=Prithvīmati.

Bhagadatta (Eastern Ganga) — Srīdatta (Western Ganga)

But this Bhagadatta otherwise known as Kalinga Ganga has not been identified in Kalinga history. In fact in the published information about the relation of the Eastern Gangas of Kalinga with the Western Gangas of Gangavadi, I have met as yet no where with an attempt to make anything out of this tradition. The Gangas of Kalinga known from inscriptions make no reference to Ahichhatrapura. But there is a place called *Chatrapur* in the Ganjam District which is the headquarters of the Ganjam Collectorate. This was possibly the place founded in the Kalinga country by this Bhagadatta as his capital, a sort of analogy to the Ahichchatrapura which was the capital in Gangavadi of his father's empire. There are widely

[1] Can this person be the Ganjam-Vizagapatam District Raja Kalinga Ganga of the Inscriptions ?

distributed inscriptions of a king called Raja Kalinga Ganga in the Kalinga kingdom, but whether he was this Bhagadatta remains to be established. Anyhow I see dimly an interesting background of Southern Ganga emigrant enterprise buried under the modern Chatrapur in the Ganjam District which is well worth earnest investigation.

From the published grants of the Gangas of Kalinganagara, it would appear that the ancestors of these rulers were emigrants from the south. Anantavarma Chodaganga's grant of S. S. 1040 states that "Kamarnava I gave over his territory Gangavadi to his paternal uncle and with his brothers set out to conquer the earth and came to the mountain Mahēndra. Having there worshipped the god Gokarnasvami, through his favour he obtained the excellent crest of a bull, and then, decorated with all the insignia of universal sovereignty, having descended from the summit of the mountain Mahēndra and being accompanied, like Yudhistira by his four brothers, Kamarnava conquered king Balāditya, who had grown sick of war, and took possession of the Kalinga Countries."

In the Vizagapatam grant of Anantavarma Choda Ganga S. S. 1118 mention is made of a prince Kolahala who, it is said, built the city of Kolahala in the great Gangavadi Vishaya. This Kolahala must be the city Kuvalala (Kolar) the capital of the Ninety-six Thousand Gangavadi kingdom which Simhanandi helped Daddiga to found. From the inscription, quoted above, describing the *Ganganvayavataranam*, we learn that when the Gangavadi kingdom was finally established with the help of Simhanandi, there arose in the dynasty a prince named Mādhava, the son of Dadiga. " His son was Harivarma whose son was Vishnugopa who associated with falsehood (or a false creed) and the ornaments given by Indra accordingly disappeared. His son was Prithvīganga who favoured the true faith." This Vishnugopa who is thus said to have associated with a false creed is thus descended from his name-sake, the progenitor of the Eastern and Western Gangas.

Vishnugopa-Prithvīmati.

- Bhagadatta. (Kalinga Ganga)
- Srīdatta.
  - Priyabandhuvarma in whose time Ahichhatrapura became *Vijayapura*.
    - Kampa.
      - Padmanabha.
        - Rama or Daddiga
          - Mādhava
            - Harivarma 266 A.D.
              - Vishnugopa 302 A.D. (who associated a false creed).
                - Prithivīganga (who favoured the true faith).
        - Lakshmana or Mādhava

The adoption of a false creed by Vishnugopa and the support of the true faith by his son seem to refer to Jaina *vs.* Brahmanic conflicts ; for the early Gangas were Jainas. From SK 176 (*Ep. Car.* VII) we learn that Mādhava's fame was very widespread on account of his renewal of Brahmanic endowment long since destroyed. Here we have evidences of the fact that Brahmanism was asserting itself in the Gangavadi country about 4th century A.D. against Jainism with whose help the kingdom was founded.[1] Matters have not been satisfactorily cleared up as one would wish them to be by this brief excursus into the prehistoric antiquities of the Eastern Gangas of Kalinga, but I hope enough has been said to indicate a southern origin of the civilisation and culture which the Gangas had brought with them into the Kalinga kingdom. Like their compeers the *Chalukyas of Badami and Vengi*, these rulers were patrons of poets and scholars and under their patronage and influence panegyrical poetry and most probably Kavya poetry were cultivated in the Kalinga mandala in Sanskrit and Andhram. Of the latter type no traces have as yet been discovered. These literary developments in Kalinga ran on almost similar lines to that in Vengi about the time when the *Mahābhārata* had just been rendered into Telugu. Of panegyrical writing from the

[1] It would thus seem that there were two distinct Ganga lines in Kalinga, the earlier one started by Kalinga Ganga about 162 A.D. and the *later* one by Kamarnava.

Vengi and Kalinga kingdoms, I add brief excerpts hereunder :— **Literary types and styles of Kalinga and Andhra.**

(1) From Madras Museum Plates of Vajrahasta III (East Ganga)

sā || prascyōtanmada gandha lubdha madhupa vyālidha gandā(ng) ajān
arthibhyassamadāt sahasramatulas sasaya (styā) ginām agrañī(h)
sa(h) (srima)n aniyankabhimanr patir ganganvayōttamsakah
·Pancattrim satamabdakan samabhunak prthvim (stu) tah parthivaih,

Malini || tadanu tadanujanmā cittajanmopamanō,
gunanidhiranavadyō gunddamākhyō mahisah,
(sa)kalamidamaraksattrīni varsāni dhatri,
valayamalaghu tējonirjitaraticakrah.

Giti || Atha vajrahastanrpateragrasutādatulaguni janāgranyah,
Kāmarnavāt *kavindrapragiyamānāvadāta* subhakirteh,

malini, viyadrtunidhi samkhyam yāti sākābda sanghe
dinakrit vrsabhasthe rohinibhe sulagne,
dhanusica sita pakse sūryavāre. trtiya,

yaji sakaladharittri raksitum yobhi-
siktah.

N.B.—The reference in these verses to a poet praising the king is important, coming from a court panegyrist of a later date.

(2) From the prasasti of rahasika Sankara Dēva, the son of Amatya Dēvachendra. (East Ganga grant of the 128th year of Indravarma) Svasti vijayavato Kalinga nagara vasakat mahendracalamala sikhara pratisthitasya Caracara gurōh Sakala bhuvana nirmanaika Sutradharasya bhagavato gokarnasvaminascaranakamala yugala pranamad vigalita Kali Kalanko gangamalakula tilakah Svasidhara parispandaadhigata sakala Kalingadhirajyah pravitata caturudadhi salila taranga mekhalavani talamalasya aneka samara samghatta vijaya janita jaya sabda pratapopanata samsta samanta cudamani prabha manjari punja ranjita carano mata pitr padanudhyatah Sriman Maharajendra Varma................

(3) From Dirghasi Insn. of Vanapati
S. S. 997.

Sī 11 Sri Sakunēndulu bhusatipai
saila namdābjabhava samkhya
nonda vengi
desambu gimidiya gosala gidrisingi
desambu yodda mari desaman-
amga
janina bhupaluran *aninocce* cala-
martti gandandai negadina
mandalikundu

bhusura vamsundu vasavanibha
bhogi janapati saujanya gunayu-
tundu
dirghasi bhagavati devi devalaya
munamumdatamgadu ghanata-
ramuga
mandapam ettimce bhandana
vijayundu gandagopalunda-
khanda varti
diviya vetten addēvikin avvalam
damamanovallabhi vanajanetri
diviya vettem badmavati yununa
ksonina sasulugalayam takunu
mudamuna
gagana bhumi camdra Kharakaroda-
kasikhi.
marutatmamurtti mahishamathana
yistapurtti phalamul ellakalambunu
meccu todam damakun iccu cumda

N.B.—It is worthy of note that the build of this verse, especially of the system of *yatis* in the major part, is exactly identical with that of the *sisam* in Nannaya's *Mahābhāratam*, a fact which indicates that Telugu prosody must have been evolving *on similar lines* in the Andhra and Kalinga kingdoms about that time.

B. From a grant of Eastern Chalukya Amma II. Poet *Potanabhatta* sakalaripunrpati makuta-tataghatita manigana madhukara nikarapari-cumbita carana sarasiruha *yugalo yugalo*cana-padakamalavilasad dvirephay *amano* (manonna-tanatoddhata *samasta* loka samsta bhuvanasrayah srivijayaditya maharajadhirajah, parama samasta bhuvanasrayah Srivijayaditya maharaja rajadhirajah parama mahesvara parama bhattarakah parama brahmanayah velanamdu visaya nivasino rastrakuta pramukhan kutumbinah samahūyettham.

(*b*) From Korumilli grant of Rāja Rāja Narēndra : Poet *Chettanabhatta.*

Sa || Yasya prajvalitapratapadahanam Sodhum na saktyabhayat
gatva kananamambudhinca tarasavidvesino vihvalah
davaurvagnipadena tatraca punas tenaiva samtāpitāh
Sripādāmara padapasya mahatīm chayam samāsisriyan
Sa 11, Rājnamarcita varcasas samuditaiyajnairvidhau tasighato
yapionama sutastatah krtadhiyo jagne krtajnah kriti
vijnatakhila vēdasastra samayah prajnah sada podita
jnatirjnana nidhirgurujna sadrso nitynatayam bhuvi

Va Sa sarva lokasraya sri vishnu vardhana Maharajadhi Raja Rajaparamesvara parama bhattaraka parpama brahmanyah matapitr padanudhyatah tyaga simhasanasinah camdikaprasada parilabdha samrajya cihnah guddavadi visaya nivasino rashtra kutapramukhan Kutumbinasarvan samahuya mamtri purohita senapati.

D. From Sannamuru grant of Aggaparaju (Bana) *Nellore Ins.* 1, 38, svasti sakala jagatrayabhivandita surasuradhisa paramesvara pratiharikrita mahabalikulodbhava krsnadchjavirajita paisacika patahaghosana vrsabhalamchana nandigiri natha parigipura paramesvara *banal ganda balikularjuna* gadusandya .... srimat *aggaparaju* samvatsara 890 yagu nendi vaisakha punnami sukra varambu pedda rajyana

.... yu konduka rajyaana cetam goni iccina bhumi....

The excerpts quoted above have all been taken from inscriptions which are either earlier than or contemporary with Nannayabhatta. They have been given here chiefly to add point to the observation that panegyrical poetry cultivated in the Andhra and Kalinga mandalas about the time when Nannaya composed the Telugu Bhāratam had *similarities of structure, diction and poetic methods.* But a comparison of them with certain features of Nannaya's poetry in the Mahābhārata may be further made to indicate how the diction, methods and structure of the *Kavya* of those times was influenced by the panegyrical poetry of the time and in turn influenced it.

First in the matter of metres—

(*a*) I have adduced examples of *sardulavikridita, malini* and *sisam* in the above excerpts.

In the Kannada Bhārata of Pampa composed at least a century earlier than Nannaya's Telugu *Mahābhārata,* I have counted among 772 verses distributed over 8 chapters (dealing with the portion of the Bhārata story corresponding to the three *Parvas* of Nannaya's Telugu *Bhāratam*) only 1. *malini* and 2. *sardulà-vikriditams.* This shows that these types of verse were not as much favoured as other types by this author.

In the Telugu Mahābhārata of Nannaya I have counted 7 *malinis* and 18 (శార్దూలవిక్రీడిత) *sardulams.* The details of distribution are as follows :—

Malini.—

I. ii, 31, 96 ; v. 127 ; vi. 309 ; viii. 196; 234.

II. ii. 75.

III.—

Sardulams.—

I. i. 69, 78, 111 ; ii. 12, 153, 227 ; iii. 11, 21 ; iv. 8 ; v. 106, 189, 257 ; vi. 9, 29 ; vii. 197, 216. viii.

II.

III. i, ii, iii. 157, 222 ; iv—

(*b*) *Sisam* is one of the most popular metres of Nannaya suited particularly to descriptive narration, for which it has been used in the excerpt from the Dirghasi inscription quoted above. It will therefore be of interest to examine closely the details of distribution of this metre in Nannaya's *Bhāratam.* Though this metre is described in Nāgavarma's Canarese prosody, we find few traces of it in the works of Pampa and Nripatunga that I have been able to examine. In 269-271 Nāgavarma gives the scheme for Sisa Padya.

In Nannaya's *Mahābhāratam* as its analysis will show, the *Sisa Padya* of this type predominates. The *Sisa Padya* from the Dirghasi inscription is also of this type.

(c) *Prasam in the Vrittams*—

Telugu Laksanikas claim their introduction of Prasam in the Sanskrit Vrittam as an improvement they have made on Sanskrit prosody. Indeed, it is a variety of alliteration which is regarded by Sanskrit rhetoricians as a special feature of South Indian compositions. Indeed, Telugu prosody has become so far fixed to-day owing to centuries of this tradition that a modern Telugu poet and pandit is horrified to see *Prasa* used in purely Sanskrit Vrittams like *Sardula Vikriditam* as merely a variable ornament in a modern composition. This tradition has become fixed well within the life-time of the second great poet of the Telugu *Mahābhārata, viz.,* Tikkana Somayaji. In the 9th chapter of *Kavyalankara cudamani,* of Vinnakota Peddana, which is devoted to a description of Telugu grammar (a chapter lately published), a work which like Ketana's *Andhrabhāsha Bhusanam* forms the earliest grammatical contribution of Telugu language, the author bemoans the disrespect of certain Sanskritists of the day to Telugu works and incidentally mentions *Yati* and *Prasa* which Telugu verses possess as improvements over the Sanskrit system of prosody.

The verse bears quotation :—

M. II. Vilasadbhāva rasādyalamkrtulace vippāru girvanabha
shala kabbambulakanna mamci tanamul samdhinchu camdambunai
Valiyum brasamulamtak aggalamulai vartillu Satkavyamul
Telugeman jevi betta lemi yudupan degalgune mamd ilan

Thus at that early date *vali* and *prasa* must have become fixed even in purely Sanskrit metres as *Sardulam* and *Mattēbham*, the type to which the verse just quoted belongs. But the Sardulam with *jna* as the second syllable in three out of four Padams, from the epigraphic excerpts quoted above, which was the composition of the Poet *Chettanabhatta*, a contemporary of Nannaya, serves to show how the *prasa system* has been creeping into South Indian Sanskrit versification. The *jna* alliteration in the verse is a fairly good type of the South Indian method of alliteration discussed in Kittel's Introducton to Nagavarma's prosody.

(*d*) *Next in the matter of prose*—

A fairly good specimen of panegyrical prose may be quoted from Nannaya's Mahābhāratam, the opening chapter. The passage runs thus :—

"Akhila jaladhi vela valayavalayitavasumati vanita vibhusanamb aina vegi desambunaku nayaka ratnambunum boniraja mahendra purambun amdu mahendra mahimato, baramanandambuna nubhavincucu Sakalabhuvana lakshmi vilasa nivasambaina ramya harmya talambuna mantri purohita senapati dandanayaka dauvarika mahapradhananta samanta vilasini parivrtund ai yapāra sabdasastra paragul aina vaiyakaranulunu bharata ramayanadyaneka purana pravinulaina pauranikulunu mrdu madhura rasabhava bhasura navartha vacana racana visaradulaina mahakavul unun vividha tarka vigahita samasta sastra sagaragariyah pratibhulaina tarkikul unun adiga agalgu vidvajjanam bulu parivesthinici koluva vidyavilasa gosthi sukhopa visthund ai yista katha vinodambulan undi. I." Bh. I. 1-8.

Just a rapid reading of this passage brings out to the ear the markedly alliterative and sonorous nature of word juxtaposition so much noticeable in the prose excerpts from the inscriptions quoted above. The other feature is the massage of long adjectival compounds and descriptive phrases towards the latter part which describes Rāja Rāja's court as in the prose paragraph quoted from the Korumilli grant composed by Chettanabhatta.

(*e*) *Next as regards diction*—

We have noticed in the epigraphic excerpts how panegyrical poetry even where it is Telugu delights in using a large element of Tatsama words to be in keeping with directly Sanskrit portions to which Telugu prose compositions have been attached. The other important feature is an anxiety to secure *sonorousness* by using literary forms (often archaic) of popular words. The same tricks of style are noticeable also in the diction of Nannaya and of his Karnāta predecessor Pampa. In fact the latter poet delighted in similating the music of his style to that of the ocean. This influence accounts largely for the very high proportion of Tatsama element in Nannaya's composition. He must have modelled it on the style and diction of Pampa's *Adi Purana*, the style of which was more celebrated in his day than that of Pampa *Bhārata*. I just take one passage of panegyrical prose which seems to have been the result in the Telugu Inscriptions and Kavyas of the panegyrical poetry of Pampa and other earlier Kannada writers.

The passage runs thus :—

" Upanata samasta samanta cudamani prabha manjari punja ranjita carano "—E. G. grant of Indravarma.

Compare with this the following from the E. Ch. grant of Amma II :—" Sakala ripu nrpati makuta tata ghatita manigana madhukara nikara paricumbita carana sarasiruha yugalo."

Compare with these the following passages from the distinctly panegyrical verses from Nannaya's Mahābhārata :—

(1) Nanavani natha kiritatativilasadratnasamghatitapadakamala II.I. ii.i.

(2) vinamad rajanyakiritamanivirajita padam bhoja— I. vi. 1.

(3) pranamadakhiladhatri palakalola cuda I kirana sri manigana manditamghri naremdragrani I. vi. 309.

(4) paranrpamanimakutaghatita pada vibudha nuta III. 1. 39.

(5) namannrpa kiritacumbi carana dvaya III. ii. 355.

Here below are references to similar phrases from Pampa a Canarese poet of great renown, a century or two earlier than Nannaya :—

(1) avanipativrata mani makuta kiranadyotita padam. — Pampa Bhārata I. 16.

(2) akhila kamapala mauli mani kiranapalita nakha mayukha ramjita caranam. — Pampa Bhārata I. 18.

Nannaya and Pampa.

Apart from these references, others may be quoted from Pampa's works which seem to have suggested to Nannaya the diction of his panegyrical verses in the *Mahābhāratam*. The similarity of phrasing is so striking that one cannot but infer Nannaya's acquaintance with the works of Pampa in their Kannada original. I shall edit here a few passages from Nannaya's panegyrical compositions in the Mahābhārata with reference to their Kannada parallelisms :—

(*a*) Vangmaya dhuramdharudun I. 24.

Pampa's Adi Purana VIII, p. 61, has reference to ' vangmaya.' An ancient division of the arts and sciences is given in this passage in which this word occurs. Three divisions of ' vangmaya' which I take it to be ' Literary art ' are mentioned (1) Padavidya, (2) Chamdo vichit, (3) Alamkara.

(*b*) Vilasini parivrtundai I. 1-8.

Pampa has in court " vilasa-vilasin janam " A. Pu. II. 4.

(*c*) *Danditahita, vira.* I. iii. 228.

Pampa has ' danditaratimandalam ' Apu. II. 14.

(*d*) Among the court officials at the court of Rāja Rāja Narēndra Nannaya mentions—

Mantri purohita senapati dandanayaka dauvarika

Mahapradhananta samanta S. I. 1-8.

Pampa in a similar passage in Adi Purana mentions—

" ati pracanda mandalika mahasamanta mantri Pradhana."

Purohitara '-II. 2.

(*e*) " Paramandalambula dharani patulan adimi Kappambula mudamuto gomcunu" I. i, 7.

Pampa alluding to a similar thing in *Adi Purana* has reference in II. 24 to '*Paramandalikar*' and '*Kappam.*'

(*f*) Describing the gifts presented to Yudhistira at the Rajasuya by various princes, Nannaya says :—

"Mada matanga turanga kancana lasan *manikya ganikya* sampadal olim goni tecci yicci mudam oppam gancisevincir ...." II. i. 18.

I have identified this phrase 'manikya ganikya' in Pampa's *Adi Purana* XVI. 8.

(*g*) Nannaya describes Rāja Rāja as '*Manumārga*' I. iii. I.

Pampa uses a similar appellation in *Adi Purana* VII, 12 '*Manumārga.*'

A theory of the early evolution of the Telugu literary dialect.

Such similarities of phrasing (both in the panegyrical part of poetry and in the Kavyas proper or sasana kavyas and prasastis) between early Karnāta and early Telugu works suggest not only that they were an expression of Karnāta type of literary culture prevalent in the Andhra and Kalinga countries, but indicate the possibility of their having developed largely under Karnāta influence in the Andhra country most certainly and in the Kalinga most probably, a type of *Kavya diction* which has left to this day a permanent influence on the growth of the Telugu literary dialect. This is my indication of the line of study of the early history of the Telugu literary dialect as represented by Nannaya. Prof. Hopkins has by a comparison of the Sanskrit *Mahābhārata*[1] and *Rāmāyana* proved beyond doubt the existence of *Epic methods and diction* well established during the formative period of classical Sanskrit to which fact can be traced the striking similarities between the epic methods and diction of the two Sanskrit epics. By a similar comparison of Pampa's works with Nannaya's Mahābhāratam it is I think possible to establish, beyond a doubt, the existence, in the Andhra mandala, for a century or two before Nannaya, of Epic methods and diction approved alike by patrons and poets.

II.

Other Jaina Works.

Jaina treatment of popular Vaidic or Puranic themes.

Dharma Pariksha is an attempt to reconsider the sacred themes of *Vaidika* literature from the point of view of Jainism. The author calls himself *vritta vilasa* (one who takes delight in verses). The work is divided into *asvasas.* It describes a city called *Vaija-yantipura* (the capital of the Kadambas). As. i, 50 describes the city as follows :—

బెళదమాన స్తంభసందోహదిం ।
బింబాడంబరరత్నకూటజినచైత్యావాసదిం ।
చెళ్వనం గంబొప్పూహాంగళిం దమె రెగుం ।
శ్రీజై నవై జయంతీపురం ॥

[1] See Prof. Hopkins, *Great Epic of India*.

Among others, the work treats of

మహీవేగపవనవేగోత్పత్తి, విష్ణుదేవతాపరీక్ష, సర్వదేవతాపరీక్ష, బ్రహ్మనజగత్కర్తృత్వవిష్ణువినపాలనశస్త్రవ్యాసనసామర్థ్యనిరూపణం, ఈశ్వరాదిసకలదేవసురార్జునరశక్తిసామర్థ్యపరీక్ష, శ్రీబ్రహ్మవిష్ణుమహేశ్వరదేవతాపరీక్ష, కౌరవ, భగీరథనభిమన్యుమింద్రజితు శ్రీవేదవ్యాసకర్ణాత్పణబిందునినుత్పత్తి, రావణకులోత్పత్తి, వాలిసుగ్రీవన, వినాయకజననభేద, త్రిషష్టిశలాకాపురుషచక్రమం, రామలక్ష్మణర సామర్థ్యం.

The stories of Rāmāyana and Mahābhārata are more particularly handled as Kavyas in Pampa Bhārata and Pampa Rāmāyana. The value of the attempt, therein, of rehandling classical material consists in the manifest motive of treating them mostly as *Kshatriya heroic tales enlivened by Jaina devotion.* The heroic element predominates the religious and cultural aspects.

The makers of Jaina literature.

A word may be said in conclusion about the makers of all this varied literature. They are, *first* the acharyas of the various mathas established in South India and their disciples and their disciples' disciples, and *secondly,* the officers of warrior chieftains who established kingdoms with the help of these achāryas and used their influence for the protection and spread of Jaina *Dharma.* The Chalukyas and Rāshtrakūtas must be mentioned as the foremost dynasties in Andhra Karnāta *dēsas* under whom Jaina architecture and literature acquired wide reputation and excellence. Jaina literature in turn is full of the praises of these sovereigns. Panegyrical chronicles, after the Jaina fashion, form the introductions to both Andhra and Karnāta Kavyas of the courtly type thus differentiating them from their Drāvida analogues. A work called *Jaina Birudavali* records the praises of these *makers of Jaina literature,* especially of the Achāryas, and tells us how by their character, attainments and scholarship they commanded the respect of even Muhammadan Sovereigns like Allauddin and Auranga Phadusha (Aurangazeb?). The following praise of such Jaina Achāryas may well form the peroration of these studies in Andhra-Karnāta Jainism :—

Islamic Patronage of Jainism.

జైనబిరుదావళి.

Jaina Birudavali.

స్వస్త్యనవరతవినయమదనిఖిల త్రిపశపతిమకుటతటఘటిత మణిగణకిరణరంజిత చారుచరణకమలయుగళ భగవదర్హత్పరమేశ్వర పరమపవిత్రతుండఖరదండవినిర్గత । శ్రుతిసుధావార్ధివర్ధనసమ్యగ చింతానాం । యమనియమస్వాధ్యాయ ధ్యానమౌనానుష్ఠానజపతప స్స్వియాసవాదిసీలగుణసంపన్నానాం । భవ్యాజన మనోహారగుణోన్నత సంనుతప్రసన్నత పాంగనాకన్నర్కుండలమండనాయమాన మునిజనవన జషండమార్తాండానాం । కర్మ . . . . కుంభకుంభిస్థల దలన ప్రచండపంచతుండానాం । నిర్జితపాదపీఠకృత వైకుంఠనీలకంఠానాం భోజపీఠమూఢసమారూఢ గర్వపర్వతసువార్ణరశావర్ణరి గర్వభర నిస్సల్యనిస్సంకితాద్యష్టాంగసమార్జిత సమ్యగ్దర్శనదినకరగుణగణ చారుచరణసమాచరదక్షణమధ్యాంహ్న కల్పవైశ్యానాం । శ్యాద్వాద కుతారవిందసాంబసాగత చవార్కమీమాంససుకరయేకాంతపక్షవైశ్వానాం । గీతవాద్యనృత్యతౌర్యత్రప్రముంఖానేక గాంధర్వకలాకుశలపేశల గీర్వాణగాయమానసర్వభాషాగేశ్వర । సంస్కృతప్రాకృత అపభ్రంశ సూరసేనమాగధియాం । పైశాచికాభిధేయషడ్భాషాశాషచక్రవర్తినాం । శ్రీమద్విమలచరణద్వంద్వారవిందవాదీంద్రవినయమర చక్రవర్తినాం । శ్యాద్వాదనీరదేందుకుందమందాకినిసుసుత్యుణో । దండహింతఘాతి

సంఘూతెంఘన । సకలవిమలకేవలావలోకాలోకిత । జినవిరూపితస్వ
రూపానూన్యనదయామయాధర్మనిర్మలస్వాతానాం । అంగవంగకాళింగ
కాశ్మీరకాంభోజసమస్తద్రావిడ ఘూటఘుజరారకర్నాటక । కర
హాటక । కేరళకుంధళమాళవమహారాష్ట్రసౌరాష్ట్రచీనమహాచీనభోట
మహాభోటప్రముఖజనపదప్రఖ్యాతవాదిభూధరభ్రాజమానానాం । కలి
యుగగణధరసమానానాం । ద్వాదశతపోనుష్ఠానగరిష్ఠశ్రేష్ఠమయా ఇష్ట
వరిష్ట విసరొబ్బలగుణమణి సింఘాయమానమార్యత్ గంధసింధూరమం
దార పాదవిన్యాసఖానసమానస్వీయమలక్షలక్ష తాకూణాక్షవ్యాపరాజి
య్యే । ధైర్యగాంభీర్యవీర్యమహైశ్చర్యశౌర్యాణాం । శ్రీమద్గుప్తి
గుప్తాచార్యాణాం । శ్రీకుందకుందాచార్యాణాం । శ్రీమయూరపింఛా
చార్యాణాం । గృధ్రపింఛాచార్యాణాం । జటాసింహనంద్యాచార్యా
ణాం । లోహాచార్యాణాం । శ్రీమధూధ్వస్వాతిసూరిణాం ।
శ్రీ మాఘనందిభట్టారకానాం । మేఘనందిభట్టారకానాం ।
తార్కికశిరోమణీనాం । శ్రీవిద్యానందిస్వామినాం । అ——ంశ
స్వామినాం । నిఃకళంకస్వామినాం । శ్రీ అతతకీర్తిమునిమగీతా
నాం । మాణిక్యనందిమహామునీశ్వరాణాం । వైయాకరణము
నీశ్వరాణాం । శ్రీ పూజ్యపాదమహామునీశ్వరాణాం । కవి
కులతిలకానాం । సమ్యక్త్వచూడామణిప్రభృతినామాంకిత చాముండ
రాయప్రశ్నానుసారప్రణీతత్రిలోకసార । గోమటసారలబ్ధసారాణాం ।
వాదిమత్తేభసింహవిశాలకీర్తిదేవానాం । వాదిగండభేరుండ మహాకీర్తి
దేవానాం । పరవాదిశరభబడబానలవరచారుకీర్తిదేవానాం । అతి
శాంతచతుఃస్రుతసమృద్ధీనాం । అరిమంత్రవాదిగిరివజ్రదండానాం ।
పరమంత్రవాదిప్రళయకాలభైరవానాం । పన్నగమంత్రవాదిసంనుత
వైనతేయానాం । కాలభోజమంత్రవాదిలోదండరుద్రాలకానాం । నే
పాళమంత్రవాదికోహడిజలధరాణాం । మాగధమంత్రవాదిమదనత్రినేత్రా
ణాం । మలయాళమంత్రవాదినవనౌఘచంద్రాణాం । మహానుభావానాం ।
మహాగుణానాం । మహోపసర్గవిజయానాం । మహామోహమల్లవిజయా
నాం । మహాపరిసహసహిష్ణూనాం । గవిగర్వవాదివాగ్మిచతుర్వధ
పాండిత్యకళావిరాజమానానాం । శ్రీమూలసంఘ శ్రీబాలతిలకాయమా
నానాం । శ్రీనందిసంఘ । సరస్వతీగచ్ఛ । బలాత్కారగణాగ్రగణ్యా
నాం । ఆచార్యవీరాణాం । పరంపరాప్రవర్తితమహాసింహాసనయో

గ్యానాం । స్వస్తిశ్రీమద్రామరాజగురువసుంధరాచార్య్యవర్య్య
మహావాదీశ్వరరాయవాదిపితామహ । సకలవిద్వజ్జనచక్రవర్తీనాం ।
శ్రీమదమరకీర్తికావ్యగప్రియాగ్రముఖ్యానాం । స్వభుజపరాక్రమోపా
ర్జితజయరమావిరాజమానచారుదోర్దండమండిత సమస్తవైరిభూ
పాలమానమర్దనప్రచండాసిధా . . . . రాజాధిరాజ అల్లవదిన సుర
త్రాతేన (Allauddin Sultan) మాన్యశ్రీమదభినవ వాదివిద్యా
నందస్వామినాం । తత్పట్టోదయాకరప్రథమవచనఖండనవాదింద్రవిశాల
కీర్తిభట్టారకానాం । తత్పట్టోదయాద్రిదివాకరాయమాన శ్రీమదభిన
వాదివిద్యానందస్వామినాం । తత్పట్టోదయాద్రిదివాకరాయమాన
నిత్యాదనేకాంతవాదిపరమత వచనఖండనవాదీంద్రవిశాలకీర్తి, దేవా
నాం । తత్పట్టోదయాద్రిదివాకరాయమాన శ్రీమద్రామరాజగురు
భాండలాచార్యవర్యమహావాదవాదీశ్వరరాయవాదిపితామహ సకల
విద్వజ్జనసార్వభౌమాద్యనేకాన్వర్థబిరుదావళివిరాజమాన శ్రీమన్మళె
బెగడసిద్ధసింహాసనాధీశ్వర శ్రీమద్దేవేంద్రకీర్తిభట్టారకానాం । తత్ప
ట్టాంభోజదివాకరాయమాన శ్రీమదభినవగజపతిభట్టారక శ్రీవాదీంద్ర
విశాలకీర్తీనాం । చండాంశుకిరణతేజోపమాన్యప్రచండా శేషతురక
రాజాధిరాజ అవరంగబాదిషావ (Auranga (-Zeb) Pādisha)
సురత్రాణమాన్యసంస్కృతప్రాకృత అపభ్రంశికమాగధియ పైశాచి
కాదియంత్రమంత్రతంత్రాదిషడ్భాషాజినచక్రవర్తీనాం । శ్రీఎండి
దేవేంద్రకీర్తిభట్టారకానాం । తత్పట్టోదయాద్రిదున్మార్గవిదూర
సన్మార్గప్రతిపాలకానాం । శ్రీమన్నలఘుభానుకీర్తిభట్టారకానాం ।
తత్పట్టాంభోజదివాకరాయమాన సమస్తశాస్త్రవిదోళ్ విశారద శ్రీ
మద్విమలకీర్తిభట్టారకానాం । తత్పట్టోదయాద్రిజ్ఞానసమయ అర్ధ
సమయగురుకులజ్యోతికర్మభకంఠీరవ । కర్మారణ్యదావానల శ్రీమదభి
నవరత్నకీర్తిభట్టారకానాం । తత్పట్టోదయాద్రి సప్రపరమస్థాప్రదా
యకరత్నత్రయముక్తభూతహితవిద్యాదేహినాం । శ్రీమదభినవబుద్ధి
సాగరభట్టారకానాం । తత్పట్టాంభోజదివాకరాయమాన సద్గుణకరండ
కశాంతస్వరూపపుణ్యప్రతాపవంత । చారిత్రధారక శ్రీమదభినవేంద్ర
కీర్తిభట్టారకానాం । తత్పట్టాంభోజదివాకరాయమాన అష్టమదమత్త
మాతంగకుంభస్థలవిదలనయపటుతరప్రచండ పరాక్రమపంచానన ।
నవవిధబ్రహ్మచర్యపాలకఃన్యాయకీర్తిఃదశవిధ ధర్మస్థాపనాచార్య శ్రీ
మదభినవచంద్రకీర్తిభట్టారకానాం । తపోరాజ్యాభ్యుదయవృద్ధి
నిమిత్తం । భవ్యజీవైః । శ్రీయామాశుభైః ।। శ్రీజినేశ్వరాభిషేక ।
సావధానాభవంతు । సర్వాజినాః ॥ శ్రీ శ్రీ శ్రీ.

SUBJECT INDEX.

CHAPTER I.

CHAPTER II.

CHAPTER II—*contd.*

CHAPTER III.

INDEX TO PROPER NAMES.

A

A—contd.

B

K—*contd.*

K—*contd.*

L

M

M—*contd*

N

O

P

P—*contd.*

R

S

V—*contd.*

V—*contd.*

W

Y